BADGES, BULLETS AND BARS

Library of Congress Control Number: 2006901273
ISBN: Hardcover   978-1-4257-0963-1
                     Softcover   978-1-4257-0962-4

To order additional copies of this book, contact:
Xlibris Corporation
1-888-795-4274
www.Xlibris.com
Orders@Xlibris.com
32023

BADGES, BULLETS AND BARS

BY DANIEL J. SHANAHAN

This book is written in Loving memory of my Dad, John (Jack) Shanahan

DEDICATION

This book is dedicated to all the fine Baltimore Police and other Law Enforcement Officers who have taught me, guided me, and helped me throughout my career and who continued to support me through the difficult times that followed.

Also, for all the love and support I received from my family, friends, and normal citizens that I didn't know. This is written for *all* the excellent Law Enforcement officers who shortened their careers by crossing that THIN BLUE LINE, into the wrong territory, sometimes into criminal territory, not being able to return to the righteous and proper side of that, THIN BLUE LINE. Therefore permanently tarnishing their badge, reputation, family, and all the good that badge stands for. This book is for the officers that could not find their way back, *wanted* to make a difference, and unfortunately, *could have.*

This book is for the honorable, heroic, and ill-fated officers that sacrificed their lives wearing that badge of courage.

Sometimes an officer cannot return to that shiny side of their badge. That badge that means so very much to a police officer; that badge that somehow gets into your blood like a disease, providing excitement, power, passion for the job, and an overwhelming sense and feeling of doing what is right, just, and proper.

Sometimes an officer cannot make it back to the extraordinary and all consuming life of, Badges, Bullets and Bars; ultimately, everyone loses out and suffers.

PRELUDE TO DEATH

After the shooting and killing of Booker Lee Lancaster, and years later when events in my life took a turn for the worse, I would spend time with my first wife Nancy, and my daughter, Jacquelyn. My present home and marriage seemed dark, dingy, and unhappy. The glue keeping me in the second marriage was my two children. Conversely, Nancy and Jackie's home was bright, uplifting, and made me feel upbeat, happy, and content. There was music, love, and contentment there for me.

I had left my second wife, JoAnne, six times over the years since my divorce from Nancy in 1985. The divorce occurred while I was incarcerated in Federal Prison. I continually swallowed my pride and returned to my second wife to be with and near my two children, Danielle, and Daniel Jr. I missed them tremendously as I did my first child, Jackie. These three children were my constant, my hope, and my life. How dare I attempt to take myself away from them! I was so very selfish.

Weeks prior to being shot, I sat with Nancy at the end of her one hundred foot pier at her waterfront home and I shared with her my incessant thoughts and desires, as well as my relentless drive to commit suicide. I outlined for her how I was mentally planning this selfish act, this heinous act, and my desire to see it through to its sad, illegal and sinful ending. Not only had I a deep dark desire to take my life, I had a burning desire to kill and maim as many blacks as I possibly could before I was to be gunned down. I wanted my own place in the annals and history books as the ruthless murderer of blacks, criminals, and bad guys, in the history of Baltimore City.

The officers and detectives that investigated my shooting and attempted suicide, never inquired as to the reason I had over one hundred and twenty 9mm rounds in my pockets and in the car. I had a dark and evil intent.

I had no preconceived thoughts or notions of killing very young or very old blacks, for I would not harm them. They are who I placed my life on the line for as a police officer. My main targets were that of the younger blacks, the gladiators. The fifteen to thirty year olds, the murdering drug dealers, the rapists, the convicts, the criminals that roamed the streets menacing the innocent, the old and very young. The blacks that I wanted to destroy were the ones I had to leave alone as a police officer, the ones I couldn't catch or arrest. It was my turn to be a violent vigilante, my turn for paybacks, and a time to end my life as well.

I had knowledge of the bad guys' whereabouts, their hideouts, havens, and shitholes. I knew the corners they loitered. I knew exactly where to go to have my murderous, revengeful, sinister, wicked and immoral plan come to its fruition. Fortunately, when I left my shop the night of the attempted suicide I drove North on Harford Rd. and not South to the Eastern District of Baltimore City. The district I had worked for so many years, the district that I became so familiar with and I connected so deeply with. It was if I had bonded with the crime, suffering, hatred, and racism. I had become part of what I hated and despised. All of that consumed me. I would like to think that my terrible desires were just racist bravado talk and not my true feelings. Today I harbor no ill feelings for any race. I have grown to realize that I was absolutely wrong in my ugly racist mind, the mindset I had when I was a police officer. That heavy burden has been lifted.

I was drinking heavily the night of my dry run to death, for I was seriously depressed. All the signs were present but not noticeable to me, my friends, or family, until a month later when I lay in Hopkins Bayview Hospital fighting for my life. A life I wanted to end but obviously didn't.

I left my car waxing shop on Harford Rd. and was driving East on 695. I turned off South onto I95 and headed for Eastern Ave. This is the same route I traversed the night I was shot. I was on my cell phone calling Lt. David Brenner, my field training officer, my friend and partner for some time. He was working the Southeastern District that night and I wanted to see him. I had a small arsenal of weapons on my front seat next to me. My 9mm Glock automatic, my .45 caliber Colt, my .22 caliber automatic, .25 caliber automatic, and the revolver that saved my life, a .38 caliber Smith & Wesson 2 inch barrel, five shot revolver. All weapons were loaded to maximum capacity. This night I had little or no idea what I was going to do with this cache of weapons. I feel as though I was beginning my ride to murder, ride to murder the undesirables, the true criminals. I am not sure why I called David that night, I feel as though I was fighting an inner struggle, a war if you will, in my mind, heart, and soul, for I knew what I intended to do was so very wrong in so many ways but had serious intentions to follow it through.

David met me across the street from the Southeastern district. As he pulled up next to my car, I exited my vehicle and began yelling at him. I told him I wanted to die and wanted to take many with me. David told me later that I looked crazed, not myself, not in control of my actions and words. I had placed all five handguns on the roof of my car where I had easy access to any one of them. I was talking crazy. I was drinking, depressed, and confused. I had no thoughts of killing myself *that* night but I would have murdered David. As I was babbling, David called my attorney and friend, Dave Love. Dave was a retired State Trooper and was familiar with my instability. He and I thought along the same lines when it came to police matters, guns, and shootings. Dave tried to persuade me to give up the handguns.

I hung the phone up on him. I gave one gun to David. The entire time I was pointing the Glock 9mm at David's head. David was standing across from the roof of my car, approximately ten feet away from possible, maybe imminent death. Dave called Tim, my brother, who in turn called me on my cell phone. It amazes me that I would take time to talk to loved ones in a serious situation like this, maybe I was reaching out for help. I just don't know.

I was ignorant to Tim which is extremely unusual and I began to cry. My eyes watered but I shook that moment of weakness off and screamed into the phone, "Fuck you! Leave me the fuck alone! I won't let you stop me Timothy!" I angrily hung up on Tim also. I didn't want to talk, I wanted to shoot. Shoot someone, something, maybe myself. I was emotionally unstable and mentally crumbling apart.

David talked me out of all my guns—save one, but made a serious mistake by putting his two way radio up to his mouth as if to call the dispatcher, call for assistance, and David threatened to arrest me. He was going to call for a paddy wagon to have me committed. He was going to have an emergency commitment warrant served on me right then and there. David was going to make an attempt to lock me up in this unstable condition and in this serious situation. *He* had a situation.

Before he could press the mic and talk, I cocked the only weapon I saved, the only weapon that he could not talk me out of, the weapon that was special and close to me, the weapon I felt safe and secure with, the only weapon that I was sure wouldn't let me down, my Smith & Wesson .38. The same handgun that snuffed out Booker Lancaster's life, the same weapon that saved my life, the same weapon I felt attached to and at ease with. That weapon! That very special .38 caliber handgun with a notch on the handle put there with a small file by my partner in the motorcycle unit, Norm Sampson. An indentation in the wooden grip that marked the death of Lancaster, a constant reminder, a tradition followed by the gunslingers from the days of The Old West.

As I stood with the hammer cocked back and the weapon trained on David's head I yelled, "You call the fucking wagon and have me put in a psych ward and I'll blow you're fucking head off cocksucker! I mean it

David, you press that button and you fucking die!" It was obvious that I was agitated and angry. There was no fear in my mind or heart. I wanted my way or someone would die.

David was cool. He did not move and he dared not touch that radio. He could see that I was extremely unstable and very serious with my threat to kill. My eyes were trained on that button and David's eyes. I watched both with death in my mentally disturbed eyes. David remained cool, calm, and collected. He said very calmly and quietly, "Okay Dan, I won't call, just give me the gun. Come on buddy you don't want this. You know you don't want to hurt me. Come on buddy, put the gun down."

I suddenly realized that I didn't want to do this. I knew I could turn back, unlike later, I knew to stop and regain control of myself. I slowly let the hammer drop to a safe position and slid my gun across the hood to David. I began to sob and sat down on the curb. David came around the car to me after placing all the weapons in the back seat, back floor, of his marked radio car, out of my reach.

The situation had ended. I can't recall how I got home that night or who I spoke with, but reflecting back, this night, this prelude to death, should have been some indication that I was having problems, serious mental and emotional problems, yet, myself nor any one else could see that this highly explosive tinderbox was slowly smoking, slowly smoldering, slowly waiting to incinerate and explode. Incinerate and explode into a horribly disastrous, actual run, *to my death.*

Shoot Me, Kill Me, Let Me Die!

I awoke to bright white lights, a tube in my mouth breathing for me, and more IV lines and monitors than I had ever seen. I began to choke, gag, and panic. I was trying to catch my breath but was unable to do so due to the life support system that had been breathing for me for the last three days. I saw that my brother Tim was at my side. Tears came streaming from my eyes. I began to move my arm in a writing motion. Tim scurried to find a brown paper towel and a pen. I scribbled on the paper. Tim took it from me, attempted to read it and said, "Can't do what Dan? Oh you can't breathe?" I nodded yes. I was fighting to get air into my lungs. I was fighting the resuscitator to see which of us would win and breathe for me. A nurse arrived, evaluated the situation, and removed the tube, the tube that had been keeping me alive for 7 days. I gasped, took several deep breaths and gazed around in bewilderment and wonder. Where was I and how in the world did I get here? I had absolutely no idea.

I began to fade back into unconsciousness. While out, I noticed two flashing objects on either side of my head, my inner peripheral vision. They were like doodle bugs that were lighting up and blinking. They reminded me of Tinker Bell. Suddenly I heard someone say aloud, Mr. Shanahan, BREATH! You must breathe! I took a deep breath and the objects faded off into the distance, continuing to flash. I calmed down. Suddenly the flashing objects were once again advancing on me. They were flashing, jittering, moving in every direction. I was amazed. Again I began to black out. Again I heard, DANNY, Breathe! You must breathe! It was the same nurse and my brother Tim talking to me. I took another deep breath and the flashing, blinking, fast moving; visitors disappeared, never to return. I will never understand what those objects were or signified. I continued to breath on my own and would be fine.

I was, in fact, in the Surgical Intensive Care Unit at Hopkins Bayview Hospital. I was suffering from eight gunshot wounds, six of which entered and exited my body. Two grazed my head and shoulder. Included in those eight shots was a blow out fracture to the femur in my left leg where one of the eight black talon police rounds shattered the bone. I was not only blessed I was probably, at that moment, lying on God's lap, head in his hand, with my guardian angel and my dad next to Him. I had survived a horrendous amount of violence, a hail of bullets, eleven to be exact, and my third suicide attempt.

Suicide is a very selfish act. It comes when one feels helpless, hopeless, and thinks of NO ONE but oneself. I feel it is a very ignorant and self-serving act and denies the family members of any closure. I have attempted suicide three times now and pray that I will not allow myself to reach such a low ever again. I have checks and balances in place to assure and insure that I go for help first and that I don't take the easy way out ever again. Former Baltimore County Police Officer Craig Kalman, and CSW Meadow Lark Washington have assisted me in these decisions. Alcohol Anonymous has played a large part, at times, thru my recuperation periods. All three, have in some way, unselfishly acted to save my life.

1996 was a very, very bad year for me, *evidently*. I was losing my business due to some improper business decisions and not knowing how to run a business, I was in a personal bankruptcy, my second marriage was falling apart, and my father was diagnosed with cancer. I was contemplating leaving my second wife for a fourth time. I kept leaving, going back, leaving and going back. My children had much to do with the decisions to return each time.

Everyday for many months I would leave my business; take my dad to Good Samaritan Hospital for his chemo and radiation therapy. I watched him fading away both physically and emotionally, as did my mom. He was fighting this horrible disease but had a terrific attitude. However, being so close to this everyday was quietly, slowly, and little by little, taking its toll on me mentally, emotionally, and psychologically. I wasn't aware. I did what was expected.

My father passed away in the early morning hours of June 14th, 1996, my mother, my five brothers, and the sister-in-laws were present, as was my daughter Jacquelyn, and other family members. Each one of us took a turn at the head of the bed holding my dad's head and talking to him. My time arrived. My dad was unconscious and was being given large doses of morphine thru an IV. His breathing became shallower with each passing moment. Suddenly he took his last small breath of life. I was right next to him. AGAIN, I witnessed death first hand and close up, close up and personal, as I had so many times over the years. However in my forty years of existence never had I experienced the death of a loved one. The first *had* to be my dad and *I* had to be at the head of the bed.

He took his last breath. I had my hand on his chin. Suddenly he spit up in my hand. I heard that damn death gurgle once again, and my dad expired. When he spit up in my hand I immediately covered it up so my mom didn't have to witness that grotesque moment. For some reason my thoughts were immediately transported to Harford Rd. and Broadway, at 9:23 a.m. on July 13, 1983. The day I was forced to kill Booker Lancaster. Then *all* the other deaths I had witnessed came back to life in my memory.

It was done! All the wounds reopened. The killing of Lancaster, the indictment, the two trials, the bank robbery, over two years in Federal Prison, all the bad and ugly surfaced at that very moment. No good was to be found that morning. I left the hospital feeling sad and empty. I went home to be alone and as I wept the phone rang, it was my mother informing me that my Grandmother had passed away. My mother had lost her husband, of over forty years, and her mother, in a twenty-four hour period. My heart was given out to her that morning. She was dealt some dirty cards, we all were.

November 2, 1996, 10:00 p.m. I was being forced to close my business of nine years due to money problems. I was to be evicted in November. I was drinking a beer with my brothers Tim and Shawn at The Bowman's restaurant in Parkville. I was in a good mood. my spirits were high. After taking my brother Shawn home I went back to Bowman's and had my second beer. I left to go home. Upon entering my home, my wife of nine years, JoAnne, approached me and said, "I'm leaving you and taking the kids, were going to Texas!" At that point in my life, my three children were of extreme importance to me. Even though Jacquelyn was from my marriage to Nancy, my first wife, I was very much attached to her. She was a beautiful little girl. My children were the glue that was completely necessary, at that time in my life, to hold me together, to keep me from taking my life.

Upon hearing those words from JoAnne, I snapped! I had a mental breakdown. I recall very little after those words passed her lips. I knelt down and kissed my eight-year-old daughter, Danielle, goodbye, and then I hugged my three-year-old son, Danny Jr., and left in a hurry. I was in a hurry to kill myself! Of course, many people thought I was drunk, but later it was found that my blood alcohol level was low. I was told that I demanded that Joanne retrieve my Smith and Wesson .38 caliber revolver. She refused. I became irritated and said, "That's okay, I'll go to the shop and get my Glock!"

I headed to my business. My wife called my brother Tim's house, he lives very close, he was asleep. My sister-in-law and her young daughter, Trina, sped to the shop to help me. JoAnne had explained to Tim's wife, Ingrid, that I may be thinking of suicide. I arrived at my shop. Not known until later, I had retrieved my life insurance policy from my file cabinet to make sure that my family would receive my $750,000.00 of insurance money if I committed suicide. I discovered that the insurance company would pay since I had been insured for over two years. I again called Nancy. I said, "Listen to this!" I fired a round from my Glock. "Goodbye Nancy!" I hung up. I have no idea what must have been going thru everyone's mind. I have not had the guts to ask them to this day. It must have been a horrendous and helpless feeling.

Somehow I came to be standing on the parking lot out in front of my business. I fired two shots from my 9mm Glock, both crashing thru a plate glass window across the street. A passing motorist immediately contacted the police department. Ingrid and my niece tried to stop me as I was attempting to leave the building to escape. Ingrid tried to get my gun off the seat. I immediately caught on to her scheme and pushed her away from the car. I had no idea where I was going. I learned later from my friend Shawn Whalen, that I had walked back into the shop and emptied my 15 shot 9mm clip into several walls in my office and into walls at the front counter. Shawn had arrived at the shop early the next morning and the Baltimore County police walked in directly behind him. Shawn was very busy and to preoccupied to even notice the arrival of the police that were investigating the attempted suicide and shooting for he was busy relocating pictures on the wall to cover up all the bullet holes I had fired the previous night. The police never discovered Shawn's excellent cover up performance and I'm sure that saved me from incurring additional criminal charges.

I was told later by my niece, Trina, that there was no life in my eyes that night, my stare was unending. "There was nothing there." She said. This eleven-year old girl saw the emptiness and sadness in my eyes. I felt hopeless and wanted so badly to die. I got into the Lincoln I was driving and quickly left the parking lot of my business with a fully loaded 9mm Glock with two rounds missing plus more than 140 rounds of ammunition in my pockets and on the front seat. I was ready to kill and to be killed.

I traveled a short distance to a bar that I felt comfortable in and had been frequenting since my teens. I felt comfortable because I knew the three sisters that owned the Linway Lounge, and was friendly with the two male bartenders. I walked into the Linway looking for Jeannie, a friend and one of the owners. She was not there. Melanie was working. She was also a friend. She walked up to me and asked what would I like? I put my fully loaded 9mm handgun on the bar in front of her. I cocked the trigger and said in a melancholy but stern voice, "Give me two beers Mel, one for now and one for the road, you won't see me again, I'm going to kill myself tonight, see you in the papers." I guzzled my first Coor's Light, and then walked directly out the back door. I have not seen Melanie since that night. I feel for her and what I put her thru.

I got back into my car, pulled up to the exit of the bar. I stopped my vehicle and slowly looked south down Harford Rd. then slowly and deliberately looked north, away from the city of Baltimore. It was at this point I must have realized that killing as many blacks as I could before being killed was wrong, very, very wrong. I don't know how long I sat at that exit in front of the small neighborhood bar pondering my next action, but eventually I turned left, or north. Then, as the movie title says, "Fate is the Hunter," fate was the hunter at that point on that particular night, heading north on Harford Road, not south.

I am fortunate that I traveled north on Harford Rd. and not south! I had very bad thoughts going thru my mind, thoughts of killing Blacks. God must have guided my hand. I drove away from the city.

During my ride to the shop from my home, I called my mom on my cell phone, told her I loved her, and then I said, "I'm going to kill myself mom, goodbye!" I heard my mother say, "No Danny, don't, I need you, come to the house!" She was frantic. I nonchalantly hung the phone up. I recall being angry because no one was going to talk me out of taking my life. I wanted to die! I was going to die! Then I called Nancy, "Nancy, I love you, I always have, and I always will. Do you understand?" "Yes Dan." She said quietly. "Let me talk to Jackie." I said. "Hi daddy!" She said happily. She was thirteen. "Jackie, no matter what you hear after tonight, I love you very much, I am not a bad man, okay? I love you Jack!" I hung up and once again pulled into the parking lot of my business. To think. It was time! Time to DIE!

I then sped North on Harford Rd. I still had no idea where I was going. I later learned that after I left my shop I crossed the center line on Harford Rd., about five blocks from my shop, in front of the Emerald Tavern. Evidently I did this because there was a police car in front of me. A police car that was looking for me! And, I was looking for him! Sgt. Marvin Haw immediately told the dispatcher that the suspect that he was looking for just passed him at a high rate of speed crossing the double yellow line. The chase was on! I was going to my death and a police officer was going to have to kill me. It was my plan. I would not deviate. I would stay the course.

I had pictured my plan many times. I would have the police chase me. I'd pull out an empty handgun and point it at the officers so that they would shoot me to death. Once I was dead the police would see that my gun was empty and realize that I would not hurt a police officer. It changed some in reality.

For some unknown reason I entered onto 695 from the Parkville exit heading east. At that point Officer Cedric Johnson joined the chase. I recall the lights and sirens but everything else about the chase was fuzzy, I cannot remember. Sgt. Haw spoke over the radio, "We are chasing former police officer Danny Shanahan, he is suicidal, armed, and shots have been fired. We reached speeds in excess of one hundred MPH. I was unaware of my surroundings, I had completely snapped.

I exited off of 695 and entered onto Interstate 95 headed south. The Maryland State Police joined the chase, as did the Baltimore City Police when I exited onto Eastern Ave. I learned later that I sped thru every intersection on Eastern Ave. until I was forced to turn north onto Eaton St. I crossed at least ten to twelve intersections without hitting another car. UNBELIEVABLE!

I recall seeing a roadblock at Eaton St. and turning right. Then I remember a white flash and my car stopping. I had driven two more blocks from Eastern Ave. to Gough St. and at the intersection of Eaton and Gough St. I hit a parked car on the wrong side of the street head on and the white air bag exploded in my face. I remember trying to get the clip out of my gun, to no avail, for that was the plan. I can recall nothing else at that moment.

Later, I was to discover that I jumped out of the car and pulled off my pager, threw it onto the ground, and stomped on it several times. I then pulled my 9mm Glock from my waistband and began to wave it around my head. I was ordered to drop the gun. I didn't point the gun at the officers because

I was unable to unload it. I yelled, **"SHOOT ME, KILL ME, LET ME DIE!** I was then shot two times in the left leg. I dropped to one knee but would not go down. I once again stood up. Again the police shouted, "Drop the gun! Again I refused, waved the gun above my head, and screamed, "I want to die! Kill me!" I began waving the gun once again. It was at that point that both Baltimore County officers shot at me an additional eleven to thirteen times. In all, approximately fifteen rounds were fired at me. I hit the sidewalk.

I remember voices, people tugging and pulling on me and most vividly I recall the overwhelming peace of mind that settled over me when my head hit the sidewalk. I can recall nuzzling the sidewalk as if hugging it and feeling as though the entire weight of the world and all my problems were lifting off of me. *I didn't have to take care of anyone's problems anymore and I didn't have to care about my shortcomings and past actions.* I was dying. It was a soft, serene, comfortable, warm, peaceful feeling. I can recall saying to myself as I lay there bleeding to death, *you did good Danny, you did good. You're dying, now close your eyes and go to sleep, it's over.* I couldn't move. I was in a state of serenity. That moment on the sidewalk at the corner of Eaton and Gough Sts. was the most comfortable, calm, relaxed, and fulfilling moment I had since I was a baby in my mother's arms. I was at peace with the world and myself; I felt no guilt, shame, embarrassment or regrets, for the first time since I was twenty years old. I was forty. I always felt as though death was a horrible experience. I had seen so much death I assumed it was horrible, painful, and unsettling. Not so. I was finally at ease.

Later after I left the hospital, I spoke to Officer Mike Ogle, Lt. David Brenner, and several Baltimore City police officers that I had worked with

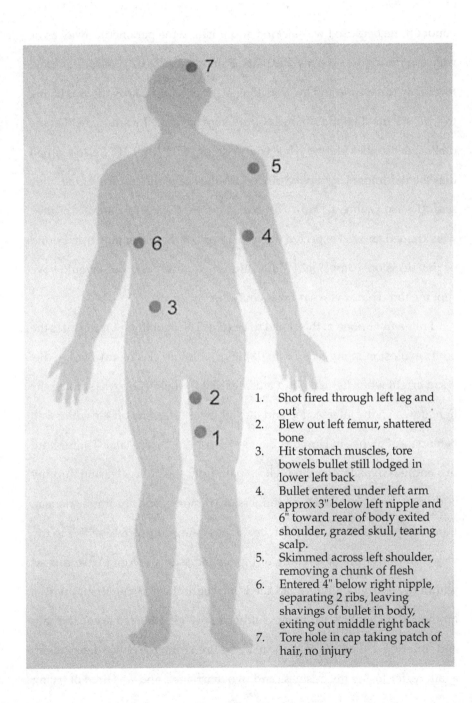

1. Shot fired through left leg and out
2. Blew out left femur, shattered bone
3. Hit stomach muscles, tore bowels bullet still lodged in lower left back
4. Bullet entered under left arm approx 3" below left nipple and 6" toward rear of body exited shoulder, grazed skull, tearing scalp.
5. Skimmed across left shoulder, removing a chunk of flesh
6. Entered 4" below right nipple, separating 2 ribs, leaving shavings of bullet in body, exiting out middle right back
7. Tore hole in cap taking patch of hair, no injury

over the years. I was so intent on dying that my former coworkers had to handcuff me because I was kicking and pushing the paramedic away as he was attempting to save my life. City Paramedic, "Doc," Watson, worked feverishly to save me and I was kicking at him because I knew he was trying to save my life. I would not hear of it! I kept saying, "I want to die! Let me die! I want to die! I know what you're doing! LET ME DIE! I also learned that the Baltimore City police officers on the scene did not fire at me, they said, "I wasn't a threat!" However, Sgt. Haw and Officer Johnson did as they were trained and as I expected them to. I was not there mentally to expound on that decision, *I* dare not Monday morning quarterback, and I would have shot me too. That was what *I* was counting on.

I remember none of this. I had to be told. The next thing I recall after the white explosion in my face, and talking myself into closing my eyes to die, was a bright white light. I found out later that the helicopter was shining the light down on the intersection and the light was reflecting off the white wall behind me. I awoke in Hopkins Bayview Hospital, 7 days later. Throughout this entire ordeal, that night, I felt no pain from the bullets tearing thru my body and shattering bones, no sadness, no remorse, and absolutely no fear. I did not think of my family, only me! I was being completely selfish to my wants and desires, not thinking of the repercussions I would have caused within my entire family if I had died that night. I cared not about my five brothers, their families, my mom, children or myself. I wanted to end the pain and suffering. I felt destroyed due to being fired from the police department, a failure, for losing my business and two marriages, and was tired of trying to pick up the pieces to go on. I wanted all of it to stop!

My brother told me that as I was being taken into surgery after leaving the ambulance and as I went up the elevator I began kicking, thrashing, and cursing, causing blood to splatter everywhere from the eleven bullet holes and cuts. There was a guard present as we traveled on the elevator. Later the hospital guard asked if I was related when he rode on the elevator with some of my family. "Yes" was the answer. "Don't worry, he's a fighter, he'll survive!" I did.

As I lay in the hospital looking at the three gaping holes in my chest and my ruined left leg, I began to fade in and out of consciousness, which was caused by the high levels of morphine I was receiving via IV to ease the pain and my body trying to heal itself from such massive wounds. I would continue to heal my body, with the help of nurses and doctors that have dedicated their lives to saving poor souls such as me. I also owe my recovery to my second mom, Ann, who nurtured me back to health. And, my mental recovery to my family and a few friends. I am blessed. I began to wonder, wonder and reflect.

I wondered how I came to be in this position. *What had happened? What had I done to myself?* I began to reminisce about my life and career. I found myself recalling, with great detail, most of my experiences as a police cadet and a Baltimore City Police Officer. Here are some of my experiences, stories, *both,* good, bad, sad, and funny, and what being a police officer is about. Maybe you can become as engrossed and enthralled with this book as I was with my job. The ups, downs, death, fun, and overall experience of performing that job. That, never knowing WHAT TO EXPECT job, of being a cop.

THE BEGINNING

FAMILY OF COPS 1973

I really wasn't 1certain I wanted to become a police officer. I was eighteen and had no idea what I wanted to do with my life. I was fresh out of high school and decided to join the Baltimore County Police Department. My brother Mike was a Baltimore City police officer and my Uncle Skip Shanahan, was, at that time, the youngest lieutenant colonel in the history of the Baltimore Police Department.

I idolized Skip. He was my dad's brother. Whenever he stopped by our house I was thrilled and mesmerized with his appearance in his uniform with his gun and gold police badge. Subconsciously I was hooked, hooked at an early age by wanting to be a cop, wanting to be a blue knight.

However, I wanted to become a *Baltimore County* police officer. I took the

test to become a County police cadet and failed. I was severely disappointed.

It would take six months in order to retake this test. I wasn't waiting. I walked

into the Baltimore City Police Headquarters and took, as well as passed, the

entrance exam in all of one hour. I was thrilled and excited. The City police

department. had walk in testing with immediate results, Good idea.

The circle seemed complete. My grandfather was a retired sergeant in the

motorcycle unit, my uncle was a retired lieutenant colonel, and my brother

Mike was a narcotics detective, now I was a police cadet. A family of cops

had emerged and was instituted.

My grandfather, John T. Shanahan, was a big man. My dad when younger

would have to stand on a kitchen chair enabling him to lift and hold his

father's large blue full length woolen reefer, or coat, onto his dad's shoulders,

seeing his dad off to work.

I don't remember much about my dad's dad other than sitting on his large

lap looking, and tracing with my little finger, the snake tattoo on his right arm

that lazily wound itself around the arm down to the wrist. My grandfather

also had a large battleship tattooed across the length of his massive chest. I

was enthralled and amazed each time I was able to look upon this ship on

my granddad's chest.

By talking to family members and mostly my mom, I have learned a few

facts about my grandfather. He was a motorcycle sergeant in the 1950's. He

drank quite often and to excess. He was inebriated the day he was bet by a

fellow officer that he wouldn't ride his Police Harley up the entire length of the steps leading to the front doors to City Hall. He was caught in the act and immediately transferred out of motors.

My grandfather was a heavy drinker and would, at times take a, "Pledge," not to drink for a five or ten year period. He did this throughout his career. He honored and faithfully took his personal pledge with a priest and wouldn't drink at all for the time stated. When his pledge time was fulfilled he drank hard and heavy until he decided it was time for another non drinking pledge.

I understand that my grandfather, Sergeant Shanahan, was an excellent police officer and loved his job. As did Skip, Mike, and myself. I know of a few war stories pertaining to my grandfather. Riding up the City Hall steps on a bet on his Harley, The night he caught a rape suspect in the act. The suspect was carving his initials in the rape victim's chest after he raped her with a pocket knife. The victim was screaming and hysterical. My grandfather hit the suspect so hard with his night stick that the tremendous blow permanently pushed the knuckle on his right thumb two inches back from its normal position. That knuckle remained far back into his hand until he died.

On another day my sergeant grandfather went through a door to arrest a man. He hit the door with such force, being so large, that he ran completely through the entire house, was unable to stop and fell out the rear kitchen window becoming entangled in the clothesline. The door was not completely closed. My grandmother, Liz, received a call from the women in the house, "Lizzy!" She said in a high pitched excited voice, "Your Johnny just fell out my back window, you better get help Lizzy!"

Donald (Skip) Shanahan was a colorful and outspoken police officer. He could run like a rabbit and as long. I've heard several war stories attesting to Skip running down a suspect or running down an escaped prisoner. Skip spoke eloquently, was intelligent, and was respected. Skip also took Commissioner Donald Pomerleau into his home when he came to town to become Chief of Police. Therefore, the remainder of Skip's career he would remain Pomerleau's fair haired boy, right hand man, and, the chosen one.

Skip was promoted by Pomerleau from lieutenant to major, passing by captain. Pomerleau took Skip under his wing. He was the police commissioner's protégé. Even though Skip was well liked and respected he made enemies and stepped on a lot of toes by rising through the ranks so quickly.

Skip had to have quite a bit of intelligence to pass the three written exams to reach the rank of lieutenant. He also wrote police procedures and he later went on to become a professor of law at the University of St. Louis. Not only was Skip Shanahan book smart, he was street wise as well. Those two entities combined add up to a top notch, well honed, police officer, able to make a difference on the streets of Baltimore and to command the men under him.

Skip retired early, in the midst of controversy when officers in the rackets squad, now referred to as the vice squad, was brought under investigation and indictment for receiving gratuities, or graft. Many officers in the Western District were fired or indicted because they were, "on the take." An officer named Llewellyn Dikes supposedly snitched on several police officers. However I am not certain of the scope of his involvement. I recall hearing his name very often when I first became a police cadet. Usually it was in a derogatory way. He was often referred to as a, "rat," by many of the older officers.

Receiving gratuities as well as cash handouts for protection of the many bars and their owners, most notably, the bars and strip joints on the then famous, Baltimore Block, where prostitution and taking numbers was rampant in such clubs as The Oasis, The Kit Kat Club, Two O'clock Club, Club 409, and The Pussy Cat Club. The block made Blaze Starr famous, or was it the converse.

Skip retired early to avoid any type of prosecution. That is, so I understand, Pomerleau warned Skip ahead of time of the sting and possible indictments, some which may have contained Skip Shanahan's name. Supposedly, Skip retired just in time to avoid prosecution for accepting bribes and taking payoffs. I personally don't believe this, however I am prejudiced. After all, he was my father's brother. I feel as though he was an honest cop.

Mike Shanahan was probably one of the most loyal, dedicated, and knowledgeable police officers I have known. Not because he is my oldest brother, but because he lived, breathed, and slept the police department. Mike had a great fund of knowledge when it came to police work, especially narcotics, which is where he worked after transferring from the Northeastern District. He contributed more than his share in the war against drugs and crime in the early 1970's. Mike was too much of a narcotics detective, he worked 24/7. On his days off he would ride through his district looking for stolen cars that were listed on the police department's "hot sheet," a sheet containing a list of recently stolen automobiles. He needed to take some time off now and then. But, he wanted desperately to make a difference, a difference by fighting crime. Mikes love for the job ultimately became his demise, along with the revenge that was taken out on him due to Skip Shanahan's quick rise through the police department ranks.

Since Skip had stepped on so many toes, Mike Shanahan was made to suffer and was about to feel the wrath of a sergeant and a lieutenant that felt as though they had been wronged and slighted by Skip. The two backstabbers ruined Mike's career and prevented Mike from becoming a police officer in any other department on the East coast.

I believe Mike has never recovered from that hit, that spiteful low blow. He tried unsuccessfully for years to become a police officer in over ten departments. He passed all the entrance tests and the oral interviews only to be rejected after his personnel jacket was reviewed and a background check was done. Of course, The Baltimore Police Department had seen to it that Mike would never be hired by any other law enforcement agency.

The Baltimore Police Department's derogatory and negative letters in reply to other agencies requests were preventing Mike from becoming an officer. Preventing Mike from doing what he loved most, being a cop. A bright young career had been destroyed and devastated all to satisfy the revenge and retribution of two imbecile officers that somehow thought that this wrongdoing would somehow pay back Skip Shanahan for accomplishing something they could not.

JoAnne Stump, later to be, JoAnne Shanahan, was another member of our family of cops. I met her in the Eastern District roll call room and fell in love. Even though I had a decent, honest, caring and loving wife, it wasn't meant to be. Many officers advised JoAnne against becoming involved with me, but I was persistent and tenacious. We became an item in 1980. While separated from my first wife, the Lancaster shooting occurred. JoAnne helped me and stood beside me through that horrible time in my life as did my family and close friends, some became false friends when I fell from grace with the bank robbery situation. It still amazes me that I had all those friends until I made a mistake, then, many turned away from me, abandoned me, and simply disappeared.

It's unfortunate that Skip, Mike, JoAnne, and I, lost our careers and were denied the chance to help the citizens of Baltimore City and to make a difference. **The Thin Blue Line** had been crossed with no crossing back in sight. Ultimately everyone loses and suffers. Especially the family, the family of cops.

Johnny, Don't Die

My first real taste of death came so very close to home, literally next door. Christmas Eve 1973, I was out partying with some friends and making my normal Christmas stops. I wanted to get home early, I was still living with my parents, I was nineteen and Christmas Eve was always so warm, quiet, loving and traditional at my parent's house. It always has been and always will be. No kids, no noise, just all six sons, their girlfriends or wives, and my parents. Soft Christmas music, candles, and a sincere feeling of togetherness, peacefulness, and joy, that was ever so relaxing and comforting.

I was driving my '69 Firebird and pulled up in front of my house which was located in a court, no intersections, side streets or cross streets, just a court. As I parked my car, I noticed Johnny's '67 Mustang parked in a strange and peculiar way. Each home in the court had its own parking spaces, and everyone in the court knew what and where each other's cars were supposed to be parked. After eighteen years of everyone parked in their own special spot, if a car was out of place it was immediately noticed. Something was out of place, not normal, Johnny's Mustang was not in its regular spot, four cars from my normal parking space and facing to the left, it was parked straight ahead almost in another neighbor's driveway. Obviously, his car was not in its normal spot.

Johnny was three years younger then I. He had just gotten his drivers license months prior to this fateful, fatal, Christmas Eve's night.

Johnny and I grew up together; we played monopoly, checkers, and chess since we were seven years old. Johnny and I raced our Tyco and Aurora HO cars together. We spent hours setting up the small tracks, racing, taking cars apart and spent hours playing Monopoly because we couldn't go out in the rain, or didn't want to. We always played together and for many years were inseparable. Our mothers fixed Johnny and I peanut butter and jelly sandwiches and our favorite, grilled cheese. We were the best of friends, were always together and always would be, or so I thought . . .

As I pulled into my own parking spot and put my car into the park position, my younger brother's Pat and Shawn raced up to my door. Simultaneously they yelled, "Johnny's not breathing!"

I raced to Johnny's Mustang. Johnny was partially in his car, feet by the gas pedals and partially out of the car lying on the asphalt. His head was approximately 3' from the driver's side of the car and to the left, he was not breathing. Pat and Shawn were unsure of what to do. I pulled Johnny's limp body completely out of his car. His eyes were open, and glazed over; it was if they had fogged up. His complexion was a light gray, I didn't know what to do, I was to upset and frightened seeing my best friend in that condition I couldn't focus on my job at hand, to save Johnny's life. My brother Tim was also coming to Johnny's car. Suddenly as if someone was reading directly from a CPR manual, it all came back to me. Tilt the head back; clear the airway, two quick breaths, five pumps with the palm against the sternum and three fingers higher than the bottom tip of the sternum. It was so strange, the Police department had trained me in CPR, I had passed the course and had evidently forgotten the procedures. But I had no idea that the procedures, and how to perform them, would so vividly and easily come back to me in such a time of pure panic and fear. I was performing these techniques perfectly. I explained to Tim what to do, he would compress the sternum/heart five times, and on the last compression I would give two quick breaths of life-giving oxygen from my lungs to the 16-year-old lungs of Johnny Sadowski, my neighbor of 16 years, my friend of 10 years, my toy race car buddy and now dying, limp, suffocating from carbon monoxide poisoning, pal.

Time seemed to be at a stand still. My brother Tim was frightened and frantic. He was so frightened and worried that Johnny would die he was exerting too much force onto Johnny's chest cavity, he would compress the chest cavity too quickly, at times not allowing me to breathe for Johnny. I had

to continually tell Tim to slow down, listen to me, and follow my instructions.

I was surprised at myself and how the training I received was allowing me

to keep my cool and do what was right. Obviously, training and repetitions

are the key ingredients to learning a procedure for recall at a later date. Tim

was intent on saving this young boys life.

I could smell a strange odor coming from Johnny's breathe and

lungs. It was a sickening odor, like that of a bad oyster or rotting crabs

and seafood. A pungent smell yet a subtle type of sickening, nauseating

smell, a smell that was making me sick to my stomach, I felt as though

I was going to vomit. I gagged each time Tim forced the dead oxygen

starved putrid smelling oyster breath air out of Johnny's lungs and into

my face. Johnny's body heaved and he vomited into my mouth as I was

ready to breathe my air into his lungs. Immediately I vomited onto the

ground just barely missing Johnny. Tim also puked and Pat and Shawn

looked away gagging.

Someone had called 911. I didn't hear the siren. I must have been so

engrossed and preoccupied with attempting to save my best friend's life. It

hadn't even registered in my busy mind that an ambulance had arrived and

a Baltimore County paramedic was pulling on my arm in an attempt to get

to Johnny. I must have been transported to *that place*. The same place I would

go to when the young cab hold up suspect pulled an automatic weapon out

of his pocket and fired it, point blank at my face, the same *place* I would visit

when I struggled for my life the day I killed Booker Lee Lancaster, that one

in the same *place*, brief but intense but also all consuming and distracting, pulling us away from what we are presently experiencing and attempting to handle or, *not* to handle.

"Let me in here son," I heard

Two hours later the phone rang. It was Johnny's mom. Evidently Johnny's mom and dad had climbed into the ambulance before it pulled off. I hadn't even noticed. I had no idea that Johnny's mom and dad watched as Tim and I attempted to save their only son's life. I had no idea they witnessed the sheer panic, the vomiting, and the fierce struggle that were taking place on that small piece of asphalt, I had no idea.

Johnny died,

Apparently, the paramedics had Johnny stabilized, after Tim and I so valiantly brought Johnny back to life. However, the paramedics had exhausted their supply of much needed oxygen before they could reach the nearest hospital and Johnny's heart had begun to violently defibrillate. When the paramedics had attempted to shock his heart and stop the heart spasms, the defibrillator had failed, it had not been placed into the charger properly and therefore could not deliver the electric shock needed to save Johnny Sadowski's life.

I couldn't believe it! The paramedics, in my eyes, had murdered *our Johnny, my Johnny!* They had killed him by their neglect and ineptness. I was incensed.

I would later discover that the level of carbon monoxide in Johnny's blood was extremely high and at a toxic, deadly level. A level that most people can't survive. If they do survive, they become vegetables, no brain reflexes, no muscle reflexes, just a vegetable sitting a wheelchair the rest of their lives. I suppose it was a blessing. I'm sure that the Baltimore County paramedics had done all they possibly could to save this young man's life, yes, I'm certain of it . . .

I received a letter of commendation from the police department and a small write up in the police department newsletter. But, I wasn't proud of myself, I didn't revel in the spotlight of heroism. I was downright sad and disgusted about the entire situation. I knew my brother's and I hadn't failed Johnny, but, after all, *he was dead*.

I will never be able to erase that disgusting odor coming from Johnny's mouth from my memory and it's been nearly thirty years. I can close my eyes recall that odor in my brain and gag, not puke like that night, but gag, like I was about to puke. The smell has not faded with the years; I want to vomit as I write this sentence. This happens to me every single time I conjure up the events of that horrible, sad, deadly night. The breaths of life, the compressions of life, the odor of death and the taste of death that won't fade. I miss you Johnny. I'm sorry.

END of THE INNOCENCE

I was born and raised in an all white typical suburban neighborhood. I never saw a black person, or never took notice, until I was in junior high school. Parkville High School had one black mentally retarded female that I saw sporadically. I really didn't pay much attention and had to press my memory to remember that. I really didn't understand prejudice or racism because it wasn't a part of my life. I had no prejudices towards anyone or anything. I didn't come in contact with that ugly creature until I became a Baltimore Police Officer. It reared its' ugly head and didn't release its horrible grip on me. I don't recall hearing the ugly words, nigger, spick, gook, spook, coon, until I was eighteen years old and a police cadet.

In my early teens I rode bicycles with my brothers, played baseball, football and just grew up in an innocent environment. My mother and father never spoke any words of racism, never used those ugly words and for all I knew these words of hatred, color and ethnicity didn't exist. My teachings were of kindness, trust, generosity, caring, giving and above all else, respect for other people. I was instilled with all the proper Irish Catholic qualities, virtues and values. I don't recall the riots of 1968, the Black Panthers, the racial tensions or the other sixties problems. I wasn't even aware that a racial problem existed and I was living in the very times. I was a young, naïve, innocent white boy. Living in a middle class innocent, naïve, all white neighborhood, in the suburbs of Baltimore County. In 1964 I was nine years old. The next nine years I would occasionally be exposed to a minimal amount of racial slurs and prejudices. To me they were just names with hollow or no meaning that I heard from other boys and classmates.

Then arrived my eighteenth birthday. I was accepted as a Baltimore City police cadet. I would, on occasion, ride to work with other, older experienced police officers that had worked the mean streets of Baltimore and were winding down their careers as dispatchers in the communications division. The communications division consisted mostly of older officers that wanted off the streets, officers on disciplinary punishment, or police cadets. These officers had an open and outspoken hatred for blacks and minorities. It was not kept quiet and I assumed it was an acceptable norm among us. The onset of my career was as a dispatcher in the communications division. I was an impressionable young, eager police cadet. I would listen intently to the war stories of the veteran officers that I worked alongside of and rode back and forth to work with. I believed most of the stories and was eager to listen to all of them. I listened intently for over two and a half years. I was extremely anxious and excited about hitting those same mean streets and to cultivate my own war stories. These officers were near retirement, injured on the streets awaiting medical retirements or just sick of patrolling the streets of Baltimore City, trying to make a difference. I guess that they had realized, attempting to make a difference, and wanting to save the world from the criminals, was a bullshit pipe dream and that these idealistic principles were out of reach and could not be achieved. Someone always feeding them shit about lowering the crime rate, saving lives, helping citizens, being a friend to the community they worked in, relating to the people, or just making that positive difference so that they and they alone could make this a better world to live in, bullshit, just bullshit. These officers were all callused, hardened, cynical, opinionated police officers that had burned out and finally realized that this job was a thankless, depressing, marriage ending, life changing, psychological nightmare that had succeeded in making them lose sight of their reason for becoming a police officer and causing them to become totally insensitive to people and their needs as well as becoming dysfunctional.

Whether it was personal desire, television, books, personal contact, or first hand knowledge of what being a police officer entails, that inspired these officers to even attempt to make a difference was a non-existent, naïve, ridiculous notion, that had somehow seeped into their minds and made them want to become a police officer.

I have yet to meet someone that this job didn't change for the worse. Male or female, makes no difference, it will eat at your inner soul and become a cancer that grows and destroys your values, beliefs, well being, and inner truth and goodness that most of us are taught all of our early impressionable years. It tears apart the inner core of goodness that we all begin with and believe in.

I am being extremely critical and judgmental and although there are some moments of satisfaction, feelings of doing what is righteous and just, and being the good guy with the white hat, I still have a firm conviction that being a police officer in a large city will ruin and destroy even the strongest willed individual.

I became very prejudiced towards blacks after being on the streets only two weeks. Of course, I was exposed to these prejudices for two and a half years as a police cadet. I had several black acquaintances, but a nigger, spick, gook, white trash and crackers, were different. I had to work with and around this element and it took away all my goodness, good faith and innocence. I just happened to work in a mostly black area, district, with some Koreans and low class white people. I began to loathe, hate, and despise all of them. This hatred would follow me throughout my career. I was not alone, officers I worked alongside of had hatred to match mine and some surpassed my prejudices by leaps and bounds. It was a very sad state of affairs. I was confused in my early years as a police officer for I had been taught to care for and to love my fellow human beings. But I had this hatred welling up inside me that became more severe as my time on the streets passed.

Prejudice for me was an inner struggle of what is right or wrong, what should or should not be, but realistically was something I could not ignore as well as something I could not escape. I was at extreme odds with my inner self. The job had exposed me to things I had not only never seen, but also, never dreamed of or imagined I would experience and see in my lifetime.

Death, mutilation, rape, murder, hatred, a blatant disregard for human life, indifference, ignorance, poverty, sickness, ruined families, drugs, blood, guts, and any other evils that I had yet to and hoped never to have to experience as a police officer.

This was a different world. *Where in the hell was I? This is nothing like my home where I was born and raised, this isn't how I was taught to act and this is like nothing I had been exposed to the last twenty-one years of my life.* I often wondered.

This police department, and police work, had taken a reserved, quiet, naïve, kind and gentle young man and turned him into a macho, cocky, cynical, glory hunting, sometimes uncaring and hateful, racist, angry young white police officer. This police department put a badge on his chest above his heart, asked him to be good and kind, to do good things, and at the same time the experiences of police work ripped his heart and soul out of his body and still they asked him to preserve peace, care and act as a soldier of goodness, fairness and righteousness.

The end of my innocence had come. It would be an irrevocable change; I would struggle thru this my entire career.

THE ROOKIE

BALTIMORE, MARYLAND
1974

My very first experience being a new police officer in the Eastern District was exciting and scary. I was not to work alone yet. I had to work side by side with my F.T.O. or Field Training Officer. Officer Dave Brenner was my F.T.O. and he was an excellent teacher. He was efficient, proficient, and knew his job. He was very good with the pen and was able to write an officer out of trouble if it was warranted.

Dave had a three-week training program. Phase one consisted of Dave doing all the paper work, driving, report writing, arrests, drug recoveries, etc. He did nearly all the work. I didn't like that part very much; I was chomping at the bit to be a real cop.

Phase two, the second week, consisted of sharing all the work. I drove half the time, I wrote half the reports, I talked on the radio, etc. We were a team and shared all aspects of the job. I enjoyed that week. During phase two we developed a small phrase that would be utilized if an arrest were to be made. If I weren't sure if I had enough probable cause to arrest a subject I would look to Dave. If Dave said to me, "I think it's going to rain," that was my key to affect the arrest. It was fun, I liked that too.

The key phrase worked well the first few times, but one day at the corner of E. Eager St., and N. Wolfe St. I ran into a situation, a dilemma. We received a call for a disorderly subject. I like the disorderly charge, it was basically, *I've had enough of your shit, you have pissed me off, and you're under arrest!* As we arrived at the location I could hear the loud mouth before I exited the car. This citizen had a bad attitude, wouldn't shut his mouth and wouldn't quiet down. I continually attempted, in a calm voice, to settle down the irate man but he continued yelling and screaming at me and cursing. I stopped talking to the suspect and looked hard at Dave as if to say, "can I lock him up?" Dave slowly and nonchalantly shook his head, "no." The citizen continued his loud antics for several more minutes and I was feeling belittled, embarrassed, *how much shit did I have to take here?* I wondered.

The suspect would not stop, after another minute I was frustrated, angry, and wanted to lock up this shithead! Just as loudmouth started up again, I looked at Dave with disgust and having lost my patience I said angrily, "WELL DAVE! Is it going to FUCKING RAIN or NOT!" Dave looked at me as if he knew what was happening inside me, which he did, and quietly and smugly said, "Yes, I think it's going to rain." I eye fucked Dave then

I mumbled, "It's about fucking time." I grabbed the suspect forcibly and handcuffed him. He finally shut up. Dave was testing me to see what type of patience I had, he said later, "very little rookie!"

I didn't particularly enjoy arresting people unless they were dirt bags. If that was the case I had no qualms taking someone's freedom. I wasn't the gentlest arresting officer; I had a procedure I followed. Once I was certain that the suspect had to be arrested I quickly grabbed the suspect around the neck, put my foot behind them and knocked them off balance, put my knee on them to hold them down and then quickly cuffed them. This element of surprise worked well for me although it wasn't pretty. This procedure never failed me, not actually proper, but it was functional and safe. That was top priority on the street, keep safe.

I learned a hard and embarrassing lesson on the corner of Eager St. and Patterson Park Ave. I received a call for an assault. I eventually arrested a black male about twenty-five years old for assaulting his wife. I was standing on the corner awaiting the wagon to take my prisoner in for booking. The suspect became angry and began calling me, "one muvafucker after another," not shutting up! I was becoming increasingly angry also. I twisted the cuffs to cause more pain so as to shut up the suspect. As the cuffs were twisted the handcuff pushed against the wrist bone causing severe pain. The suspect just looked at me in defiance and smiled.

He continued to mouth off and pull away from me. I again retched the cuffs tighter to a point where I absolutely was certain there was an unbearable amount of pain. The suspect said nothing but I knew I was hurting him; he was standing on his toes. He again looked back at me in defiance and began to pull away, I was pissed I clicked the cuffs two more times; I couldn't get them to go any tighter. *I'll fix this smartass fuck; he thinks he's so fucking tough, let's see!* I looked this guy directly in the eyes, put my foot on his foot and twisted the cuffs as hard as I possibly could. *Fuck this bastard, how bad does he really think he is? I'll fix his ass!* I thought.

By now I knew that the suspect was in great pain. *Good, Fuck him!* I thought. As I looked at his face I could see the pain I was inflicting. The suspect didn't flinch. Then it happened. I looked directly at his face and I could see tears dripping from his eyes and down his face, tears of pain. He was a proud man, a stubborn man. I couldn't believe it, not a word, just tears.

At that moment I realized that this man was more determined and more of a real man than I could ever dream of being. He out classed me and I felt bad. *How could he handle the amount of pain I was doling out to him?* I thought a moment and realized I was nothing; I was a little mouse in this lion's shadow. I was a piece of shit, I wasn't professional and macho, I was being a chump! I was disgusted with myself for doing this to another human being, It mattered not that he assaulted his wife, I was wrong!

I reached back and gently released the cuffs to where they almost fell off. I rubbed his wrist as I placed the cuffs in front of the suspect so he would be more comfortable. I looked at him and said, "I'm sorry, I'm sorry, that wasn't right."

He and I never talked as we stood waiting for the wagon. He had, with NO words, merely his actions, caused me to feel belittled and embarrassed by my actions. *I'll never forget this.* I swore, and I never have.

The wagon man, Joe Slate, arrived and as I placed the suspect in the back of the wagon I explained the whole story to Joe. Joe had the knowledge, wisdom and reputation of being an excellent officer. He had worked the streets for many years. He said to me in his soft subtle voice, "You're learning Dan, you're learning son." I admired Joe. I did not however feel very good about myself. But, I had learned a valuable lesson, or should I say, was taught a valuable lesson by a man much stronger in character than I.

Catalytic Converter

Phase three of field training was by all means the most enjoyable of all phases. I was able to learn so much. I was also becoming comfortable being on the street and was really enjoying being a fresh new police officer.

Since Dave was one of the first Field Training Officers he received a lot of respect and clout. Here was an officer willing to take his time to train another officer how to survive on the street and how to properly function as a professional, a professional police officer. He underwent special training to make this grade. The title also had its perks. Every time a new police car was sent to the district it was usually given to a F.T.O. This was an honor, everyone wanted the newest car.

On this particular day, Dave and I were driving a brand new 1977 Ford LTD. It looked, smelled and drove, new. Dave is an excellent police officer but he doesn't know shit about cars or their workings. I knew something about cars. I definitely took advantage of this edge to pay Dave back for being so rough on me and making me rewrite an entire report because I scratched out one letter. It was payback time.

The night before our 8 a.m. to 4 p.m. shift I had been out drinking and had eaten cabbage, corned beef, beans and Mexican food. This mixed with the beer I consumed made me a very unpleasant person to be around each few minutes. The smell was horrible.

Dave was proud to be in the newest car and showed it off to the other officers. He was rubbing it in their faces, all in fun. We began to patrol our post and after approximately fifteen minutes I passed gas. Dave has severe allergies and always kept the windows closed and the air conditioner on high. This clears the air of allergens and continually recycles the air in the car. Okay for me, definitely not for Dave.

"What is that?" Dave blurted out. "What is what?" I answered, laughing in my head. I knew damn right well as to what he was referring. "That smell!" He said. "My God that's disgusting!" I had to think quickly, what was I going to say? "Oh yeah, that's the catalytic converter. It smells like sulfur when a new car is breaking in, also, if you run the car hard it smells too." "What's a Cadillac converter for?" Dave asked. "It's not a Cadillac converter, it's catalytic, it burns all the excess gas fumes, and it's good for the environment, its pollution control." I went on to explain that the converter is located under the car and that the fumes come up from under both sides. Dave quickly interrupted, "Quick, put your window up so the fumes don't get in." Of course I had just ripped another one and the smell was BAD.

Dave seemed to be dealing with the smells as I sporadically dropped the bombs on him. Finally I mellowed out for nearly a half hour, all was quiet. I could feel a monster brewing. I let loose! "Jesus Christ Dan, what's that thing called again?" "Catalytic converter, Dave". Meantime, this putrid smell is recycling itself thru the A/C vents and A/C system.

Ten minutes later the smell arrived once again. "That's it!" Dave screeched as he looked at me with his face all twisted like someone had stomped on his toes. "We're going to take this car to the police garage, this smell is terrible!" I played stupid as Dave attempted to explain to the mechanic that the Cadillac converter was malfunctioning, causing a horrible stomach turning odor. Dave knew the mechanic and immediately the car was placed onto the lift for inspection.

Ten minutes later the car was let down and the mechanic explained, as I had done earlier, that new cars with the converters have to break in and until then they smell like sulfur. Dave had no idea what sulfur smelled like and I knew this. Relieved and now knowledgeable we got into the new LTD and drove away. I couldn't resist! I was holding this one for over fifteen minutes. I farted. Dave's face cringed as he checked to make sure that all the windows were shut tight. He shook his head as his eyes began to water from the horrible odor.

Fifteen more minutes passed and I let go the worst one of all, after all these things were brewing all morning. Suddenly Dave yelled, "Fuck this new car! I can't stand this horrible fucking smell anymore! It's unbearable Dan, I'm shopping this fucking cesspool of a car!"

We took the car back downtown and put it in the shop. We were given a 1976 Pontiac Lemans. Of course as Dave was filling out the necessary paperwork I had a chance to take a well-deserved SHIT. All was well now. No more gas.

As we headed back to the Eastern District from downtown, Dave seemed content. He looked at me, I smiled and said, "Okay?' He smiled back and replied, "OKAY!"

Years later I confessed to Dave all that had taken place that day. I had set him up. He didn't talk to me for days, I laughed as long.

Cap'n Crunch

My first midnight shift was only my third month on the street. I worked three shifts. 8:00 a.m. to 4:00 p.m., 4:00 p.m. to Midnight, and Midnight to 8:00 a.m. The second shift was always my favorite because it was the busiest and most violent. Alcohol, drugs, the unemployment rate, and family pressures, combined with the large amount of citizens confined in the small area that consisted of the Eastern District and their poor surroundings, contributed to the excitement and violence of this shift. All these variables seemed to come together and erupt in a violent, busy shift. At times I would fill up two or more run sheets. Each run sheet contained sixteen calls for service that I had handled. It was crazy and exciting.

Usually in the summer months the excitement and large amount of calls would continue to spill into the midnight shift well past 2:00 a.m. when the bars closed. By 4:00 a.m. all was usually quiet no matter the weather. I would find out as the years passed that the morning shift was boring, all the upper echelon worked, no time for play. The citizens were either at work or still sleeping off the previous night's abuses. With all the bosses at work, this meant all business and no play. The 4:00 p.m. shift was extremely busy, and the midnight shift was usually quiet. The midnight shift would intimidate me and cause me to have a feeling of apprehension and fear for the first hour of each midnight shift. I would get nervous and feel uncomfortable. I feel it was the change from the hectic pace of the prior shift, then the quiet and solitude of the midnight shift causing a shift in gears both emotionally and mentally. I had more time to contemplate what I was doing, what might happen to me, and the dangers involved. On the other shifts I was to involved fighting crime and answering calls for service to stop and think of the repercussions, the repercussions of the job. Injury, violence and maybe death, could take me. Each midnight I was scared for a very short time, this fright didn't last long but each change of shifts to the midnight, it appeared. The same alleys I had chased bad guys thru and walked thru performing my duties on other shifts, seemed to hold hidden, imagined dangers. *What if someone was hiding up the alley and ambushed me? What if there was a bad guy lying in wait for me? What if I was shot or cut tonight? What if I die tonight?*

All these horrible thoughts would appear at the onset of the midnight shift. Why? I don't know. This occurred every year throughout my career, but only on the first night. I guess God was humbling me and making me aware that I was not invincible as I sometimes thought, that real danger lurked behind each corner or trashcan in each alley I passed thru.

On this particular night, I was working the midnight shift. I was about two weeks into the shift and was comfortable with my surroundings and was not apprehensive. The midnight also held its own life, as did the other two shifts. The quiet and solace of the early morning hours was at times soothing and relaxing. No hurry, no fast pace, just slow and easy. This was a time to reflect on the job, enjoy my partners, and interact with them with no interruptions.

We had a tight knit squad that cared for one another. We not only worked together, we socialized after work and became friends. Some of us became close friends. We enjoyed the same hobbies. We drank beer, shot our guns at the range, fished, rode motorcycles, attended parties at one another's homes and became a family of cops. A family not related, but held together by camaraderie, respect, and the fact that we all experienced the same pain, suffering, violence and excitement of working alongside one another in the most violent district in the city. As a family, we depended on one another.

We each patrolled an area six blocks by six blocks and were constantly with one another, especially on the busier shifts. We depended on one another for our safety. In a violent struggle, back up could save a life. We all were aware of this and we functioned as brothers. We functioned as a well-oiled machine, a crime-fighting machine. We shared everything. We knew each other's faults, strengths, fears, and work habits. We were brothers. Black or white didn't matter. There was no room for any type of racial hatred or tension. We were all the same. We were one. Very few, if any, prejudice or racial tensions existed between the white and black officers. Even with my prejudices slowly growing, they seemed nonexistent with black officers. I would have laid my life on the line for any officer, including a black officer. It made no matter to me of the officers color or sex.

On this unforgettable night shift, I was somewhat sleepy and felt drowsy. I was sleepy but awake. It was three a.m., I was driving slowly down Milton

Ave., South on Milton Ave. from East Preston St. As I approached East Biddle Street I thought I noticed something sitting in the middle of the street directly in front of me, just thru the intersection. It appeared to move. It was sitting on the center double line of the street. I wasn't sure what I was seeing and stopped to rub my eyes and to shake my head to clear it. As I peered up thru the windshield I saw this object move slightly, once again. *There! It moved again! What is it?* I thought bewildered.

I put the car in the park position and this noise caused the object to move again. It moved from left to right. *What was it?* I wondered. I exited the radio car and slowly and cautiously approached the object. It was a Cap'n Crunch cereal box. The box didn't move back and forth or move any distance, it just turned left then right. Then it was motionless. Each time I made a noise the Cap'n Crunch box again moved left then right, as if looking for something. I didn't move. I was perplexed as to the contents of this box. *It's not a rat. They can get out of anything. What could it be?* I again thought. I didn't move. It was 3 a.m., I was standing on the corner of Milton and Biddle Streets watching a damn cereal box. I wasn't touching it, no way!

I called for another unit to meet me. Harold and Lee showed up momentarily. They observed me standing in the middle of the street, twenty-five yards away from my car, watching a cereal box. "What are you doing Dan?" They asked warily and simultaneously. "SHHH." I pointed at the box and they too saw it move from right to left. They stepped back.

Since the midnight is sometimes boring, officers listen to the radio to hear what's happening. This night was no different and out of curiosity or just for the hell of it, officers ride by to see what is going on. Another car pulled up and stopped. Pat Henley observed three officers standing in the middle of the street, all watching a box. As Pat approached the box moved again. He slowed. Hearing me call for a car to meet me, two additional officers converged on the corner to see what might be happening. Charlie and Martin exited their radio cars and walked towards us three.

At this point there are five police cars stopped at this intersection all parked in different positions. Usually five police cars would occupy an intersection only if a shooting or violent crime had occurred or if a horrific vehicle accident had taken place there, only if we were all needed. Not this night. Five police cars and six seasoned police officers including one rookie, me, were cautiously standing around a cereal box. Cautiously watching to see what might be causing this box to turn left then right at any slight sound.

We had the box surrounded. Six flashlights shone on the box attempting to illuminate the contents. To illuminate us as to what made this box move in this manner but not moving in distance. The next time the box moved Charlie pulled out his revolver. Martin, who was black, jumped back. "Holy shit! What's in there?" He sounded scared. We all knew Martin believed in ghosts and we knew he was frightened. He moved back a few feet once again. "It's a ghost!" He exclaimed. "Jesus Christ Martin it's not a fucking ghost, it's a box" Said Lee. Charlie had his gun pointed at the box and stood there staring as he chewed on his pen. "Let's shoot the fucker!" Said Charlie. Charlie never seemed wrapped too tight to me. He was aloof and strange. This night it definitely showed. "This beats the shit out of me" Said Harold. "You guys are pussies". "It's a box, do you understand, a box!"

"Wait! Yelled Martin. "It's moving again." "Kill it quick!" The box had moved as we talked. It's as if the box knew we were staring and wondering. Staring, wondering and scared. Especially Martin. Suddenly, Lee said loudly, "Assholes!" Lee then reached down to grab the top of the box. All six officers stepped back in fear. Charlie cocked back the hammer on his revolver. "What are you doing Charlie, you asshole!" Pat said. "Shut up!" Came the reply.

The scene was set. Three a.m., the corner of Milton and Biddle Streets, five parked police cars, six seasoned police officers, with flashlights shining on one box, one officer with his gun drawn, another fearing a ghost lurked about, four more unaware of what to do or what was in store for them, stood around this unusual and perplexing cereal box arguing, bickering and looking absolutely ridiculous, looking absurd as we surrounded this Cap'n Crunch cereal box. *This is crazy! I can't believe this!* I thought.

Lee pulled the box completely off of its inhabitant. Four of us stepped back, Martin jumped back. The truth was out. The secret was exposed, the riddle solved. The box revealed a small black puppy. The puppy looked up at Lee, looked at us. Looked at us with sad eyes. The puppy seemed frozen except for his head turning. The same head turning that caused the box to move from side to side. The puppy looked at Lee as if to say, "Thank you! Thank you for pulling this fucked up box off my fucking head!"

The puppy had gotten its head stuck in the box. His body was still small but the head, being larger, was stuck. Each time the puppy heard a sound only its head moved causing the box to move from side to side also. The puppy had gotten tired from attempting to escape from Cap'n Crunch and his terrible box. He had given up trying to break away and was resting on the centerline of a busy street corner. The puppy was exhausted, tired and had evidently given up trying to escape the confines of the cereal box.

We all began laughing. "Put your gun away Charlie, it's only Snoopy." Said Lee. "You guys are such assholes! I can't believe this!" Said Harold. We all felt so stupid. It was one of those experiences when everyone feels stupid and idiotic. Six morons, imbeciles, we were. But we were morons and imbeciles together.

Together we were a family of dysfunctional police officers that stood surrounding a Cap'n Crunch cereal box at 3:00 in the morning for over ten minutes waiting to take whatever action necessary to protect each other. To protect each other from the sinister, Captain Crunch and his possessed little black puppy.

As I sat down in my radio car and looked at the recently vacated Cap'n Crunch cereal box lying in the gutter, I wondered what was in store for me. What did this job hold for my future? Would it be fun and good? Would it be bad and evil? I had no idea, but I had a gut feeling that I would look forward, maybe in anticipation, to whatever being a police officer would entail and would push my way. I was ready, willing, and able.

Darryl

Not all the experiences on the streets of Baltimore City are negative. I met numerous types of people who respected police officers. Some I tried to show the meaning of respect.

I was working a foot beat on East Oliver Street and walked up to a crowd of people, including women and children. I nodded my head and said hello. Some citizens turn their heads, some nod back discreetly for they fear that one of their peers would witness the fact that not only did they acknowledge a cop, but a white boy cop, like me. Most of the older people in the area still respected the badge and were glad to see me. As I walked past the crowd, swinging my nightstick, I heard a little person's voice, "Honky pig!" I stopped dead in my tracks and turned around to see why such a youngster would say that to me. Where did he hear that, I wondered? He's only five or six-years old. How could such a young boy have learned this racial hatred that existed, at such an early age? Why did it have to be this way?

I asked the boy if his mom was near. "Yeah." Was his reply. not a respectful reply, but with an attitude, an attitude intended for me. I looked up and saw a young black women, maybe twenty-five, also looking at me with a surprised look. When she realized what was said she immediately looked away from me and said to her son, that's not nice Darryl. I quickly spoke and asked her if I could walk up the street to the store with young Darryl. She said yes and I took this opinionated and prejudiced five-year-old up to the candy store.

As we were walking, I said to Darryl, "did you call me a honky pig because you know what it means, or just because you heard it on the street or in your house?" "I heard it!" He replied disrespectfully. His eyes were innocent looking and he appeared somewhat scared of me.

We walked into the store and I took him to the candy section. Pick out what you want son, I said. He didn't hesitate as he grabbed three different kinds of candy. I felt the racial gap narrowing between us when he asked me, "Do you like ice cream?" I replied with anticipation. "I sure do, why don't you get one of your favorites, and get one for me too?" We walked out of the store and we sat down on the steps of an abandoned row house across the street.

Darryl opened his ice cream as I was opening mine. He seemed to be watching my every move. As we sat there, I tried to explain to him that police officers are people too. That police officers pick this line of work to make a difference and to help. But sometimes that means arresting bad guys, people that have broken the law, and sometimes people he might care about and it really didn't matter what color their skin was.

Of course, trying to explain all this to a five-year-old is quite ridiculous and senseless. After all, as I sat there talking, I wondered if I knew what was happening in this world myself. I felt confused. His world was structured and safe. Mine, on the other hand, was full of sadness, death, violence, racism, loss and very few, good things. I just tried to be his friend and make him see me as something positive and friendly in his life, not a honky pig or someone to intimidate him.

I could see his mother down the street watching us. I helped him open his lollipop and we walked back to his mom. Darryl and I were hand in hand. It was somewhat nice to see his small black hand inside my large white hand.

The contrast was so very evident, but for that short walk in wasn't as obvious to me as it had been. My street learned prejudice seemed to subside and slightly diminish. I felt warmth inside that really opened my eyes to the sadness and senselessness of racial prejudice.

I said nothing to his mom as I let go of Darryl's hand. I looked at him and said, "Thanks for going to the store with me, it was fun." He glanced at me, then his mom, then back at me. Darryl said, "Thank you." But in a much kinder and softer voice then when we had first met. I smiled and walked away.

Days later I saw little Darryl standing on the street as I rode by in my radio car. He ran to the curb and waved to me while flashing a big smile. This little boy's actions had somehow started cutting through that thick, hard, seemingly impervious layer, of racial prejudice that I had adapted as a young white police officer in an all black neighborhood. I was the one that wanted to make a difference, but was it Darryl or I?

I went home that night and put Karen Carpenter's soft, soothing, melodic voice on the record player so I would be ready to face another day of not knowing what was it store for me, good, bad, or ugly. I stared at the wall and drank beers.

The tone arm didn't always hit the first song on the vinyl record. As I sat down in my chair I expected the first song to play, "We've Only Just Begun," But it wasn't meant to be. Instead, "Bless the Beast and The Children," began to play. "Bless the beast and the children; for in this word they have no choice, they have no voice." I sat back in my chair, replaying my experience with Darryl and felt warm and fuzzy. I had heard his voice that day; maybe it could change a few people for the better? May be it could change me? A good thing had happened to me today. I thought.

D.O.A

I was only on the street six months when I began to learn that all cops aren't

honest. I had heard that dishonest cops existed, but I didn't believe it. *All*

cops are honest, *right*? At least I thought they were.

It was only my third call that night and my fourth, D.O.A. call of my

career. *Dead on arrival*, meant just that. Usually when responding to that

type of call, I would find a dead body upon my arrival. Usually the cause of

death was of a nonviolent nature. Usually the body had not been discovered

for some time. On this particular call, the victim had hanged himself one

week earlier. It was summer, and the body had started to rot. In the summer

months when the temperatures are highest, the human body decomposes

and breaks down much faster than in the colder months and tends to smell

much worse.

I walked up the steps and was immediately taken aback at what I was

seeing, a giant! *This giant was eight feet tall!*, I thought to myself. The body

stretched from the ceiling to the floor, one huge, stretched out grotesque

form of a body. Each limb was swollen to nearly three times it's normal size

including the fingers and toes. It reminded me of a hot dog that was boiled to

long. It looked as if it would explode at any moment. The eyes were popping

out, as were the lips, there was no hair. I got closer. I was startled by a voice

coming from behind the plump, stinking corpse. "Don't touch him Shanahan!

He'll pop" said the medical examiner who was already there.

I couldn't believe it. I was amazed! The body smelled so bad I had my nose buried deep in my hat the entire time, attempting to mask the foul stench. The medical examiner noticed this and gave me some Vick's VapoRub. "What's this for?" I asked. "Put it in your nostrils."

Ok I thought! I put a small amount of the strong smelling rub up both nostrils. Suddenly, relief. I smelled no foul odor, just the comfortable familiar aromatic VapoRub my mom used to put on my chest when I was sick. *Cool, I learned something else, what a job,* I mumbled.

From then on I always carried Vick's VapoRub in my briefcase. No more sickening odors or stench filled houses, no more smelling dog shit in the back yards, no more mysterious smells from trash filled alleys. All of these offensive odors could now be handled, with just a little Vick's.

Some officers smoked cigars to mask the smells, others used Vick's or their own remedy. I didn't care as long as I could alleviate the nasty odors.

You cannot permanently alleviate the smell of a dead rotting body once the first smell makes it's mark in your brain. After I smelled my first dead body, the smell never erased itself from my memory; it would be this way the rest of my life. If I was exposed to that same odor, the odor of death, I knew something was dead somewhere. I can't explain it, it's a learned smell that never disappears from the memory. It is a one of a kind distinctive smell.

The medical examiner put the body into a large bag, a body bag. As we cut him down, I heard a pop. The skin had popped, the smell got heavier. I stopped in my tracks puked and ran downstairs, only to puke more outside. No VapoRub, cigar, or home remedy could mask that concentrated dead body smell along with the smell of body fluids that had been stored inside of the body for nearly a week in the summer heat.

Once outside as I was catching my breath and clearing the puke from my nose, I noticed an officer from another squad. *What was he doing here,* I thought, as I collected myself and wiped my eyes dry? It's unusual for an officer from another squad or sector to show up on such a boring call. This was a routine D.O.A., not a shooting or homicide.

"Hi Dan." He said, as he walked past me and into the house. It was Jim Johnson, a quiet cop from sector one. On a D.O.A call usually no other police officers appear or they stop by if it's a boring shift. *Just curiosity,* I thought, so I brushed it off. I thought he was just curious or maybe he knew the medical examiner and was stopping to say hi.

Harold Stanton pulled up about ten minutes later. Harold was one of my partners when I worked a 2-man car. He was in my squad. "Just riding by Dan, hey what's Johnson doing here?" He said, curtly and with an attitude. "I don't know Harold, why so shitty?"

They say they are stopping by out of boredom. Just stopping by to be curious and to see a dead body. Not so, these thieving bastards go through pockets, bureaus, clothing and belongings of the deceased and the entire house looking for loot, or anything small that they can steal. Such as money, rings, jewelry. They know they must get there as quickly as possible before the family arrives.

I couldn't believe it *police officers don't do that,* I thought in disgust. I then remembered that this same officer had been at the last two D.O.A calls I had responded to I assumed it was out of sheer curiosity and the excitement of death and seeing a dead body. *Shit, do these guys think I am a thief too? I'm not!*

"*No shit.*," I thought to myself. Harold drove off and so did Officer Johnson

upon seeing Harold arrive. They knew what the deal was, but not me.

I never let Johnson or any other officer from outside my squad enter

another house involving a dead body again. My squad may not have been

always thinking legally but we knew where to draw the line. Stealing

possessions from the dead and their families definitely crossed that Thin

Blue Line. How could someone do that to the dead? Especially a police

officer? *What a job . . .*

MY FIRST
YEARS . . .

Officer Daniel J. Shanahan
the Streets of Baltimore

Thanksgiving Day

My first year on the street I had seen a few dead bodies. I hadn't actually touched any yet and I certainly hadn't witnessed death in progress. I had yet to see a human being struggle to take their last few breathes of life, to see the fear in their eyes for they know they are on deaths doorstep, and to hear that death gurgle that sends chills down my spine.

It was Thanksgiving Day, 1976. I received a call for a family disturbance on Durham St. This street was also located in the Eastern District of Baltimore City. I arrived alone.

Thanksgiving to me was a day for family, a day to be with brothers and sisters and to be thankful for all we have. Also, to share, to love, and to reminisce about the fun and good times experienced as a family over the previous years. *This* was what Thanksgiving meant to *me*. This is what I was taught and lived, for as long as I could remember. Like Mother's Day it was a day to reflect on the wonderful mother I had, the wonderful family I had, and to thank God for blessing my family and me. Then I reached Durham St.

As I walked up the steps and into the row house, I could hear screaming and wailing. I heard shouting. I couldn't make out the words but a problem was brewing in this house on this Thanksgiving Day. I had no idea what to expect. I was nervous because I was fairly new to the crime-ridden streets of this district and because I had learned and witnessed many officers being injured, or even killed, handling family disturbance calls. As I walked thru the front vestibule and into the dining room I saw a table set for a nice Thanksgiving dinner with all the trimmings including something I had never seen before, collard greens.

Four people were yelling at one another, two were actually screaming incoherent words. "Quiet!" I yelled. I startled the four occupants; they had no idea I was there. "What's going on here, who called?" I asked in a loud tone. As I was speaking two men stepped aside clearing a space for me to see a young black male approximately thirty years of age sprawled face up on the kitchen floor. I immediately noticed, to my horror, a fourteen to sixteen inch butcher knife sticking out of this man's chest exactly where the heart is located. I knew it was a very large butcher knife by the length of the wooden handle that was protruding up from the flesh, approximately eight inches. His shirt was ripped open, his hands and legs were quivering. I immediately called for and ambulance and back up. I could see the knife moving slightly with the beat of the heart, the rhythm of a heart beating was quite noticeable. It was odd watching the knife handle move rhythmically back and forth with each beat of the dying man's heart. *Damn, this is strange, I cannot believe the size of that knife that must hurt, and this guy isn't going to live thru this.* I thought.

The victim was a black male but his complexion was actually light gray or charcoal looking. I knew that a black person turns this shade of gray when sick, dead, or dying. Just as white people turn pale white, no color is present. As I approached the quivering body, it jerked one time and then another. Then the victim took one big breath and gasped. His body became motionless. I could hear a gurgle, a death gurgle. It's a sickening low fading gurgle that I had never heard before. I didn't at all like it; it was unnerving. Suddenly there was no gurgle just an escaping of air like the last seconds of escaping air from a balloon before it's completely empty, quiet but constant. This, I would learn and experience again, was the last seconds of a dying human being's actions.

Blood was trickling out around this knife wound. *Not much blood,* I thought. I would also learn thru experience that a knife wound doesn't bleed much unless the knife is thrust in and out of the body forcefully and violently. Just one stick doesn't bleed much. The knife had been thrust thru this man's heart, killing him on Thanksgiving Day! This man had died before my rookie, virgin, new to the real world, naïve eyes. I guess it's true, death knows no boundaries or holidays. I was absolutely shocked and appalled by this sight, but also enthralled with experiencing the final moments of a dying man's life.

The ambulance arrived and the paramedics pronounced the victim D.O.A., dead on arrival. My back up arrived and began to calm the hysterical family members. I learned that the dead man's brother had stabbed his own flesh and blood in the heart with this monstrous butcher knife because they argued over who was to get the turkey legs. Turkey legs! This was unbelievably difficult for me to comprehend. *I can't believe this! Christ, its Thanksgiving Day! Don't these people know it's supposed to be a family day, a warm caring, and giving, family day! Shit, it's Thanksgiving Day! What the fuck!* I thought in amazement.

I have five brothers, we argue, but when one brother is in need, all of the brother's come running to his aide. We're at our best when things are at their worst. My brother Tommy always says. He's absolutely correct. To deliberately and savagely shove a sixteen inch butcher knife thru your own brother's heart was almost impossible for me to conceive, especially over a piece of meat and on this particular holiday.

I didn't handle the call. I was in a daze. I heard sounds, saw movements, but it was as if I wasn't present, wasn't present in that moment. I felt numb and confused. *Where am I? Is this the United States? Were my mom and dad wrong teaching me about loving, respecting, and caring for my brother's and family members? This is just like Mother's Day! Damn!* I talked and talked to myself trying to make sense of this scene. To make some sort of sense out of what the past fifteen minutes of being a police officer had dealt me. I just couldn't fathom this.

I would go on to experience violence and death almost on a daily basis throughout my fantastic career. These experiences change a person. Unbeknownst to me I was becoming, *dysfunctional to be functional*, I thought, *Dysfunctional to be functional? How true.*

I went home that Thanksgiving night after going to my mom's house and eating a fine turkey dinner. I was with my five brothers, their wives/ girlfriends, my mom and dad and my wife, Nancy. I was extremely quiet the entire time, *I* knew why. My family had no idea. I couldn't share the experience yet. We left earlier than usual. *Once again,* I stared at the wall, listened to the Carpenters on the headphones, drank beer, and made everything *right* again so I could go back to work the next day and be able to function and be able to do my job as best I could. This *was* the job, and *what* a job!

Mother's Day

I feel as though the incident that occurred in the 1200 block of North Washington St. was the final experience, incident that caused me to become totally and completely callused and indifferent to all I was to observe and experience throughout the remainder of my career. I cannot forget the incident that occurred on this particular Mother's Day.

I was now a veteran police officer of one year and three months. The call was broadcast as an assault report. *No big deal, just an assault report, I'll take my time.* I thought. It was 10:00 a.m. on Mother's Day. I was feeling good having just had breakfast and purchased a nice gift for my mother whom I have always been extremely close to. She is understanding but opinionated. She is my confidant and friend. She was often my support system as I learned of the real world, not the sheltered one I had lived in for my first eighteen years. The sheltered life that she and my dad had provided my five brothers and me.

I walked confidently but cautiously into the address on Washington St. I had a spring in my step and in my heart. I was happy this day. When I pushed open the partially opened front door what I observed I would never forget. At that moment the scene I was seeing burned itself into my lifelong memory quickly and forever. A women in her sixties, graying hair, small build, frail looking, curled up in a the fetal position lying next to a wheelchair, bleeding from her mouth and face, holding on to the phone handset. She was actually cradling this phone for dear life, or it seemed. Her clothes were ripped, exposing her small little bra. She had scratches on her upper chest and face. Also, her face was swollen. She had heard me enter and looked up slowly and cautiously as a dog looks up when it thinks it will be beaten again. She began an attempt to crawl towards me with her arms outstretched and her hands open to grab onto me. I noticed that her hands looked odd. Her fingers were bent in an unnatural way and they were crooked. I then realized that she belonged in the wheelchair. She wasn't screaming but she was moaning and wheezing. She was definitely upset, *had she fallen? Had her wheelchair broken and she fell to the ground?* I wondered. *What had happened here? Why was she all beaten? Maybe she had fallen out of her chair. No way.* I again told myself.

She had not fallen. After I picked her up and placed her back into her wheelchair I was able to settle her down enough to hear and understand the story of why she was in the condition she was in and how she had come to be on the floor, upon my arrival. I was to hear exactly what I didn't want to hear but I was unable to escape the inevitable.

Her drug addicted drunken son had beat her, knocked her to the ground, and kicked her because she refused to give him more money. Evidently she had been giving her son money and finally figured out what he was doing with the funds. She didn't like it and decided to say no, no more money! I was to learn that she could take the punches no more and handed her son a small amount of money. Evidently it wasn't enough for him. He grabbed her hands and twisted and pulled breaking four fingers on her right hand and three on the left, taking the small amount offered. He then took what remaining money she had from inside her bra after ripping her shirt. This was done, as she lay helpless on the floor after being forcibly thrown out of her much-needed wheelchair. She went on to explain that it took her nearly ten minutes to crawl to the phone to call 911 and get some help.

How, on Mother's Day, could a son do this to his mom? Where was I? Is this America? Am I in a different country, a different world? This is not what I had learned as I was growing up, it's not supposed to be this way! I was outraged, appalled and totally disgusted. I could not then, and still cannot now, comprehend how a son could commit these acts on his own mother, let alone on Mother's Day.

I had the elderly women taken to the hospital. After the ambulance left I was alone in the house for approximately five minutes. I was looking over the scene standing wondering, staring, and attempting to sort this out in my mind. My thoughts were interrupted by a black male about thirty-five years old, thin, unshaven and with very few teeth. "Who are you?" I asked "What are you doing here" he asked. Neither of us knew why the other was there. "I live here with my mom, where is she?" He asked. A surge ran thru my body. A surge of hatred, disgust, and revenge. "I'm her son." He stated. "Are you her only son or do you have a brother?" I asked indignantly. He stepped back and said, "I'm the only son, just me." He and I both knew why he had stepped back. I wanted a piece of his ass and he could see it in my eyes. I must have looked, as I had felt, furious. I glanced at his hands. The right hand was slightly swollen and had abrasions on the knuckles. The left hand seemed normal. *You bastard! You're mine asshole!* I thought. I grabbed him forcibly and handcuffed him. I immediately called for a paddy wagon to transport him to the Eastern District for booking. I did this for a good reason, a purely selfish reason. I had called for a paddy wagon as soon a possible so I wouldn't accidentally maim or kill this shit. I knew I would be beating him, a beating I felt was street justified, street justice at its best.

As I waited, I shoved his head into the wall, stomped on his toes with the heel of my boot, and twisted the handcuffs to cause as much pain as possible, for I had clicked them as tight as I could. I struck him several times in the ribs and shins with my nightstick. *I had to stop myself.* I thought. I was almost unable to cease with the brutality. He fell to the floor. I walked outside to await the arrival of the wagon. As I stood half in the doorway and half out in order to watch my suspect, I could see the wagon approaching. I looked at this piece of shit one more time, and I spit in his face and on him.

The wagon pulled up in front of the door I was standing in with the back doors open. I dragged the son of a bitch down the steps and threw him headfirst into the waiting paddy wagon. I was relieved when Joe Slate, the wagon man, closed and locked the wagon doors. *This was good! I couldn't get to this guy anymore. I couldn't get my hands on him to inflict more pain. Enough pain to equal the pain he had caused his mother, on Mother's Day!* I screamed in my head. Joe asked no questions about the suspect's condition after I explained the scenario to him. He too was infuriated.

On the way to the station to write the necessary paperwork for assault and attempting to maim, I stopped at the phone, located at Washington St. and Federal St. I stopped to call my mom. "Happy Mother's Day mom!" I said cheerfully, as my own mom answered the phone. "I love you mom." I then said. "Thanks Danny." Was her reply. What she said next caused tears to well up in my eyes, stream down my cheeks, and drip onto the phone and my shirt. "How's your day so far son?" All that I had experienced that past hour came rushing back to my memory. The sadness and disgust of it all leaped out of my memory to the forefront of my conscious thoughts. I paused briefly, covered the phone with my hand, sniffled, and replied, as upbeat sounding as I could, "Fine mom, fine." "I'll see you later tonight then son, I love you Danny." She said softly. I hung up the phone and sobbed quietly as I opened the car door. *I love you too mom.* I thought warmly. There was no spring in my step and no happiness for me the remainder of that day, Mother's Day.

Just A Kid

After the Mother's Day incident not much affected me, or so I thought. The occurrences on the street were exciting but I was now confident and comfortable working in the Eastern District, which was notorious for being the district with the highest crime rate in Baltimore City. I still had emotional ups and downs when a small child or elderly person was maimed or injured. They among *all* should be spared from the hatred and violence of a big city. I can vividly recall the twelve-year-old boy playing on the railroad tracks under the bridge on East Eager St.

There were several sets of tracks belonging to CSX and Amtrak railroads running under the bridge. The young boy had crossed the small field and was playing on the tracks. This is a common sight in the Eastern District. This, and kids playing in trash laden alleys, small streets and if fortunate enough to find a small grass plot, they would still be playing in broken bottles and glass. It was a given, no one thought twice about a child playing on the tracks.

Evidently this child had climbed up on top of a railroad car and inadvertently touched his head on the overhead main supply line, or had grabbed it with his hand. Since he was standing on a metal car, he was grounded. This wire carries thousands of volts of electricity to the powerful engines that pull the trains. The shock was so powerful he was immediately and savagely thrown to the ground.

When I arrived, his small limp body was still on fire and the Fire department was carefully extinguishing the flames. So much current passed thru his body that he was still smoking and smoldering almost twenty minutes later. I was amazed at the severe damage that the electricity had caused to this boy. His sneakers had melted off of him; there were no feet, just two charred stubs where his feet should have met his ankles. The power of the electricity had shot out of his extremities with such force that his hair was gone, his eyes were gone and his hands were gone. I stood there in amazement and horror. I had never seen this before, his body was shriveled and the stench of burned flesh permeated the air. It was a terrible stench, a smell that burns itself into your nostrils and brain, a smell I will never forget. Just like that of a decomposing body, After one experience the smell is always discernable no matter what length of time has passed since that first putrid smell embeds itself in your brain. I just stared at this sad sight and became unaware of what was transpiring around me. Suddenly I heard someone say, "here comes the mother." As the mother approached, I expected her to scream, become hysterical, and unmanageable. She did none of these; she just slowly knelt down next to her dead little boy and muttered something in his ear. I could not hear what she was saying to this charred, burned, horribly deformed body that was her twelve years old son, but my heart and soul were feeling her agony, her sorrow. I thought I had become hard and callused enough over the years that even this would not have an effect on me, it did and it was obvious.

After a few minutes she stood and looked directly in my eyes. I was becoming somewhat uneasy because she wouldn't look away. Finally she lowered her head to her chest and said softly, "he was twelve years old today, today is his birthday." Her eyes were looking thru me, into my heart, my soul, and she knew I cared; I was sharing in her pain. She then turned away from me and slowly stepped into the ambulance with her dead little boy. The ambulance had arrived unnoticed by me, for I was consumed by this sad and horrible scenario. I felt sick and queasy.

As the doors to the ambulance closed, I walked over to the railroad tracks, looked down to the ground and wept. *I hate this job,* I thought. *I should send flowers and attend his funeral,* I thought again. *Yeah, I should and would do that.* I never did, but I will never forget, I will never forget him. To this day I wish I knew what she had whispered so calmly to what remained of her little boy. I wish I knew.

A Monster

After the experiences of Mother's Day and Thanksgiving Day, I had numbness in my heart and soul, a numbness that I could not overcome or eliminate. For the next six months of my newfound career, I would see more dead and dying human beings than I ever imagined. The experiences would continue throughout my career but these six months seemed the worst for bloodshed and violence. The dead and suffering, the violence and disregard for life and everything connected to it, were definitely changing me as a person and also changing my perspective about the world and people, as well as my attitude towards the world and people. I felt like I was becoming a monster. I had no idea of the magnitude of what I was about to see and experience over the next eleven or more years as a Baltimore City Police Officer in the crime ridden, violent, and unforgiving, Eastern District.

The violence was unbelievably gruesome and gory. It seemed as though each incident became more violent than the last, but that really wasn't the case, it was just that I was in no way ready for that world, that world of indifference, death and sadness.

I pulled onto the northwest corner of East Lanvale St. and North Bradford St. to write an entry onto my run sheet, it was 7:00 p.m. The run sheet is a sheet that details the calls you are given during your shift, the location, the times these calls are received and finished, the nature of that call, and the outcome. This sheet is basically a history of each officer's eight-hour shift and his activities.

As I sat in my radio car writing, I heard a disturbance and happened to look up and see a man stumbling out of the front door of the bar, The Bradford Lounge. This man was holding his throat with both hands. The amount of blood spurting thru his fingers and out from under his hands was immense. I was nearly mesmerized. *Holy shit, I can't believe all this blood would come from one individual! What the hell happened to this guy?* I had never seen that much blood in my life! The blood was spewing out of his neck. His hands, fingers, neck, and the entire front of his shirt were soaked in blood as were his pants. It was a constant flow, not letting up or slowing. It kept squirting and spurting, squirting and spurting. The victim was pumping arterial blood. This type of blood is dark red and very thick. It coagulates quickly due to its thickness and because it comes from a major artery, not a vein or from a capillary, the much smaller vessels that carry our blood. This bleeding was continual, non-stop.

This unfortunate man collapsed about ten feet in front of me onto the sidewalk. I called for an ambulance and immediately ran to this man's aide. I had no idea what I was going to do. This man was seriously cut and was in dire straights. The straight razor incident flashed in my mind. *How had this man come to be so mortally wounded?* I wondered. I knelt beside the victim and applied direct pressure against this jagged, deep, grotesque wound. All I had for gauze was my handkerchief. The handkerchief was useless. It was like putting a band-aid on a blow out. The man gagged, choked, and gasped one last living breath. He died right then and there! That quick, a human being had died. That's it, just gone. He would never see his family and friends again, would never see his children. He was just . . . gone.

This all happened so quickly. I was not ready for what had transpired directly in front of me, transpired right before my very eyes. It's not unusual but it is infrequent for an officer to experience a crime that occurs directly in front of him. That was the case this night on East Lanvale St. at Bradford St. I had witnessed a homicide. One human being taking the life of another.

Suddenly, and as fast as the dead man walking had burst thru the front bar door, and once again without warning, the front door to the bar burst open. This time a black female came out thru the door yelling hysterically, "I loves him! I loves him! I cut his throat with a beer bottle because, I loves him!" In her hand was half a beer bottle that had been broken and had sharp, jagged, terrifying edges of glass protruding from it, edges of death, edges that were stained with blood, blood that was still dripping from the base.

It was this dead mans wife. She had cut his throat wide open with a broken beer bottle because she had caught him with another woman inside the bar. She had stuck a broken and jagged beer bottle into her husband's carotid artery. This is the main, or jugular vein. The vein that runs from your heart to your brain. The artery that supplies the major blood flow to the brain.

The murderess had uttered a Res Gestai statement, or outburst of what caused her husband's untimely death and demise, in front of, and, to me. This utterance was enough of a statement and was spoken clearly enough to me, that I was allowed by law to arrest her on the spot. On the spot where she murdered her husband and he gasped his last horrible blood gurgling breath. I immediately handcuffed her.

The paramedics arrived, looked around the victim's body in disbelief, saw the huge amount of thick blood surrounding the man's limp and dead body, and took only a few seconds to pronounce this man, D.O.A. or, as on Thanksgiving Day, dead on arrival. *Does this shit ever stop? Does this death and destruction ever take a fucking break? I need a fucking break!* I said to myself. The paramedics stood alongside the man's dead body and just shook their heads. I guess they too were amazed at the amount of blood spilled on the street, these mean streets of death.

As I stood at this deadly scene wondering and questioning what I had witnessed, I could see his blood, his life sustaining blood, running from this mans throat. It was as if all had quieted down and was allowing me to take this time to track this trail of blood with no interruptions or outside interference.

Time to watch the life flow out of this man and onto the sidewalk. I could see the path it had traversed after it left this man. I could see that the blood followed the crack in the sidewalk, backed up in a small pool shortly, flowed over the curb, and into the gutter. Then the thick dark red blood again became dammed as a twig, cigarette butt, beer bottle cap, or piece of dog shit stopped its flow momentarily. The blood slowed and pooled. It formed a puddle and pooled until the pressure of the blood continually pumping from the body behind it, broke thru this blood dam and then continued to travel its final few feet down into the sewer. I was amazed and could only correlate these last few inches of life giving blood flowing into the sewer, with the ending of this dead man's life. It too had just been washed into a sewer. Just as a piece of garbage would be washed or thrown unnecessarily into a sewer, this mans life was ended. He went into the sewer a dead man. This was sad.

This was very sad indeed, a sad and morbid scene. As the life flowed out of this man I feel a little life flowed out of me also. I had a blank stare on my face I felt little emotion and no sorrow. I was numb. The numbness overcame the death. It was also overcoming my feelings and me. I became cynical and unconcerned. *Let's see, she has lost her husband, the girlfriend lost a lover, the wife will spend many, many years in jail, his kids have no father, and this guy merely lost his life, merely his life. Gee! Poor Bastard.*

I gathered myself and looked up at the murder suspect, again, she muttered, "I loves him!" I looked at her in amazement. I could feel the anger welling up in me just as the blood welled up in front of the cigarette butt in the gutter. I grabbed this woman by her shirt, pulled her down forcefully to her knees close to her husband's lifeless and bloody corpse. I yelled, "You loves him? Look at Him! Yep! You really loves him! You asshole. You just fucking killed him! He's fuuucccking dead!" I know this was wrong but I could care less. I had something to say to this bitch and I was going to say it. *Piss on all of it!* I thought. I was incensed and it showed. I placed the suspect in my radio car to take her in for murdering her husband. As I drove away the morgue wagon was placing the dead man's body in the back of the wagon. He was zipped up inside a body bag. *No more worries for him,* I thought. *No more worries indeed, fuck it . . .*

I was becoming hard and callused. I was becoming dysfunctional to be functional. As I mentioned, I was becoming a monster. A monster that was uncaring, unconcerned for others, but also a monster who was developing a voracious appetite for this job and the violence it afforded me. The death I was seeing was so interesting and appealing I was thirsting for it. People were killing and maiming each other and I was sitting by watching. The police department had given me a front row seat with an unobstructed view.

She received a twenty-year sentence for manslaughter. I would remember the look on this dying man's face as his eyes searched my face and quickly found my eyes and his opened wide, as if to ask me if he was going to die, he did. His look, *I* would remember, for twenty years.

Taking Down Doors

Sometimes on the city streets, we as police officers, have to laugh at ourselves. I was only on the streets three weeks or so when this situation presented itself to my coworkers and me. I was feeling at ease, was learning my streets and directions. I actually showed up as a back up unit and found the proper street by myself. It's quite embarrassing when a hot call comes out over the radio, or another officer calls for assistance and in your eagerness to help or just get involved you go to the wrong street.

When a call is broadcast and you know you're close to the location you mentally picture the street, if you've handled a call there before you instantly map out the route and go. Sometimes, you inadvertently map out the wrong street. Some look alike and it can be confusing.

Several times in my early career I've driven to the address broadcast and was the first one there. I advise the dispatcher I'm "10-23, or have arrived," and I become full of myself because I found it by myself and was there first! You talk to yourself constantly, *Ain't I something! I'm the first one here! I know my streets! Yippee!* I walk up to the address and when the door opens I ask the occupant if they called the police. "No officer, no one called." I immediately go back on the radio. "Dispatcher, no one called at 2200 E. Biddle St." Always, always, one of the other officers in the squad would get on the radio for everyone to hear and say, "Hey Dan, you turned onto 2200 Oliver St., not Biddle St., I was behind you when you turned off, thought you knew a shortcut, ROOKIE!"

Of course you don't answer back, you just keep quiet and tuck your rookie tail between your legs and slowly drive a block or so to the proper location, now being the last one to arrive. Everyone points and laughs at you for they too have experienced and suffered thru the same embarrassment when new to the streets. You have to laugh at your shortcomings and misgivings. It eases the tension and stress.

I think in every young, aggressive, police officer's career that deep down inside they can't wait to kick in someone's door, not with a battering ram but with your body, feet, and shoulders, The MACHO way. Just can't wait to kick that door completely off the hinges the very first attempt, the manly way.

My first month or two on the streets I normally rode with Lee or Harold. They were experienced and had the desire to help the F.N.G's, (fucking new guys). My second month on the street I was feeling extra tough and macho and really wanted to take down my first door. I had this burning desire to obliterate a door and my entire squad knew it. I was beginning to become one of the boys now. I was slowly proving myself. I had on several previous occasions been on calls where we had to take a door down or it was okay to go thru a door. Chasing a suspect, serving a warrant, or on a drug raid. I really enjoyed watching the other officers kicking the doors down. It was rough, tough, cool, macho, kick ass good stuff. I was infatuated. I must kick in a door or use my entire body to flatten one. I absolutely had to do it myself, no help just ME!

2400 block of Ashland Ave., warrant for armed hold-up suspect, and information that the hold up suspect was in the house. My post! I get to do the honors. My entire squad knew I was about to take down my first door. Several other coworkers arrived at the location because they had heard the call and knew of my excitement to prove myself by kicking in a door for the very first time.

This is it! We all met one half block away, around the corner. We planned our strategy, passed around the suspect's picture and off we went. I was to pull in front of the address, but across the street, exit the radio car and run up the three marble steps and *kill* the door. The officers in my squad would come running directly behind me and enter the house to affect the arrest. Good plan. I was more excited about the door killing than I was about capturing the hold-up suspect.

I pulled my radio car in front of the address, exited and ran in front of the radio car. I was double-checking to make sure I had the proper house, I did. I ran across the narrow street, up the sidewalk and up the steps. Most row houses in the Eastern District have three white marble steps leading to the front door, a vestibule, or landing, then the first floor of the dwelling is one step up from the vestibule. I bounded up the steps, pounced onto the marble step landing, put my right shoulder down and hit the door with all my might. All my excitement was in that forceful blow.

No one had given me directions on how to hit a door. I was supposed to hit the side of the door with the doorknob on it; it was much weaker than the side I hit, the side with the three hinges, which held all the strength of the door. I bounced off the door, fell down the steps and flopped onto the sidewalk, sideways. Fortunately, no officers were behind me, in my haste to be macho and to prove myself I had forgotten to wait for my helpers, the officers who were supposed to enter behind me and make the arrest. They were still getting out of their cars. The suspect ran out the back door and was arrested, certainly not by me. I was still on the sidewalk wondering who hit me with the door. As I looked up from the sidewalk I could see my three co-workers hanging onto their car doors doubled over laughing. Lee and Harold had tears in their eyes from witnessing what I had just done. Two other buddies were standing over me telling me wisely that I hit the wrong side of the door and that this story would most definitely follow me throughout my career. I was the laughing stock of the squad, no doubt.

After another officer arrested the suspect, I took control of the suspect and placed him into the paddy wagon for transport to the district. I walked to the driver's door of the wagon to talk to the wagon man, Joe. As I was speaking to Joe, I noticed that soda had been splattered all over the windshield and dash of the wagon. Soda was everywhere! I had to ask, "What the hell happened Joe, spill your soda responding to my call?" I snickered. My answer, "No Dan, you asshole, I had just taken a big drink of my soda when you ran up those steps. You came back down so fast and looked so fucking stupid I choked on my soda and spit it all over the windshield and dash after it came out my nose! He pulled away laughing hysterically. *Real funny! Ha! Ha! You dick!* I thought.

It wasn't long after this horrible disaster I was to have my second chance at kicking in a door. *It would be done right this time, I know it!* I said to myself. It was on my post once again; therefore I was to handle the arrest, therefore MY DOOR!

Once again we met around the corner from the house in question. This time it was a drug raid. Officers would go thru the back door and thru the front door at exactly the same moment. This would confuse the occupants giving us the element of surprise. All this would be done over the radio. I would give the okay and all would proceed. As I was going up the steps I was to notify the officers in the rear to proceed. Three officers would be directly

behind me. We were to go thru the door, split up as quickly as possible to

cover all areas of the house, and make arrests.

I would be the first in the door, Lee behind me, Harold behind Lee, and

Pat behind Harold. Four men acting as one battering ram all going into the

house simultaneously, as a team of one. All within close proximity of each

other, all acting as one.

All four of us walked to the house to be raided. It was on the corner of

Washington St., and Eager St. As we came closer Harold said, "Go ahead

Dan, we'll be right behind you, you go for it Danny Boy!" I broke into a trot,

then a full run. My three comrades were less than five feet behind me. One

well oiled piece of equipment, four men acting as one! I continued to run,

as I cleared the curb, I had a surge of energy; a burst of adrenaline hit me. I

was, beyond a doubt, going to redeem myself and take down this door, No,

I was going to hit this door so hard I was going to take it completely off its

hinges, and destroy the doorframe in the process.

I cleared the first step with ease; I could have bounded over anything

at that point. In my haste and excitement I skipped the second step and

landed solidly on the top step landing. *Okay Dan, you got it, hit that door!*

Go for it. I said to myself with encouragement. There we were four officers

molded into one force, ready to take down this door and complete this drug

raid successfully. Suddenly, I tripped on the landing, and fell into the door.

"OHHH SHIT"! I yelled aloud. I felt Harold fall onto my back, and then Lee

fell onto Harold and onto me, Pat finally lost his balance and fell onto Lee.

There we were, all four of us lying in all different positions all over these three steps and landing. Pat was actually on the sidewalk on his back. "Jesus Christ Danny! Jesus Christ! Shit! What the Fuck!" Everyone had something nasty to say but me. I was quiet, very quiet. I just lay there saying nothing waiting for Harold and Lee to get off of me, and get up.

They were all pissed off at me, especially Pat; He hated being made a fool of. About ten to twelve bystanders witnessed this fiasco, this chaos. They were laughing as we all unraveled and attempted to regain our composure. It wasn't going to happen, not THIS day. I felt so very bad. I would eventually get a chance to go thru a door, but only with help and a battering ram, also, I was usually alone or with just one officer, go figure!

I will not soon forget the scene of three experienced police officers, one rookie, me, flopping around all over these steps trying to get into a house, trying to, *take down a door*.

A Little Fun

There are times when police officers break thru the sadness and stress of the job by having a little fun. Pat Henley and I had been working together for six months. We were full of ourselves. New partners, own car, shotgun, 100% police officer, worked hard, and were completely enthralled and pleased with being rookie patrolmen in the Eastern District.

It was January we were working the day shift. Pat and I were bored. We drove off our post and out of the Eastern District boundaries to the Jeppi Nut Company located in the Central District. We purchased 2 pounds of red pistachio nuts. We quickly drove back to our proper place in the city. We turned our hats upside down and over the hours we shelled and ate both pounds of nuts, saving all the empty shells in our hats. There were hundreds of broken in two red pistachio nut casings in our respective police hats.

As we drove around our post we pondered what to do with all those red shells. "Something productive could be done with these, throwing them away would be boring and a waste. We must be productive." I told Pat. Pat agreed and we decided after much deliberation to play a prank on our best friends and teachers, Harold Stanton and Lee Gregory. They were working 335 car, the post next to Pat's and mine.

Harold and Lee were constantly playing pranks on us and other unsuspecting young officers. They would drive the young officer's radio car around the corner from where a call was being handled, *if* one of us left the keys in the ignition. An officer would leave the location of his last call only to come out of the house to find his radio car GONE! This is a very lonely and empty moment. Losing a radio car or you gun was a very bad scenario not to mention embarrassing. No officer wants that reputation. They would rip reports in half if left unattended or just sitting on the seat. This also was a lesson to us not to leave the keys in our cars or the doors and windows open or unlocked. These two, referred to as Batman and Robin, were the pranksters of the squad as well as two of the best police officers I had a chance to work with. Our squad was full of heroes as well as brave, dedicated, helpful and excellent police officers.

It was now payback time! Pat and I called for 335 car to meet us behind the Super Pride Supermarket located at Patterson Park Ave. and Chase St.

Most of us slept behind this market during the midnight shift or if we were bored. We all met there after leaving roll call to drink our sodas, coffee, or occasional beer. Each day at the beginning of the shift one of us was appointed to pick up the drinks and to 10-11, or meet, behind the Super Pride. We ate our free Chinese food we picked up at Jimmy's Chinese store located at Hoffman and Milton Ave. We also drank beer, pissed on the walls, met women or removed our gun belts and threw them on the hood of the radio car when the belt seemed extra heavy. We would straighten ourselves out and tuck our shirts in and brush ourselves off so we could take a deep breath and get back to saving the world and chasing bad guys. Super Pride was our general hangout.

After I left the department I would sometimes stop at Jimmy's, buy some Chinese, and pull my personal car to the same spot I used to park. I would sit there and recall all the fun, danger, and exciting times. I missed it so. I haven't been there in a year. I still go there. Life without the Badge is difficult for me.

As Harold and Lee pulled onto the front parking lot, Pat and I both exited our radio car so the two pranksters couldn't pull their radio car very close to ours as we usually did to talk about a call or to bullshit between calls. As usual Pat walked over to Harold's side of the car and I was at Lee's car door. Both had their windows completely open. Pat and I had our upside down hats on the roof out of the unsuspecting view of Harold and Lee. Pat nodded at me and we both quickly threw all of our shells into the radio car. We scattered them on Lee and Harold, on the dash, on the back seat, and as we left, in a hurry, shook our hats onto the hood of the car, making certain they were empty, every last shell was on or in their car. Pat ran around the front of our car, I jumped into my seat. The entire time we were singing, "Frosty the Snowman."

Before we sped away we threw two snowballs in the car. The snowballs had a few carefully placed red pistachio shells embedded all around them. We made our getaway laughing and snorting, giggling and screaming, like two little girls excited about going to a rock concert.

We weren't bored any longer but we had to find a place to hide in the foot and half of snow we were playing in, it had snowed all the previous night and most of the morning.

We continued to laugh as we opened the door to the firehouse located on North Collington Ave. and slid our radio car out of sight, just in case. We always stopped by to check on the firefighters and to say hello. We told them about our triumphant scheme they too laughed as we did for minutes. Police officers and firefighters have a closeness. We look out for one another. We work in the worst areas and handle the worst of calls for service from the public. Just as nurses, we have a special link to one another, a special camaraderie.

We left the firehouse after thirty minutes with tears in our eyes and with certainty that the victims were in the station house basement vacuuming out their car and cleaning themselves up. Getting DE-PISTACHIOED!

As Pat and I rode around our post warily, I said to Pat, "We better be careful, I'm sure they're going to get us back, I'm certain of it." Pat agreed and we sneaked around for over an hour. Looking and laughing, looking and laughing.

"336," came the call. "336 go." I answered. "Respond to North and Gay Sts. For a bogus check at the Dept. of Social Services." "10-4 dispatcher." I replied. We arrived minutes later. As we closed the doors I reminded Pat of our dirty deed. We both double checked to make sure that all doors and windows were completely closed, locked, and secure. I also made sure that the emergency brake was set and that the car was in park. We entered the building to handle the bad check call with a confidence and a smugness of two smart-ass, cocky, rookie patrolmen. We were safe.

Twenty minute passed as we handled the call. As we left the Social Services call, I happened to look over to our radio car. Something was amiss. The windows were white. All the windows were fogged up or just plain white. Pat and I were puzzled. *We* looked white. "Fogged up Pat?" was my query. "Looks like they're fogged up Dan." Came Pat's curious sounding reply.

As we came closer to the car it was obvious that the windows were white, but how, when? My mouth fell open as we closed in on the car. The entire inside of the car was filled with fresh snow. Front windows, back, and side windows, were entirely white. The snow was piled up on the rear and fronts seats and the dash was snow covered as well. The snow went up to the headliner! The inside of the car was one big fucking snowball! "The doors are still locked Pat!" I said. "Holy shit Dan, how did they do this?" Pat uttered. "My briefcase was wide open with my reports, run sheets along with everything else we have!" I yelled. "Those rotten bastards!" said Pat. "Fuckers," said I. We were astounded, pissed off, and perplexed all in one moment.

I noticed one other piece of evidence as to who perpetrated this dastardly crime against us! Two small red pistachio shells pushed up against the glass being held there by a handful of snow. We were most definitely paid back by Batman and Robin. "This was the best payback of all times. One for the books" Pat said. I just stared at the radio car in disbelief. "Fuck Frosty the Snowman! Let's find some shovels Pat." I was pissed.

A loud siren blast shattered our complaints and cursing. Pat and I simultaneously looked up the street. Harold and Lee were leaning against the front of their radio car. Lee was swinging a set of car keys. Harold was doubled over laughing. They had witnessed the entire payback from a close distance.

They had gone into the station to clean their car out and decided to call the sergeant and ask for the spare set of car keys that belonged to our car. While we were handling our call for service this payback was fiendishly carried out with two shovels from the station.

The smart-ass, cocky, not to be foiled rookies were ruined, devastated and the brunt of many jokes over the next few days. But, we had *a little fun* being laughed at. *What a job!*

Nicole Hopkins

A cold wintry day, February 5, 1978. I was patrolling my post, which encompassed a six block by six-block area. 336 post was one of the busier cars in sector three. 334 car, 335 car, the shotgun 2 manned car, and 336 car were the posts in sector three with the highest crime rates and the most activity. Drug sales, murders, rapes, armed robberies and any other type of violent crime that existed, existed on these three posts. Actually, sector three of the Eastern District was notorious and well known for its violence and high level of criminal activity.

This was a perfect area to learn how to become a good cop, how to handle any situation that may arise, and most assuredly, how to survive on these mean streets, including how to stay alive, not to, as we used to say, "not wake up dead."

On the southern boundary of my post was E. Madison St., the Northern boundary was E. Biddle St., the Western was N. Broadway, and the far Eastern boundary of my active and violent post was N. Milton Ave. This six block square area also included such streets as; Ashland Ave., Chapel St., Chase St., Chester St., Federal St., Duncan St., Lanvale St., Lafayette St., and one street that will never escape my memory of being a policeman, the 900 block of N. Castle St., yes, the 900 block of N. Castle St.

The fifth day of February was a very cold day. I was slowly patrolling my post, it was approximately 10 a.m. I was sent to the above location to investigate the problem. As usual, this call could entail any sort of situation from a shooting/stabbing, to a woman being locked out of her parked automobile. An officer never knows what to expect.

I acknowledged receiving the call from the dispatcher and pulled into the 900 block of N. Castle St. It was cold but clear that morning. As I exited my radio car I looked around for someone or something out of the ordinary, or, just someone. I observed 335 car pull into the opposite end of this long narrow street. I waved, Harold waved back. We each knew the other was there in case of a problem. My actions were slow paced that morning, even though I was in a laid back mode I still was alert, aware, and wary.

I never knew what lurked around corners and alleys in the Eastern District that was part of the excitement and thrill of the job. It could be danger or nothing at all, I never knew.

Harold began to walk to the rear of the Eastside of Castle St. I slowly walked thru the alley and to the rear of the Westside of Castle St. The alley was strewn with trash. Trash bags, soda and beer cans, empty food containers, old mattresses, headboards, box springs, and some items I couldn't recognize. Dog, cat and rat shit were everywhere I looked.

It was a slow process trudging thru these alleyways, even in the light of day, not to mention the difficulty at night. It was a major accomplishment traversing these alleys in the darkness of night while chasing a suspect and not knowing where we were going, or where we would end up. The suspect knows the route he is taking but the pursuing officer does not. Just keep running, dodging the piles of dog shit, trash cans, garbage, and hope not to fall or stumble into the small alley full of waste and shit.

I became frustrated walking thru this crap because I could find no one needing assistance or no crimes occurring. I was disappointed. I began kicking cans and bottles as I slowly turned and headed back in the direction I came from, being careful to avoid the various types of shit at my feet.

Suddenly, something moved and quickly caught my eye. A bag, a small brown paper bag. *There it was again, it moved.* I thought. It moved slightly once more. This time I was certain. *Must be a fucking rat, or hopefully it's a cat, I hate cats. Yeah probably a big fucking dirty disgusting RAT. This place is full of rats and full of SHIT.* I thought in disgust. *That's why I wear army boots with extra thick tire tread soles.* I said to myself. *To walk and run thru these alleys of*

putrid smells and nasty garbage without slipping and sliding and falling on my ass.
I stopped and studied the bag. It was a grocery bag and it was neatly closed,
folded nicely. *Why is that? Why would this clean bag be neatly sealed yet be lying
in this dirty filthy shithole?* I was perplexed.

The bag moved again. "FUCK THIS." I yelled in exasperation. I pulled
my right foot back and with the force of a pissed off, bored, walking in dog
and rat shit young cop, I kicked the bag which I was certain contained a rat,
mouse or cat, thru the goal post of heaven, approximately ten feet up the
alley of shit. *Aah, that feels better, not such a bad day after all.* I thought happily.
I walked the ten feet looking to kick the bag again for nothing had exited or
made any type of noise from my wondrous kick. As I approached to kick
the bag once again, for I had every intention of playing football with this
supposed RAT for several yards and satisfying field goals. What I observed
and witnessed at that moment caused me to crumple and fall to my knees,
to all fours, into that disgusting alley of shit.

I was astonished, astounded, appalled, and became flushed and numb.
I felt so very, very bad. They're moving ever so slowly was a small, frail,
tiny, pale human hand, an INFANT'S hand. I, ME, had just kicked, with
vengeance and anger, the small limp body of a new born baby, ten feet up
the alley from hell, rat mouse, filth, and shit hell.

My eyes widened my heart skipped a beat as I ripped open this brown
bag. This beautiful, brown, neatly folded, makeshift crib for this innocent,
quiet unsuspecting newborn. As I gently tore open the bag, I had conjured
up pictures of horror, make believe scenarios in my mind of what I would
see as the bag unfolded. Pictures from a hardened, sinister, cop mind. *Was*

the baby dead! Was it mangled! Was it bleeding! Did I break bones! Did I, ME, harm this poor infant? Please be alive! Please Dear Lord, Please.

As the bag opened completely, roaches scurried out of the bag, one came out of this little angel's mouth. I finished opening the bag and more roaches ran out. I nearly puked. I hadn't been on the street but a year or more. Yes, I had seen some horrible, violent sights, but this wasn't violent or extremely dangerous and bloody, this was heart wrenching.

All the angry thoughts and feelings drained from my mind and body. I felt like I did when I witnessed my first killing of a baby deer. As I watched the life flow from this beautiful creature I felt emptiness, sadness. That passed as I left the hunting area that evening and especially when I ate deer stew and venison that night. Those feelings and thoughts passed. But this! This did not compare. The deer paled in comparison to finding this newly born infant in a brown paper bag, in an alley, in fifteen-degree cold February weather, in THAT alley. THIS WOULD NEVER PASS!

I felt my heart drop onto the ground and shatter into small pieces, small crying, disbelieving, hurting pieces of my heart surrounded this miracle from God, this infant in the alley.

I gently pulled the infant from the bag. The warmth coming off the infant in the dirty towel clashed with the cold February air and caused steam to encompass this baby. The umbilical cord was still attached to this dying infant. The cord was still leaking fluid. Neither it, nor the baby was warm.

The baby was light charcoal in color, not black, as it should be. White people turn white when sick and pale, blacks appear light gray or charcoal in appearance. This beautiful being was light gray and cold. Still, no cries, no tears, nothing. It just lay there quietly and seldom moved. I became mesmerized watching her.

I quickly snapped out of my feelings of being alone and peaceful as if sitting in church and realized I must act and act immediately. I called over the radio to Harold. "Harold 10-11 me in the rear alley behind 914 N. Castle St., I've found a baby"! No answer! "Dispatcher, give me an ambulance here"! "10-4, 336". I waited for which seemed minutes, hours, to hear a siren, nothing! *DAMN!*

I had the baby stuffed inside my reefer, my long woolen winter police coat. I waited, waited and waited. Time dragged, I guess due to my amazing find, time was distorted, minutes seemed like forever. I couldn't stand it! *You cannot wait Dan! Where's Harold? What should I do? I know! I'll RUN! Yeah, RUN DAN RUN!* I ran to save an innocent new life.

I was aware that I was very near to Hopkins Hospital Emergency Room; it was only four to five blocks away. I wasn't waiting. I jumped to my feet, bag and baby in arms, tucked the two-foot umbilical cord into my coat and pulled the baby close to my chest. I ran south on Castle St., West on Ashland Ave., to Broadway and right into the emergency room at Broadway and Monument Sts. I left my radio car and Harold behind.

I didn't think of much as I ran, I only hoped that this little one would survive. *How long had this infant been in that alley? Who was the mom? Why would a mother discard her baby? I don't know this world, I don't like it either! It's so cruel, violent, uncaring and unforgiving! This is not a good experience.* I thought.

I burst into the Emergency Room at Hopkins Hospital. Two ER nurse friends of mine, Ann and Ann quickly looked up at me searching me and my body with their eyes. They were experienced, professional nurses I was out of breath, was gasping for air, and could barely talk. They waited. They searched for injuries, problems, and any medical emergency. They found none. "What Danny! What's wrong?"

I ripped open my coat and everyone in the Emergency Room gasped. "A baby! I found this baby in the alley in a bag!" I blurted out. I was nervous and excited. Someone said, "Oh my God!" and the infant was quickly removed from my arms and the warmth of my chest. The baby was taken away in a hurry.

I didn't see the baby for an hour or so. I was left alone and felt abandoned. *That's okay; they're fixing the newborn baby.* I said to myself. During that hour or so I discovered that Harold was talking to a citizen about a young woman and a baby, he had not heard me. I then realized that this baby might not survive. *It was fifteen degrees outside and it was February, how could a newborn, less than an hour old, survives these elements?* I worried.

After nearly an hour and a half I was called to respond back to the hospital. I had walked the five blocks back to my car because I needed the time to contemplate and decipher what had just happened to me, what I had just experienced and how I was going to deal with this atrocity.

As I walked into the neonatal section of Hopkins Hospital I suddenly heard someone yell, "Look there's the dad, the father!" I spun around to look behind me. I wanted desperately to find the dad. If I found him, then I could find and prosecute this so called mother. I wanted her badly. How dare she do something like this? It was totally unacceptable.

As I turned a camera flash went off and bright TV lights illuminated the entire room. *Where is the dad? I want to see him too! Where is he!* I wondered.

"You're the dad, Officer Shanahan!" Said one of the reporters. I laughed. I guess I was the dad. "We named her," NICOLE HOPKINS," said Ann, one of my friends. "Why that name?" I asked. We named her Nicole, which is like nickel, because it was the fifth of the month, and Hopkins because of the hospital. "Nicole Hopkins? "I like it Ann."

I made the news that night and the papers the next day. I was a hero for a very short time, and I liked it! Over the next month or so I put approximately $200.00 of my own money on the street to find Nicole's mother. Twenty dollars here, forty dollars there. I went to all my snitches and stoolies. Nothing turned up. I even told suspects I was about to lock up for misdemeanors, that I would let them go if they knew whom the mother was or could find her for me. This too was to no avail. I was upset, I tried so hard to find the animal that dropped this baby in an alley, not just any alley, thee alley, thee alley of shit and disgust.

Nicole Hopkins will always be in my memory and will always own a piece of my heart. She must have reached down and grabbed a small piece as I whooshed her out of that alley of death. Are you out there Nicole?

Tiny

There existed an ominous and frightening figure that lived in the Eastern District. His nickname was Tiny. I never learned his real name, but Tiny was definitely not small. Tiny was black, as most all the residents of my post were. He had a very dark complexion, stood 6'6" tall, and weighed all of 380 lbs. He was large! He loomed over everyone.

I would see Tiny quite often as I patrolled my post, for Tiny lived on my post. He had a nasty look about him and I never saw him smile. He would watch me every time I rode by, never breaking his stare. He was intimidating. I say at times that a police officer cannot allow someone to intimidate him, or let someone know you're intimidated or fearful of them. Tiny scared me. Each time I saw him I prayed that I would not have to confront him.

The call came out as investigate the man selling drugs at Eager and Duncan Streets. No big deal, just another drug call, or so I thought. As I rounded the corner onto Eager Street, this call became a *big* problem. It was Tiny on the corner. "Oh shit not Tiny."

I stopped my radio car and exited. I knew Tiny wouldn't run, he couldn't, he was too large. I walked up to him with my nightstick in my hand and ready to grab my radio and call for help. All I could picture is this behemoth, throwing me over the top of my radio car and leaving me in the street wearing my own handcuffs. "You're Tiny, right?," I said in my deepest manly voice. "Yeah" was all he said, or maybe it was a grunt. I didn't care I wanted to leave, maybe he'll let me live through this I thought. "My name is Officer Shanahan," I said. He replied, "Shades Shanahan right?" His voice wasn't at all what I had expected. It was gentle and soft. I was amazed by this but still scared. He was so big, yet had such a small voice. On the street I was sometimes called Shades Shanahan because I wore these purple/blue-mirrored sunglasses. I could see you but you couldn't see me. Macho stuff.

I told Tiny. I got a call for someone selling drugs and that I had to frisk him. I was sweating. It wasn't even hot out. I said to him, "look I don't want to do this and I know you don't want me to either, so just tell me what drugs and how much you have on you." In the late 70's cocaine and heroin were the drugs of choice. Marijuana was no big thing. I usually threw marijuana away and let the suspect go unless they possessed a large amount. But I abhorred heroin, and coke was almost as bad. I locked up anyone with these two types of drugs. Tiny reached into his pocket and pulled out a small amount of marijuana and two rolling papers. I took a sigh of relief, no heroin or cocaine. Tiny looked at me and said that he wasn't selling drugs, I believed him. I took the marijuana and papers out of his hand and threw them down the sewer, which was five feet away. Tiny looked surprised. I told him to leave, but not before saying to him, "you owe me." He nodded and walked away. I got back into my radio car and pointed the air-conditioning vent at my face. I was *still* sweating It wasn't but three weeks later that I had four suspects against the wall to a bar. The Castle Inn, located at Castle St. and Ashland Ave, Tiny territory. I was frisking them. Two suspects were mouthy and loud. I was not far from being in trouble. I had a feeling that at least two of these guys were going to fight me. I made sure that the dispatcher was aware of my location as a precaution that I always utilized. As I was searching the second loud mouth and belligerent suspect, I found a concealed weapon, a knife. I grabbed the suspect and he immediately pulled back and away from me.

Two of the four suspects ran, one I had a hold of and the other was pulling at my arms. I was in trouble. I reached for my radio to call for help. Suddenly a large arm came over my shoulder and knocked me aside. Another shot of adrenaline surged through my body, for I could not get to my radio to call for back up. An eerie feeling came over me. I was going to get hurt, I thought one of the suspects that ran had come back to join in the fight against me. Just then the two suspects were thrown against the wall and pulled away from me. Someone had their forearms against their throats pinning them against the wall. Come on Shades, handcuff em! It was Tiny! He had come to help me. I handcuffed both suspects together and called for a paddy wagon. As I was taking that big breath, that sigh of relief that you take when all the scary shit is over, I noticed Tiny walking away. Thanks Tiny, I said. He turned around slowly and said, "we're even Shades," and walked around the corner. Just then the wagon pulled up, and I stood there all-full of myself and beaming in front of this other officer. I had two suspects for him and needed no help! I had arrested two suspects all by myself. What a cop! But I knew that I had a *Tiny* bit of help, so did he.

I would see Tiny now and then over the years and we would just acknowledge each other discreetly with a slight unnoticeable nod. Words were unimportant. Thanks Tiny . . .

Straight Razor

I was working 334 car, in the vicinity of East North Ave. and Broadway. I hadn't been on the street very long, about three years. As I was patrolling my post a call was broadcast for an armed hold up at the grocery store located at Washington St. and East Lanvale St. "Suspect armed with a knife," the dispatcher announced. It was icy and cold out; I was working alone and began driving up and down different streets searching for the hold up suspect. *I'd really like to find this suspect*, I thought to myself. I was driving down Durham St. towards Lafayette Ave. I noticed a black male standing on the Northwest corner in a three quarter length denim coat with orange stitching. For some unknown reason I just stopped my radio car and stared at this man. He was dark skinned, tall, thin and he would not turn to look at me, I waited patiently. "334, give me the description of the hold up suspect from the grocery store again, I'm at Durham St. and Lafayette Ave. with a possible suspect". I said. The dispatcher began to rebroadcast the description. The suspect still refused to look in my direction; I even revved my car engine to attract attention to myself. *Why won't he look at me?* I wondered. I had a gut feeling he was the suspect. *Something just isn't right.* I was thinking to myself. There was strangeness in the air, a weird uneasy, *something's not right,* feeling. Maybe this feeling is something that comes naturally to some police officers or maybe it's in the training, it's hard to say. I have to think it's a natural uneasiness or feeling, an awareness of something out of the ordinary. My thoughts left me. The suspect still would not look my way and NOW I knew why. I heard, "three quarter length denim coat with orange threads". *That's it, he's my man.* I thought quickly. I opened my car door, our eyes met, we both knew, the chase was on! *That moment was so cool,* I thought. It's a good guy bad guy thing, the suspect knows he's being watched, he knows he's guilty, he thinks I know too. A short, quick, meeting of the eyes, it all becomes clear to me and to him, he's *bad,* I'm *good, he's fucked.*

"334, I'm in foot pursuit west on Lafayette Ave. towards Broadway," I yelled into the radio. The suspect crossed Broadway, a four-lane street with a fifteen-foot wide grass median strip. The suspect crossed the median easily.

Two vehicles nearly hit me. I was running around the vehicles tripping across the grass median. There was ice and snow on the grass, running was difficult for the suspect and me. The suspect ran north up the next alley. He slipped on the ice and fell. *I've got him now,* I thought. Just then I too fell. *SHIT!* We both got to our feet and started running again. It was as if I was getting nowhere. I felt as though I had a ball and chain around my waist. I was getting tired and running out of energy. I couldn't give up. *Keep going Dan, just keep going!* I was telling myself. I was continually calling out my route on the radio so the dispatcher and my fellow officers knew my location as I was running. I came within twenty feet of the suspect and observed him throw something into a trashcan as he passed it. We continued running up this trash laden ice covered alley. I kept running not bothering to stop and look into the trashcan, I wanted this guy.

Suddenly the suspect stopped, turned and whipped out a straight razor. It was long, sharp, shiny and scary. *Shit, not a straight razor! Fuck me!* I thought. I was deathly afraid and intimidated by straight razors. I had taken a few razors off of suspects that were closed and safe, but when I would open the blade a chill ran up and down my spine. I was petrified. I'd rather have a gun or knife pointed at me. I could imagine this guy cutting my throat, severing my jugular vein, and knowing I was going to die and I had a few seconds to think about it. I had pictured this morbid and frightening scene before. I could see him carving up my face with this horrible weapon that placed so much fear in me.

I already had my gun out, I don't recall pulling it out of the holster. When I saw the razor, I yelled, "FREEZE! FREEZE MUVAFUCKER!" At that same instant I fired one shot at this figure that had frightened me to the bone. I was petrified.

As I yelled these words my Motorola radio that was attached to my left shoulder loop had the microphone open. I must have held it open in that moment of sheer fright. The entire district heard my words and the single gunshot. I would learn later that no one knew what officer was in pursuit until they heard me yell, "Freeze muvafucker!" I had a fault of holding my mic open when in distress or in a dangerous situation. Maybe this was a blessing. The officers in my squad heard the voice, recognized it was mine and advised the dispatcher it was 334 car. The dispatcher remembered where I was and the troops were on the way.

Simultaneously as I put pressure on the trigger of my .38 caliber revolver and it fired, the suspect slipped on the ice. My bullet hit the brick wall that was the back wall to Samuel Gompers High School. We referred to it as Little Alcatraz. The timing of the suspects' fall was split second good luck. He fell; the bullet narrowly missed his head. He continued running west, only it seemed much faster, I'm certain he too was petrified. He came out of the alley onto Bradford Street, A dead end street ending at another brick wall. Just as the wagon man, Joe Slate, came up Bradford Street in the paddy wagon. Joe nearly ran over the suspect and forced him into the wall with nowhere to go. The suspect was trapped, the chase was over. This gave me just enough time to catch up to him. I forcefully pushed the suspect against the wall and shoved my gun into his ear, I was pushing hard. I continued pushing the barrel of my gun into his ear canal. He was screaming. "Don't shoot me, don't kill me, don't, don't!" I wouldn't take the gun out of his ear, I kept pushing he kept screaming. The adrenaline was pumping thru my veins, my body was extremely tense and my mind was psyched. I was breathing so heavily, I was having trouble catching my breath. I was holding onto the suspect so I wouldn't fall on the ice. I was wide eyed, staring. Joe grabbed the suspect's hands, I stood there gasping and gagging. "Don't shoot Danny," said Joe. "Don't shoot!" Joe must have seen the intensity or intense fear in my eyes and wasn't certain of my presence of mind. "Dan!" I heard it this time. I had come back to reality, the fuzziness was subsiding and I became focused again. I had returned from *that place.*

It's at this point in a violent or tense, seemingly deadly situation that you become so very close to your fellow officers. You depend on each other to stay alive or not to get seriously injured. Several men together in a moment of life or death become drawn together, it's a weak vulnerable time but also a time when heroes emerge and lifelong friendships are forged. I've had officers save my life and I too saved other officers lives. An officer doesn't realize how close each of us becomes until the commotion, the near death experience has ended and the seriousness of that situation surfaces, just as the trembling and shivering surface. It's as if something inside helps you do what's proper and correct at that given moment. Then that awareness of the closeness to death or serious harm you have just experienced ultimately sets in and you realize that you should be stabbed, shot, cut, or dead, you're not and you shake uncontrollably.

The reality of the situation sets in. Your entire body quivers and it won't subside. There were times and instances when it took a half an hour or more for me to settle myself down enough to write my report of the incident. I would attempt to write but the pen merely scribbled. It's odd though, other officers notice the shaking and fear but no one says a word. Its okay to become unglued afterwards, not during, it's okay. This is not taught or learned, it just exists. I never mentioned the shaking, it was never mentioned to me. It's uncontrollable but it must be temporarily acceptable. It's an unspoken acceptance. It's a part of the job, a necessary part, I guess?

The suspect was cuffed, taken back to the store he had robbed with the straight razor, positively identified and transported to the Eastern District for booking. It was the cash that the suspect had thrown into the trashcan.

The trembling subsided somewhat as I drove to the station. I had a chance to walk the fear off as I backtracked to my still running radio car. I had lucked out again, or was it God's plan. Again I went home that night, put on my headphones, listened to Karen Carpenter's soothing voice, stared at the wall, and drank six beers. Tomorrow was a new day, new experiences awaited, hopefully no straight razors were in those unknown experiences.

Two Small Words

As a police officer I really didn't expect many words of thanks or appreciation from the general public. However, there were times when I was acknowledged by the citizens and even praised and respected.

Courtesy and respect were not something that I experienced much of as a Baltimore City Police Officer.

It was a warm spring day and I decided to walk my post rather than drive around in my radio car. That way I could get to know the people on my post personally, plus it was a nice day weather wise. As I neared the corner of E. Biddle St., and N. Milton Ave. I observed an elderly black man reach into his jacket and take a drink from his liquor bottle almost directly in front of me. I assumed it was liquor, he was sneaking it and he was standing in front of a liquor store. He jumped as I surprised him with my stern police officer voice, "Okay what's in the coat pocket?" He replied nervously, "I'm sorry *ocifer*, I only had a taste. It's only knottyhead. I didn't see ya. If I had a seen ya I wouldn't have tasted, I respects the police." I was taken aback by the respect part. I really didn't expect that, it's not something I heard often.

"What's knottyhead and what's a taste?" I asked, "Knottyhead is vodka and a taste is a sip ocifer. "He explained. I had no idea. This older man was actually from the old school, the school where people respected police and showed it. I wasn't used to being respected by the citizens I saved, looked out for, protected, and laid my life on the line for these past 5 years. I was quite pleased. I didn't let the old man know of my pleasure. He had no idea what was going to happen. I took advantage of this and said in a harsh tone of voice, that tough guy, somewhat loud cop voice, "stay here, don't leave, I'll be right back!"

I walked into the liquor store and purchased a pint of knotty head, which turned out to be Smirnoff vodka that came in a yellowish tinted bottle with bumps all over. I was to find out that it was referred to as knottyhead for two reasons; the bottle had bumps on it and if you drank too much the next morning your head felt like it had been hit several times with a baseball bat and it had knots all over it, hence, knottyhead!

I paid for the pint, walked out the door and handed the pint to the nervous old man. "Here, this is on me, thank you for the respect and for making my day, have a *taste* on me." The elderly black man smiled with delight. I smiled back and we parted ways. We both parted ways with a light heart, a spring in our step and a good feeling inside. I felt good. *I have learned so much in these past five years."* I thought, as I continued my foot patrol with a smile in my heart.

Now for the two small words I eluded to earlier in this chapter.

It was a slow, drawn out 8x4 shift. The rain had been pouring down all day. I had been inundated with several uneventful, boring, rainy day calls. Lost wallet, flooded basement, hit and run car accident with minor damage, etc. However, I was able to remain dry even though I was working in torrential downpours most of this dreary, wet, and damp morning. I did get a little wet but the heater in my Pontiac Lemans radio car served as a hair dryer, hat dryer and shirt dryer all in one.

The rains continued causing minor flooding and causing the gutters to become small streams. If I stepped into the gutter inadvertently the water immediately rushed up, over, and into my boots. I made a right turn onto N. Bradford St. just West of Milton Ave. This street was located at the lower end of the Eastern District and all the drainage was rushing down Milton Ave., and Bradford St., from five blocks up the hill. I really didn't care as long as I was able to jump over the small streams and reach the dryness of the sidewalk; besides, I had no reason to get out of my car.

As I neared the bottom of Bradford St. a cab that was driving slowly down the street stopped in front of me. I couldn't go around as many streets in the district can only accommodate one vehicle. But, all are not one-way streets, they're just narrow: i.e., 900 N. Duncan St., Madeira St., Castle and Chapel Sts., and of course, N. Bradford St. The cab slowed, I stopped.

I noticed the trunk pop open automatically and observed nearly twelve full brown paper grocery bags in the trunk of the cab. My view was blocked preventing me from seeing who the passenger was. *Shit, this poor bastard is going to get soaked. I'm not getting out of my dry car, no way.* I murmured. I had no intention of getting out into the pouring rain and chance stepping into the small rivers the rains had caused.

The driver's rear door opened. There she was. My foot soaker of the day. A frail, elderly, black woman stepped out of the cab and onto the sidewalk. At least the cabbie had pulled close to the sidewalk. I sat in my warm radio car and pretended to be doing paperwork. I was certain the cab driver would, at any moment, exit the front and begin carrying the twelve large, full, grocery bags into this fragile woman's home for her, in the rain. I wasn't about to. I didn't feel like being a helpful civil servant that day. My bad attitude wouldn't allow the goodness to win over.

I sat as I watched this old woman, this grandmother, take one bag at a time into the vestibule of her row house, struggle to place each one on the floor and make her way back into the rains, walk thru the rushing water and retrieve another grocery bag. As bag number three was hoisted slowly and carefully out of the cabs trunk I could watch no more. *Why isn't the cab driver assisting this lady, it's his fare, it's his responsibility, not mine!* I thought in disgust. I was angry. I exited my radio car traversed the small river at my feet in one carefully planned jump and reached the sidewalk.

I walked past grandmom not hearing or saying a word. I knocked hard on the driver's window, startling the cabbie. He was approximately thirty to thirty five years old, and he was black. He looked up at me but did nothing. "Put the window down!" I said loudly. He opened the window just enough to hear but not enough to get wet from the raindrops. "Aren't you going to help your fare with her load?" I asked sternly. "No way am I getting wet!" was his nonchalant reply. I became indignant and incensed. "Hey asshole, she's old, she's one of YOUR people, and she needs help. Where's the WE BE ONE PEOPLE AND HELPS ONE ANOTHER SHIT I HEAR ABOUT ALL THE TIME?" I said with indifference and indignation. "I ain't getting wet!" was his reply once again. That was not what I needed or at all wanted to hear as the rain dripped off the brim of my hat and into my ears then traveling down my neck. "Let me tell you something FUCKHEAD, you make me sick! I patrol this area all the time, I see you at anytime on my post I'm pulling you over and I am definitely FUCKING with YOU, BRO! UNDERSTAND?" My fist slammed into the top of the cab and I went to the trunk.

I had no idea if this poor old lady heard my conversation with the cabbie, I really didn't care. I advised the hunched over soaking wet old black lady to get into her house as I removed the grocery bag from her arms.

I placed the bag into the vestibule and went to retrieve another bag. I was pissed and disgusted. I forgot to jump the river and stepped ankle high in this six inches of water that was rushing down the gutter from a six-hour deluge. "FUCK!" I said loudly. By now I was completely drenched. The water was dripping into my ears, down the back and front of my neck. I could feel it traveling down my lower back and down the crack of my ass.

Both feet were soaked as were my shirt and pants. The rain didn't subside or let up, it continually poured down, no break, no pause, just kept pouring down. Neither did I.

I carried eight more bags from the trunk, up three steps and into the house for grandmom. As I pulled the last bag from the trunk I slammed the lid and kicked the rear quarter panel. "Leave asshole! And don't dare attempt to make a complaint against me!" I yelled, actually, *gurgled,* as my mouth filled with rainwater. The cabbie quickly drove off.

I sloshed up the three steps and placed the last bag on the floor. The old lady stood there motionless and speechless. After all I had just done and after being a helpful civil servant/police officer I wanted nothing, nothing but to hear two small words. Two small words would have made all this effort and sacrifice worthwhile. Those words would have warmed my innards and my heart; no matter how wet I was on the outside.

Two small words for all I had been thru when I didn't have to and certainly didn't want to would have settled me down and soothed the beast. The old lady looked directly into my eyes for the first time and merely stared. She said nothing, she made no thankful gestures, and she did and said absolutely nothing. I was not going to hear my two precious words. Those two small words that now seemed so large and important at that moment in time.

I stood in front of this woman as I dripped all over her floor. No words were uttered. I turned and left. To my amazement and confusion she slammed the door behind me. *Why, why did this happen like this?* I wondered.

As I stepped off the bottom step of the lady's house I intentionally walked into the rushing water. I kicked at it; I kicked at it like a little boy throwing a tantrum. The water went everywhere. I didn't care I was pissed and pouting.

As I sat in my radio car, I could feel my underwear was also soaked. I moved my feet and I could hear them sloshing. I threw my hat onto the dash hitting the windshield and splashing rain on the window. The car heater was of no use to me; it was senseless to even turn it on.

I slammed the car transmission into reverse and sped backwards up the street, the bottom of the street was flooded out. I couldn't pass. I wondered as I called out of service to the station to get a dry shirt and to take off my now thoroughly drenched bullet proof Kevlar vest what this woman was thinking, what was going on in her mind as I carried her bags into the house. I realized that probably, just probably, some white person had offended, insulted, or mistreated her at some point or points in her life. This was her chance to pay whitey back, pay me back. *Why did I have to suffer? Why did she have to suffer? This racial shit really blows!* I thought.

I changed only my shirt; all my other clothes remained on and remained wet the duration of the shift.

The rest of the day my attitude matched my appearance, wet, soggy, disgusted, pissed off and bewildered. Two small words could have cured all that, but those two small words would not be spoken today, I would not hear those *two small words.*

Ice Cream Boy

The often looked forward to 4 p.m. x 12 p.m. shift had finally arrived. This was the busiest of all three shifts. The bosses were off, out of their offices, and on their way home. The job became much more fun and enjoyable. This shift was every young police officer's favorite. Especially in the warmer months, there was plenty of activity. I could count on one to two good fights, a foot chase, or a domestic melee on this shift. I was usually put back in my place and humbled on this shift. I would wind up in a fight where I would win or sometimes I'd be forced to call for help because I was losing, being humbled. This shift offered lots of violence, fighting, drinking and arrests.

On a normal shift I'd fill out one run sheet. This shows how many calls for service an officer handles during that shift. On a violent and busy second shift, I'd have two or three sheets. That's over thirty calls for service handled by one officer. There were thirty officers on the shift. Once the good citizens of East Baltimore began drinking and returning home from work, the fights, shootings, stabbings, and complaints started. My calls for service rose sharply. I was extremely happy on this shift. It was thrilling and exciting.

This shift was preceded by the 12 p.m. x 8 a.m. The past month the midnight shift had been an unusually quiet one. I was looking for some excitement and felt bored. But, sometimes when you get what you ask for it is more than you can, or want, to handle.

It was late afternoon on a Sunday. I hadn't had many calls for service. I received a call to the 2900 block of E. Oliver St. This is a quiet neighborhood located at the far east end of the district. I had handled very few calls in this area in the past years.

I walked up the six brick steps to the porch and knocked on the door. I was sent there for an, investigate the problem, call. I had no idea what the problem was. As the door opened a short black male in his late twenties opened the screen door. He was much smaller than I, so I mentally relaxed. This guy can't cause me any harm, he's small. I had properly sized up the situation, or so I thought.

"Did you call the police?" I asked politely. The reply surprised me. "Fuck you, ICE CREAM BOY!" *Ice cream boy! Fuck this little punk, who's he talking to!* I thought. At that time police officers wore blue pants and white shirts, evidently I resembled an ice cream boy to this punk. His attitude was bad, it was obvious to me that I was going to lock him up for some reason before this was over. "What did you call me!"? I asked. "I called you a fucking ICE CREAM BOY! Now get the fuck off my porch!" He pushed me.

I was elated! You have fucked up now, Boy! I grabbed little smartass by the collar and pulled him out the door. That was easy enough, now I'll just cuff the little one. I was so mistaken and took so much for granted. I needed to be, and was going to be, humbled. The suspect punched me approximately ten times before I got my second punch in. He drove me back six feet and I began to fall over the 3 foot wall that surrounded the porch. My mind was whirring with questions and exclamations. *Jesus Christ, this little fucker's hitting me hard and fast! How does he do that? I'm going to be in trouble if I fall over this porch!* The suspect continued pummeling me and I fell over the wall and hit the grass ten feet below. But, I had reached out and grabbed the suspect by the collar and pulled him over the wall with me. We flipped in mid air switching positions on the way down. As we hit he was on the bottom. My police radio had shoved into my left hip and caused my entire left leg to become paralyzed. I was extremely upset! I was frantic! I was losing and paralyzed! I definitely needed help. I knew I had only a few seconds to get on the radio to let my partners know where I was. "333, Signal 13, 2900 E. Oliver St.! NOW!" BamBamBam! I got punched again, several times.

The police department mandates that an officer's use of force can be raised by one level. I.e. if the suspect uses his fist or body a police officer can use a nightstick or chemical mace. If a suspect uses a stick, pipe, hammer, etc. an officer can use his gun. I was at that crossroad. This suspect was obviously a great fighter; I was paralyzed and could not get up to defend myself. I had to raise the ante in this near deadly game.

I pulled out my revolver and pointing it at the suspect I yelled, "Get up against the fucking wall asshole, you're under arrest, I'll shoot you muvafucker! Move!" I was not in control of this situation by a long shot. I managed to stand up utilizing the step railing to my right. My right leg was fine and I propped myself up against the railing. The suspect was calming down, after all he had a six inch barrel .38 caliber revolver about six feet from his head! I could hear sirens in the distance as I attempted to catch my breath and gain control of this chaotic melee. My overall senses were returning. I was coming out of the zone.

Suddenly my gun discharged! BANG! *Shit! What the fuck! I didn't pull the trigger, did I?* Again the adrenaline began pumping. The suspect's father had been on the top step of the porch, I hadn't even noticed, I was preoccupied.

The father had jumped off the top step and his fist had come crushing down on my right forearm instantly causing my weapon to fire. I grabbed the father with my left hand and pushed him to the ground kicking him in the head as many times as I could while I was watching the first suspect's actions. I was in a very serious situation, a family disturbance turned around. Instead of the family fighting each other they were now fighting me. I was well aware of the fact that most officers are seriously injured in these exact circumstances.

Did I shoot him? He's on the ground! Jesus! Where's my help? I need help! Danny, your in trouble, now think! The bullet had missed the little fighter. It hit the brick wall behind him. He was petrified and had ceased and desisted! He was done. He stood up and put his hands on the wall. At that time the first car arrived. It was Jimmy. He was a scrapper too, and small. "Jimmy the one against the wall, he's a fighter, he assaulted me Fuck Him UP! My leg's paralyzed!" I yelled. Jimmy began to kick, punch and cuff the little one. Jimmy was doling out the street justice that I couldn't. However, I still had a chance with the father. We rolled down the front hill and under a tow truck that was parked against the curb. I had no idea how we rolled those twenty feet as we were kicking and punching each other. He was mad because I had kicked him in the head, I was furious, nervous, pumped and scared after my gun discharged.

Finally I had enough. I had to street fight. All fairness was out of this game. I was still paralyzed and was not going to be hurt anymore. I changed the rules. I could! *Fuck this bastard, Dan, fuck him up and don't stop until you're safe* I told myself. I had passed that plain of being fair and following police department rules. My rules came into play, rules of survival. I slammed dad's head into the muffler over and over and didn't stop until he slumped down next to me. He too was on top for I was still paralyzed from the waist down on my left side. After he slumped next to me, obviously unconscious, I was still furious. I spit in his face and hit him with my gun butt. I was going to get my revenge. I had no time to holster my gun and I thought I might need it. I was not about to let my gun go.

Three more radio cars arrived. Jimmy had pretty much busted up my little ice cream kid. Two officers threw my suspect into the arriving wagon, head first. Another officer dragged me out from under the tow truck. I had asshole dad by the hair and was dragging him along also, still unconscious. An ambulance had been dispatched. A neighbor had called in and told the operator that shots were fired, I needed help and was hurt. By the time I stood up there were ten radio cars, a wagon and an ambulance parked in all directions all over the 2900 block of E. Oliver St. I definitely needed help and help came. It just seems to take forever when in dire straights as I was. In actuality, I had only been fighting two minutes. That seemed a lifetime to me.

All three of us went to the hospital. I went first and the two bad guys had to wait for a second ambulance. Of course. The sensation in my leg slowly returned in about thirty minutes. The radio had slammed into the nerve in my upper leg incapacitating the entire leg. It was a horrible feeling; I was scared out there alone with two bad guys. As I was being wheeled down the hall past the first suspect, who happened to be handcuffed to the bed and controlled, I reached out and punched him one last time. I needed that.

The next day I discovered who my little fighter was. He was a United States Marine! He also was a professional boxer for the Marine Corps. I never had a chance. He made a mess of me. The Marine Corps apologized, I dropped the assault charge so that the Corps could handle the fighter, and I was avenged. The father was fortunate. He too was charged with assault on a police officer and if the bullet had of hit his son it would have most likely killed him, leaving the father to face murder charges.

Another war story from the 4x12 shift. As I said, it was a shift that was the most violent and dangerous. But, I did enjoy it especially when I was the one to survive and I had help just around the corner. I guess the Ice Cream Boy had won another battle.

Deadly Pressures

The pressures of police work can and does take its toll on a police officer, they are human. Some handle the violence, pain, thanklessness, worry, apprehension and plain fear very neatly. Others, like myself, tend to drink away the bad scenes, sights, smells and experiences by abusing alcohol and sex. Almost all the officers in my squad of about ten officers, in sector three of the Eastern District, drank beer and liquor at sometime or another. Drugs were abhorred and considered unacceptable among us. Drinking a few beers or drinks was almost a given in my squad during the four to twelve-shift and the midnight shift. We usually met on the vacant lot behind the Continental Can Company at the foot of Biddle St., or under the bridge in the 900 block of N. Linwood Ave., The Linwood Ave. Bridge, as it was referred to. This is where we usually slept also. We slept in the same, few known, spots so each of us knew where the other officer was, a safety measure. None of us ever became intoxicated to a point that any of us were put in jeopardy, we just had a good time drinking a few drinks, and it was acceptable.

One early spring afternoon (the four to twelve shift) I heard the 344 car driven by Officer Benny Brinkman break the silence on the radio, "I'm shot!" "Signal 13". "I'm shot!," "Signal 13 Sinclair Lane and Patterson Park Ave." I was only three blocks away! *Oh shit,* I thought. *I hope Benny's okay, please, God let Benny be okay!* I drove at an excessive speed west bound down Sinclair Lane. As I was traveling down the street toward the injured officer, I could see Benny's radio car sitting in the middle of the street at Sinclair Lane and Patterson Park Ave. No other vehicle had passed me en route to the shooting scene and I noticed no other persons on any side streets or running away from the scene, as I raced to Benny's aid, I knew then that this call was genuine. Benny wasn't known to be one of those officers that called for help for unwarranted reasons, he didn't have that type of reputation as some officers do, a pussy that shouldn't be on the streets.

Police officers are trained or maybe just learn to notice and make mental notes of what they are seeing on the way to a call, especially as you get very near to the actual scene. When I was a rookie police officer there were incidents where I had actually passed the hold up suspect or the hit and run automobiles, but was so intent on arriving on the scene I had overlooked or missed exactly what I was supposed to look for from the onset of the call. It was very frustrating to arrive on the scene of a *hot* call only to learn that I had missed my mark, I learned this thru frustration and a desire to be the best officer I could be, or was it to be a hero, to be respected and to be liked?

In this case, I had learned thru experience to notice a car or person that may be fleeing the scene of this crime, as I mentioned, it's a learned response. It can also be of monumental help in catching a criminal or solving a crime. I saw or noticed nothing as I responded at a high rate of speed, to this horrible call for help from one of my own.

I felt an empty feeling in my stomach as I slammed the car into the park position and ran to Benny's side, blood was everywhere, but Benny was alive and coherent. He had a bullet wound in his left hand; the bullet had passed completely thru the palm. He also had a bullet wound in his right leg, which was spurting blood all over his pants and the radio car. I was severely concerned about this leg wound for if the bullet had nicked or severed the main artery near his femur bone, located in the upper thigh, Benny could bleed to death right in front of me, and that would be unacceptable to me.

Officer Pat Henley's radio car pulled up on the scene as did Officers Lee Gregory and Martin Snyder. They had arrived from three different directions within moments of my arrival. By now Benny was unconscious, or I *thought* he was. The dispatcher had called for an ambulance as I was responding to the scene, I had heard the dispatcher advise me and the other officers responding, but at the time with so much going on and so many things racing thru my mind I half remembered. So much goes on in your mind and physical body when responding to this type of call or any type of call with that magnitude of excitement and danger connected to it.

As I sped away from the station house responding to this bone chilling call, my body, mind, and psyches were racing at top speed and in high gear. There was so much to do and so little time to do it in. I had to activate my emergency lights and siren which caused me to bend over toward my right side and down to the siren box, simultaneously pay attention to my driving, look for pedestrians and other vehicles on the same roads that might be in the way of this speeding police car, advise the dispatcher that I was responding, listen to see if the other officers had heard the call for help, listen for a possible description being broadcast as to a suspect or suspect car and attempt to keep my pounding heart, rising blood pressure, sweating palms and racing mind in complete check and control so not to become involved in a car accident and so I could be at my best in case my experience or help was needed. In addition, try to think ahead of what I might encounter upon reaching Benny.

My mind always played out the most exciting and dangerous or worst scenarios I could conjure up responding to a call of this importance. I had already pictured myself shooting it out with a criminal that had shot another police officer, a criminal that had enough bravado and balls to actually shoot a police officer. I pictured Benny shot to pieces and already dead or dying as I watched helplessly. The imagination goes totally into high gear as a police officer thrusts himself into the life of violence and terror that he faces now and then. All of this was happening in my head in nanoseconds as I was responding. There is a lot going on in those minutes it takes to arrive at the scene. The adrenaline rush is spectacular. I lived for that adrenaline rush, any cop that says he doesn't live for that rush is either lying, has never been on the streets, or doesn't like the job. It's hard to describe the feeling. I would say it's like driving too fast, slamming on your car brakes and making an evasive maneuver to avoid a imminent accident. Most of us have experienced that; the body gets an instant surge of adrenaline to handle the situation. The eyes become like binoculars, the ears hear every sound, and the mind is a huge processing machine, missing nothing. It's almost as good as a sexual orgasm! Running down an alley chasing a suspect with a gun and trading gunshots gives the same type of rush. It's fabulous, scary, exciting, and most of all fun! It's especially fun after the danger has passed and you are still in one piece and unharmed, uninjured. I sometimes feel that a lot of the troubles that occurred after I left the Police Department, and that wonderful life I cherished so much, was caused by not being able to achieve that adrenaline rush that I love so much, in my daily life. I feel as though that's the reason I enjoy, or feel it a must to drive my Harley and my cars at excessive speeds, why I used to drink too much and drive, and why I got into trouble. I miss my job. I miss that rush!

I had the driver's door open and was assessing the situation as Pat, Lee and Martin raced up to me. Now, Benny was unconscious. "Fuck the ambo Pat," I yelled. Lee and I put Benny's limp body into the back seat of Pat's radio car. Lee was holding Benny's head and I had my finger inside the hole in his thigh. Blood continued to spurt out of this wound. "Not the artery," I yelled. Please don't let him die! "Come on Pat drive this fucking car!" Time slowed, I half watched as we passed the street signs heading for Hopkins Hospital located on Monument St. Lafayette Ave., Preston St., Eager St., Ashland, Ave., Madison St. I knew these streets and knew we were drawing close to the hospital. The street signs passed by so very slowly I couldn't hear any of the sounds of the moment, the crackling of the police radio, Pat calling out streets as we passed some of them to alert the hospital of our location, Lee talking to Benny to keep him calm. I may have been hearing these sounds of stress, excitement and desperation, but I wasn't comprehending these sounds. It was as though I was watching a movie, and I was experiencing a fast moving emergency scene being played out in front of me but in super slow motion with the volume turned down and the lights turned off so all I could focus on was the tiny screen directly in front of me, nothing else. I was in *that place,* that place I refer to often. That place I go to in order to survive what is transpiring at that moment, that horrible, present moment.

I was watching Benny breath, short quick breaths. I whispered in his ear, hang on Benny, hang on. That place I often refer to is a place we go to in times of severe stress or great pleasure. What and where is *that place?* I've experienced its warm and fuzzy feelings often. It's not knowing or realizing what you're doing as you're doing it, no perception or clarity. It's difficult to explain, but one way to describe it would be for you to recall what feeling your body experiences when you reach a sexual climax. You actually hear the song on the radio, the dog barking, the drone of the lawn mowers, or the kids far off voices, but you don't acknowledge any of the sounds. Nothing registers but that sensational, warm, all consuming feeling, or the extreme real or imagined danger of death or severe injury you are presently experiencing. None of your aches and pains hurt any longer, your sunburn doesn't seem to burn, your headache temporarily subsides, you feel an overall rush of warmth and comfort. A feeling of separation from your whole being. When I go to, *that place,* out of fear or apprehension, such as Benny's life threatening gunshots, It's not as warm and fuzzy, it's a feeling of not being totally in that moment, a total unawareness, a *place.*

The car slammed to an abrupt stop. I snapped back to reality with such quickness it seemed like the blink of an eye. Sounds became loud, sights normal, I had returned to reality. We had arrived at Johns Hopkins emergency room. The staff was waiting for us. They took Benny from me. We had done well. He was still alive. Benny would survive.

Rumor's circulated almost immediately that Benny had shot himself. *No way.*

Pat and I searched all the private garages from two blocks south of the shooting, two blocks east, two blocks west, and the railroad tracks that were directly north, all four possible escape routes had been covered, and no vehicle could have gone up that hill North of Sinclair Lane, it was all fenced in, there was no break in the fence, no damage. No vehicle had been hidden and abandoned so as to continue to flee on foot. Benny specifically stated that the car went east, right at me! I know what I saw and observed, I had no doubts of my recollections, I have an excellent short term memory, it wasn't failing me, *NO* cars or pedestrians passed me as I responded to that call . . .

As of the completion of this chapter, and as far as I am aware, Homicide Division still hasn't closed this case. I couldn't ask Benny if he had shot himself. That's not a proper question to ask a fellow police officer. There was no black car, there was *no* two black male suspects, and no attempted homicide.

I know that when I was asked if it was possible for a car to have passed me. I told the detectives that it was possible that the car could have turned left or right onto Belair Rd. because I told them I was 10 blocks away and even though I was extremely close there was a slight possibility that Benny had told the truth, and the black car may have turned before I reached the first possible intersection. The only possible intersection that the suspects' could have turned onto from the shooting scene, I was lying.

If Benny's story was as he explained it and that's what he wanted, then that's what I was supposed to testify to, it was the proper thing to do . . . Benny retired from the police department using the shooting as his reason, and, stress, he said, deadly stress. Deadly stress that can cause, *deadly pressures.*

WAR STORIES

War stories are just that. Stories from police officers, of incidents or experiences that they have witnessed or been an actual part of. Most officers feel as though it is an actual war on the streets. The good guys versus the bad guys. A war on drugs, war on crime, or just plain war. Therefore war stories are accounts of incidents or occurrences that other officers remember more clearly than most. Stories that stick out from the others due to the added danger, excitement, strangeness, bizarre nature, or just plain being a weird out of the ordinary story. A war story.

Officer Michael Shanahan, patrolman, Northeastern District, Baltimore City, 1972. Mike was investigating a series of home burglaries that were occurring on and around his post, in the then, usually quiet, Northeast section of the city. The Northeast District was predominately white and normally considered a quiet district.

This burglar and his burglaries were, by any stretch of the imagination, not of the usual type. I.e., break into a home, steal property, and leave quickly and quietly. No deviations from the norm, just get in, steal, and get out. Mikes war story had many a strange twist in a perverted and sick sort of way.

This burglar would usually strike late at night or in the early a.m. hours. The burglar's M.O., Modus Operandi, or Method of Operation, which means a suspect's normal routine of pulling off his crime, was to break open or jimmy open a first floor window and gain entrance. Unlike most burglars, this perverted psychopath would break in the home while the occupants were home; also, the occupants were always women.

The suspect would somehow tie up or incapacitate the female victim and inquire as to where she kept her panties, clean and soiled. The suspect would then retrieve the panties and commence to cut out the cotton crotch panel with a pair of scissors he carried on his side. He would first cut out the panel of a soiled pair of panties, discarding the remaining ruined panty on the floor wherever they happened to fall. The suspect would then place the soiled cotton crotch panel in his mouth and chew and suck on the panel in front of the victim. The suspect would do this while showing obvious signs of complete bliss and satisfaction.

This aberration would then carefully, slowly, and deliberately cut out the cotton crotch panels out of each remaining pair of panties and carefully place them in a small cloth bag attached to his waist.

The suspect never harmed the female victim. But I can only imagine the horror and fear that would over shadow a victim that was tied up, helpless and debilitated, watching this strange and sick behavior that was taking place directly in front of them by this sexual deviant.

When finished his sickening ritual, the suspect would either remove the pair of panties the victim was currently wearing or order the victim to remove the panties for him. The suspect would tuck the entire pair of panties in his bag, no cutting. The entire time in the dwelling and while all of this was taking place, the suspect was busily chewing away at the very first pair of soiled cotton crotch panel panties, the whole time he was quite noticeably making noises of satisfaction and delight as if tasting his favorite brand of chocolate for the first time, in some time.

The perverted burglar would then exit the premises with all his goodies including his fresh pair of warm panties. He left out of the same window he entered but not until he left his signature on the windowsill. A personal signature that never left Mike's memory, nor mine now. This perverted individual would drop his pants and leave a big pile of shit, feces, poop, on the windowsill before leaving his den of iniquity. The suspect never changed his method of operation and was never apprehended.

Mikes war story!

Not all war stories are sick and perverted. Some are comical, many sad. Most are just strange and somewhat unbelievable. But, truth is stranger than fiction, especially in the police officer's world.

Officer Charlie Ball, patrolman, Eastern District, Baltimore Police Dept. Officer Ball was a small individual, thin and frail looking. However, this in no way compared to his A plus personality, his temper, his flair for wanting to be a top notch police officer, and his Napoleonic complex.

Charlie was a typical red neck, street fighting, and kick ass kind of guy. That's why I believed this war story that was related to me by another police officer and which I also confirmed personally from Charlie not long after learning of this story. Plus, I worked alongside Officer Ball for over seven years and had first hand knowledge of his demeanor and personality. He was an excellent policeman and taught me much over the years we worked together.

1959/1960; Police work was much different in the late fifties and early sixties than it was in the late seventies, when I worked, and I'm sure it's much different today. The citizens respected police officers, there were very few radio cars, most patrolman were foot patrol officers. Usually only sergeants had radio cars and of course the paddy wagon was motorized.

There were no two-way Motorola radios, only a call box that was located on certain designated corners. These boxes were solid steel, dark green, and an officer needed a call box key to gain access. These boxes were still in use when I went on the department in 1973 and I had many occasions to use the call box. However nothing could replace the efficiency of the radio.

In the earlier years, officers had to stop by a call box on their post at certain times and check in with the desk sergeant. This was done to assure that the officer was okay, to make sure he was awake, on the midnight shift, and to give any special information to the officer. In those early years officers hung around and slept at the firehouses. They had access to a phone there and I'm certain the firefighters were good company on cold and rainy nights.

In those old days, if an officer needed help or assistance he had to rap his wooden nightstick forcefully on the pavement or street making a distinct sound that traveled for blocks. Officers worked only blocks apart and that sound indicated that help was needed. Everyone that heard the sound came running.

I've heard war stories where an officer actually stuck an unruly or violent prisoner's head into the call box and held the heavy steel door against the prisoner's head to control him as he called for a paddy wagon. It was survival of the fittest or maybe the smartest that ruled in those days, an officer had to make his own way and build his own reputation on the streets.

This war story begins, as Officer Charlie Ball is a new officer with a foot post on Harford Ave. in the Eastern District. Harford Ave. is now Harford Rd. This occurred very close to where I was forced to shoot Booker Lancaster, at Harford Rd. and Broadway. Actually Harford and Broadway was Officer Ball's post back then.

There was no Internal Investigation Division, and very few complaining citizens. IID unit investigated police brutality complaints and allegations of police misconduct. Commissioner Pomerleau established the IID unit in the mid seventies. Police officers ruled with an iron fist. The public was apprehensive of police officers and usually feared them as well as respected them.

Charlie's sergeant dropped Charlie off at the corner of Harford Ave. and 25th St. The area was beginning to turn predominantly black, the time was just prior to the riots and racism was high. Charlie's sergeant delivered a pep talk to Charlie about not taking any shit from citizens and making sure that the people on his new post knew that Charlie meant business as a rookie and that he was a force to be reckoned with. He was instructed that no *booze, coos, or snooze,* would be tolerated. Of course this meant no alcohol, women or sleeping on duty.

Charlie was set out onto the public like a hungry tiger. As he exited the radio car his sergeant yelled to him, "Let them know you're the boss out here, just because you're a F.N. G., (fucking new guy), and a rookie, makes no difference! Kick ass Ball!"

Being a small guy and a scrapper, plus being a F.N.G., Charlie took all his sergeant's harsh words and pep talk to heart. He walked two blocks to the very first bar he could find. It was late Saturday afternoon, Charlie was working the 4 to 12 shift and this occurred after 5 p.m. The bar was packed with customers.

The forty to fifty foot bar was jammed with men and women drinking and listening to the loud music playing on the jukebox, which was located at the far end of the bar. It was located at the far end of the room, the farthest point from the front door. Charlie opened the door and stood in the doorway. He didn't enter yet he stood in the doorway for nearly thirty seconds saying or doing nothing. He was barely noticed.

Full of himself and having a fresh bad attitude, of kick ass and take names, given to him by his tough guy sergeant, Charlie slowly walked the sixty plus feet to the rear of the bar directly to the loud playing juke box. Charlie abruptly and deliberately kicked the plug out of the electrical socket. This caused the playing record to scratch loudly and the loud music to come to an abrupt stop causing an eerie silence. This was followed by all eyes being concentrated on the new officer with the bad attitude. Officer Ball had a captive audience.

This wasn't enough of a, "Hi I'm here, the new guy in town, look at me!" gesture. Charlie had to take things one-step further. F.N.G., rookie, Officer Charlie Ball placed his new wooden nightstick on the wooden bar and slowly walked the entire fifty foot length of that bar knocking off bottles, glasses, cups, mugs and ashtrays, causing them to crash onto the floor both in front of and behind the bar, smashing into pieces.

The breaking glass and flying debris made loud sounds as it hit the floor. It was obvious that this was definitely intentional. When the F.N.G., rookie, reached the end of the bar by the front door, completely clearing it of any containers or glassware, He turned, faced the entire bar and it's occupants, and said quite nastily, "I'm the new officer on this post, my name is Officer Charlie Ball, and anyone that has a problem can meet me outside. I'll be out on the sidewalk waiting. Charlie waited outside, no one followed.

I was enthralled and thrilled by this war story. I would have loved to have witnessed that occurrence. Such big balls for such a little guy. I asked Charlie why he did it. After removing the toothpick he always had in his mouth ever since that night on Harford Ave., and then putting the toothpick back into his mouth, he then switched it from side to side in his cocky kind of way, he cocked his head and shoulders back and placed his hand on his .38 revolver and stated, "I was a bad ass and I wanted everyone to know it."

I learned much from little Napoleon, Officer Charlie Ball, over the next seven years I worked with him, but nothing I learned from him nor anything I witnessed him do could match this War Story.

Charlie Balls war story!

Police officers are a strange breed of individual. Both male and female officers must lighten, or make light of, certain situations with comedy, to enable them to function properly and to get by. Also, to maintain their sanity, which assists them in dealing with the sadness, pain, horror, boredom, death, and strange situations associated with their job. Officers must find a coping device.

Sadly, I feel as though, alcohol is among the top coping mechanisms, however comedy and laughter is ranked first. After all a police officer must be dysfunctional to be functional in his or her line of work. Facing and dealing with criminals, crazies, drunks, and also their own administration can and does take a serious toll on an individual if no release is available.

"We have a jumper sarge!" The seasoned officer stated to sergeant Melner upon his arrival in Towson at a busy business area located in Baltimore County. Usually an area quiet and void of any serious crime. The jumper was standing on a ledge approximately twenty stories up on a Towson office building. Routine police procedure mandates cordoning off the area to keep the rubbernecking, gory hunting, public away from the jump area. This keeps the public from being harmed by the falling body and keeps them from being splattered with blood, guts, brains etc., if the jumper decided to follow thru with his threat.

It was early in the morning in Towson, on a slow and uneventful shift, so several other officers arrived to watch the spectacle. Police officers are curious. Also, they always get the front row seats. They are a curious bunch and like to witness what society throws at them. After all, police officers get to see it all. Gunshot victims, car accident victims, suicides, homicides, etc. Not to mention an occasional jumper, suicide attempt, in progress.

After twenty minutes or so the crowd had become larger including five officers from the same squad watching the event. These officers had worked side by side for several years. After time, officers get to know one another. They learn each other's attitudes, demeanors, work ethics, and mannerisms. A police officer can become seriously callused and hardened, which tends to make an officer macho and tough, rough around the edges.

Which officer is more callused, who can experience the most devastating circumstances and rather than fall apart and cry, or crumble under the stress or sadness, remain macho and tough and handle the episode. Usually the officers that persevere are making fun of the situation, person, in their mind or aloud. That is their coping device.

One sergeant, five seasoned police officers, six radio cars parked bumper to bumper all waiting for this poor unstable bastard two hundred feet above the street to jump and get it over with, or come down alive. The police officers up on the ledge were attempting to talk some sense into the deranged man and persuade him to come in off the ledge. Time passed ever so slowly. It's a waiting game, time must crawl.

Police officers become bored quickly, usually events unfold quickly in their line of work. These five comrades, amigos, friends, partners, were becoming bored and listless. The usual jokes and sick remarks abounded. "Hurry up and jump, I'm hungry." "Either do it or get down." "Jump asshole!" One officer whispered to his buddies. "You can dooo it!" like the nut in the movie, Waterboy.

These antics and remarks weren't crass enough for one of the five amigos, he pulled out five sheets of report writing paper turned them to the blank side and after retrieving a thick black marker from his briefcase he scribbled something on his, 81/2 x 11 inch, piece of paper. He then nudged the officer standing next to him. He then showed what he had scrawled on his paper to his partner, handed him the marker and the remaining four sheets of paper.

It was quite obvious that the next officer was to scribble on his paper, keep his paper and pass the last three papers and the marker to the remaining three bored officers. Once all five officers knew what was transpiring their facial expressions lit up and the laughed uncontrollably but quietly. A perverted type of devious smile came across all their faces.

One officer had to get in his car and put the windows up because he couldn't contain his laughter. The public must not become aware of their sick antics. Sgt. Melner had no idea what was happening or what was about to happen, if the man jumped.

A large crowd had gathered but was orderly and quiet. It seemed as though the crowd was getting jittery and was impatiently waiting for something to take place.

All five officers had completed their required tasks that the first officer had initiated. They put their sheets of paper on each driver's seat of their respective radio car.

Time passed slowly, everyone waited and waited. Suddenly and without notice, the poor suicidal bastard jumped. He plunged nearly two hundred feet and smashed onto the concrete below, full force. Splat! The crowd ooohed and aaahed, the paramedics ran to the crumpled mangled body. All eyes were on the action and the paramedics.

All eyes, except the five amigos. They waited for the nod from the first amigo, and simultaneously reached into their radio cars and immediately called to sergeant Melner. Sergeant Melner shifted his attention from the bloody, gory scene in front of him and looked up to see exactly what makes these officers what they are, sick and perverted. But sick in a silly sense. Sick and perverted in order to keep their sanity and composure Dysfunctional to become functional.

When Sergeant Melner looked up he saw five individual police officers holding up five individual sheets of paper. On theses separate sheets were these numbers: 8.7, 9.5, 9.7, 9.9, and 10.0. There they stood, five police officers, acting as Olympic judges, grading the jumper's fall as if it were an Olympic dive competition! Each score was the officer's grade for the suicide jumper's precision jump.

His mouth wide open, Sgt. Melner was speechless. He was attempting to control himself. He asked in a cynical way, why did you give him such a low score of 8.7, John? The first amigo, which initiated the entire fiasco, said, "His feet came apart before he hit Sarge!"

The five placards with the scores written on them didn't stay up very long for fear that a citizen would see the scores or, God forbid, a late arriving news station would notice the papers. That would be devastating and would definitely result in six police officers being fired.

Sgt. Melner told me later that he couldn't recall in his entire life laughing so damn hard and long. After he realized what his men had done he had to get into his radio car, tuck his head down and after putting the windows up laughed and chuckled uncontrollably. He laughed until he had tears in his eyes and his stomach muscles hurt. It took five minutes for him to gain his composure.

I can only imagine, no, I know what drives police officers to these extremes. The comedy of a situation must be found and discovered in order to keep them sane and somewhat normal. Sane, collected, functional, and psychologically sound, OR, maybe I'm wrong. Maybe the job takes its toll on all police officers making them cynical and hardened.

Sergeant Jim Melner, Baltimore County Police Department,

Towson Precinct—late 1990s.

Safe Again

I worked with many officers over the years especially when I was in the Eastern District. Most of the time I worked a radio car alone. Before I was given my own post to cover, I worked hand in hand with Officer Pat Henley. Pat didn't have to work at being manly and macho, it came naturally for him. In his mid twenties, like me, but he was taller, six feet two inches. He was also leaner than I and in great shape. Pat was an excellent cop and we complimented each other wonderfully. We were one of the best team workers and set of partners I had seen in my career. We knew each other's next move, we weren't afraid. Sometimes we felt invincible, but apprehensive. We did wind up in some wild off the wall situations. We were fearless, most of the time.

We took no shit from anyone, we both drove like maniacs, up sidewalks, down one way streets the wrong way, sliding around corners with tires squealing and engines roaring. We always wanted to be the first ones there, the first officers to assist. Especially on a, "Signal 13," officer needs assistance. It was no holds barred, get there first! We were, one would think, super cops.

Summer, 1977. I was driving west on Eager St. and thought that I had seen a black male walking west with something large protruding from his upper back. I stopped the car and leaned across the roof. "Come here" I said in a gruff voice. He walked towards me. I looked at him strangely and turned him around. There I saw a very large Stanley screwdriver protruding approximately five inches out from his shoulder blade. He was calm and cool. I asked him who had done this to him and he nonchalantly pointed up the street to the 2500 block of E. Eager St. I placed the victim in my radio car and called the dispatcher. "336, I'm transporting a stabbing victim to Hopkins Hospital from the 2400 block of E. Eager St." "10-4, 336 out to Hopkins." I heard.

I told the twenty-year old victim not to lean back and that he was going to be okay. He was more relaxed than I was. This guy is more laid back than I am, and he's got a fucking screwdriver shoved into his back. I thought I was macho. This guy is too cool. I thought.

As I pulled into the 2500 block of Eager St., I saw a young black male sitting on the steps in front of 2523 E. Eager St., alone. Suddenly the victim said, "That's him! That's the muvafucker who stuck me!" I always like a good felony arrest and I became excited, my heart began to beat faster. I exited my radio car and confronted the alleged suspect. "Did you stab this guy in my car in the back?" I asked loudly. He said, to my surprise, "Yeah Why?" I thought to myself, *what an asshole! He never should have told me that. He just admitted to a felony, dumb fuck!* I quickly grabbed his left wrist and with one easy swipe I placed one cuff on the suspect and simultaneously advised him that he was under arrest.

All was calm at that point; usually a suspect or arrestee will go with an officer without much of a fight. They might pull and yell to look cool in front of their, "homies". But they usually come along quietly. Not this *Gladiator!* He was a young black male and hated cops, especially white cops. He wanted to be bad.

He swung at me and attempted to pull away and we began to struggle. He was resisting arrest. The fight was on. Using the one-cuffed wrist, I yanked him off the steps and onto the ground. I was doing well on my own and didn't feel as though I needed help at this point. I nearly had the two wrists together to cuff the other wrist when I observed another black male, young black male, coming out of the house and down the steps. He began pulling on his brother and at the same time was attempting to kick me away. At this point I needed help. "336, signal 13, 2500 E. Eager St., signal 13!"

The officers that worked with me knew that I never called for help unless I was definitely in *deep shit*. Most assuredly I was in dire need of assistance.

Some officers were marked as wimps, pussies, always calling for help at any slight sign of trouble. You only call for help if you really need it, not because you're scared. There is no place on the streets for scared cops! Some officers were scared on the streets, we knew who they were, they always *cried wolf* so we always took our time getting to them.

This was not the case with my squad and me. If any one of us called for assistance it was because we were in serious trouble and were about to be injured. When I called for help I struggled briefly then I made sure that the dispatcher knew my location. I heard the dispatcher repeat, "Signal 13 2500 E. Eager St., 336 is calling for a signal 13, 2500 E. Eager St.!" I knew help was only moments away and I could concentrate on fighting and not losing my halfway-cuffed stabbing suspect. I was mistaken!

I had forgotten it was a hot, Friday, summer night. A very *busy*, hot, Friday night. Calls for stabbings, shootings, family disturbances, fights, etc. were rampant and coming out in rapid succession all night.

I felt as though my back up was taking longer than usual getting to me. It seemed I was struggling for quite sometime. Usually you can hear the sirens and see the procession of radio cars approaching. You can really start fighting then because you knew that the troops were coming. You could look your best for you co-workers, you were safe. Again, not this time!

I had to call for help once again! "336 I really need help down here!" Again I heard, "Signal 13, 2500 E. Eager St. second call, Signal 13,2500 E. Eager St!" This was unusual, but not unheard of. After all, it was Friday night, 4x12 shift.

By now I was getting worried, I might get hurt here. I had hold of and was scuffling with both brothers, but had absolutely no control of the situation. Next I see an older woman come out, I assumed it was the mother. She tried to kick me in the groin but missed and hit my leg. She was attempting to pull her sons away from me, interfering with an arrest. I instinctively punched the mother in the mouth letting go of the second brother, the one not handcuffed. I was not letting the other go! Very bad move with the mom. The two suspect's mother hit the curb and struck her head. I was now in deep trouble and I knew it! I was losing. Three younger boys and two girls emptied out of the row house and came down the steps; it was the remainder of the entire family.

About five minutes had passed since my first call for assistance. *It never took five minutes! Where was my help,* I was seriously concerned and knew that this is how officers go down.

There was no help close. I yelled, "336 I need some fucking help 2500 E. Eager St, NOW!" A third signal 13 was called this time; it was aired over the entire city. *Any* officer from *any* district, *any* detective, plain-clothes officer, *anyone* who could hear their radio knew I needed help and fast.

As all eight members of this family were kicking and beating the shit out of me

I felt a rush of air, a large rush of air above me. It was the police helicopter, Foxtrot, above me. The pilot and observer were approximately thirty feet above me. They could see I was in trouble and was being beaten. The little bastards were pulling at my nightstick, mace, and most fearful and scariest of all, my gun! The observer wanted to jump out of the helicopter but couldn't endanger his life or that of the pilot's. I could hear the observer say, "Dispatcher, get this officer some help. He needs help!"

It had been about seven minutes by now but it seemed like thirty. I was continually kicking and punching, anything to get these fuckers off of me. Suddenly I looked up and saw two sets of shiny boots running in my direction. *Thank you God!"* I thought. I got a surge of energy, a renewed strength, the troops were here. I saw Lee grab the handcuffed suspects head and jerk it back, Harold then kicked the bastard in the face. Blood squirted everywhere! It seemed like everything stopped. I heard another thud and more blood came squirting from the other suspect's face. How happy I was to see that, that blood. Two more officers ran up, two more radio cars arrived, and so did the paddy wagon. I was safe. *I love these guys I do!* I thought. *All this for me!*

We locked up ten people in the 2500 block of E. Eager St. that night. Including the mother. It was a violent five to seven minutes, I did like it. Especially after it was over and I wasn't seriously injured.

I was a hero once again, Why? I never let go of my half handcuffed suspect. It was a bad time. I found out later that Lee and Harold had come over four miles from the station to reach me. Four miles and they were the first to reach me! Normally we only work eight to ten *blocks* apart. Each other officer in the squad had serious calls. Two other officers had two separate arrests and another officer had called for help as I had. Not a typical Friday night, but close.

FOUR *signal 13 calls, unheard of!* I felt great, another first! I learned that the stabbing victim had gotten out of my car and ran away. He was too scared to even stay in my police car.

After the signal 13 was called off, I walked around, somewhat dazed but feeling good. I walked around as a captain walks around the battlefield after a major skirmish. I picked up my nightstick, radio, mace, hat, and even found the contact lens that came out during the fight. My things were strewn all over the street. I went to the hospital for minor repairs; *I love this job, what a rush!* I was, once more, safe again.

Choir Boys

When the Joseph Wambaugh book, THE CHOIR BOYS, hit the shelves the younger and more aggressive officers in my squad read the book. We passed it around to each other; all of us had it read in a week. We began to act out the book. We were, CHOIR BOYS. About eight officers were fitting into, or becoming, the personas in the book. After work on certain nights of the 4 x 12 shift we had our very own, CHOIR PRACTICE. We also had a 'church key', or bottle opener, that was given to a different officer after each CHOIR PRACTICE for safekeeping until he handed it over to another CHOIR BOY to keep safe.

In the book there were two women that were cop groupies and hung out with, and partied with, the choirboys. We gave our girls the same names. Oralee, (orally), Tingle and Carolina Moon. The girls loved their choirboy names and made nearly every choir practice. They would supply goodies and eats as well as beer, on special occasions. All of us sat on tailgates of officer's trucks. We drank, talked about the previous shift, ate chips and pretzels, and just partied. After all we were choirboys and we were at choir practice. Every beer had to be opened by our church key and *only* that church key.

One night during choir practice we met behind the Tastycake Company on Edison Hwy. We would meet there or under the Linwood Ave. Bridge. These spots were somewhat secluded and out of the way. I challenged one of the choirboys to attempt to shoot the American flag off of the antenna of my 1969 Firebird. He was approximately twenty feet away. I knew he couldn't hit the antenna, it was dark, the antenna was only a 1/8 of an inch thick and he was twenty feet away with beers in him. I bet $10.00, as did the other choirboys.

Mark took aim, stood very still, took a breath and held it, and fired! We thought he missed, but then the American flag slowly fluttered downward to the hood of the car. We couldn't believe it! He had nicked the antenna and the speed of the bullet snapped the antenna with such force the flag just fell off. It was the topic of conversation all week. We drank and laughed. Mark pocketed his $80.00.

Weeks later we were again at choir practice behind Edison Hwy. It was a boring practice. No one seemed in the partying mood. Suddenly we saw red and white flashing lights. It was an ambulance with all its lights flashing backing up to our little circle of pick up trucks. "What the hell is that someone yelled?" The ambulance came to a quick stop, the siren blasted one time and the back doors flew open. Oralee Tingle and Carolina Moon jumped out of the ambulance with a six-pack of beer in each hand. They were only wearing flimsy nightgowns. The choir practice started and the party began. Jerry was one of the choirboys and also a part time ambulance driver. He had surprised us. Great surprise, another night to remember.

That was not to be upstaged, we thought, until Jerry came by to visit us during choir practice. He was working overtime. Jerry was a wild man he did things that most of us wouldn't dream of. He was a true, full blooded, 100%, choirboy! Jerry was working a slow, uneventful midnight shift and was bored. It was about 1:00 a.m. when he decided to sneak up on us by driving his radio car over the railroad tracks. Bad idea! His car became stuck on the iron tracks and he couldn't move it. We could hear noise down the tracks but had no idea what was going on and had *no idea* it was Jerry. We heard an engine approaching off in the distance but it slowed and stopped, we paid no attention, we were in choir practice. After a few minutes we heard the engine begin to accelerate again and gain some speed. Then we heard a horrendous crash and crunching of metal. The screeching, scraping, sound of metal against metal continued. We were bewildered. "What the hell is going on?" someone said.

All of us looked down the tracks and coming into our view was a large locomotive engine. As it slowed and passed us we noticed that the locomotive was dragging something along the tracks by a thick length of chain. "Jesus Christ it's a fucking radio car!" Tom spurted. "What the fuck is going on?" Another choirboy yelled.

Evidently Jerry had, in his haste to surprise us at practice, gotten his radio car stuck on the railroad tracks. He had stopped a passing locomotive, put a chain on the front end of the car and attempted to have this huge locomotive engine that normally pulls fifty to a hundred railroad cars free his 3900 pound police car from the tracks.

The entire front end of the car had ripped apart from the firewall, or windshield of the vehicle forward, and it was being dragged down the tracks directly to us. We were amazed, flabbergasted, and dumbfounded! "How could you be so *fucking* stupid? You are a *fucking* moron Jerry, an imbecile!" Tony was pissed at Jerry. There was nothing we could do to help Jerry this time. We walked down the tracks about fifty yards and stood in amazement as we watched gasoline, oil, and transmission fluid spewing from the remainder of the radio car, what was left of it.

We waved good-bye to Jerry and fled! We wanted nothing at all to do with that chaotic situation. We followed each other to the Linwood Ave. Bridge and continued our choir practice; of course there was ONLY one topic to speak about the remainder of our meeting, TRAINS!

Now and then at choir practice an officer, choirboy, that's on duty, will stop by and visit the other choirboys. This particular night all of us had finished our choir practice and left to go home. We left Oralee Tingle with the officer that was working the midnight shift. She climbed into his radio car and we left. It was approximately 4:00 a.m.

The following day there was a buzz at the district. Amtrak Train Authorities had called to complain about the officer-working car # 7832. They had seen the number on the trunk of the radio car. These numbers are very large and are used to identify radio cars, especially used by the helicopter unit to assist the officers on the street when in a situation. The

Tastycake Company is located near the Amtrak train route. The train goes past the company, which is also one of the locations for our choir practice. It seems as though a certain choirboy was sitting on the hood of his radio car with Oralee, (orally), Tingle on her knees in the dirt, with her head buried in the officer's lap. This wasn't so bad, but add into the fact that the Amtrak *commuter* train goes by only at about thirty miles per hour and that the train was only twenty-five feet away from this sexual encounter, and a problem, dilemma, arises. Several commuter passengers witnessed a portion of choir practice in session and were offended, someone complained.

Fortunately, for that choirboy, and the rest of us, the numbers that were reported from the trunk of the radio car could not be matched to any one car in service that night. Needless to say, CHOIR PRACTICE was moved to the Linwood Ave. Bridge for good!

The CHOIR BOYS eventually faded into history but will not soon be forgotten. The, 'church key,' was retired. There were some wild and strange occurrences that took place at CHOIR PRACTICE, that's why they are in this book also. Thanks Mr. Wambaugh.

Pearlman Place

The 1900 block of Pearlman Place consists of just one block. There is no 1800 block and no 2000 block. That single block, street, merely sits there all alone and frightening, always looming over the Eastern District of Baltimore City. It's an eerie street sitting there all by itself; it even looks strange compared to other streets in the district. It looks scary and evil. I cannot explain why but driving onto that block always affected me in a negative, ugly, sort of way. Maybe because my first week on the street I witnessed an unusually gruesome and gory homicide, the victim had been repeatedly stabbed in the upper chest and torso. I guess the crime had impacted me more than I wanted to admit, evidently this block *did* scare me. I had to force myself to patrol, *the 1900 block of Pearlman Place.*

"332," radioed the dispatcher. "332 go," I replied. "1900 block of Pearlman Place, investigate the problem." *Oh shit, not Pearlman Place, why does it have to be Pearlman Place?"* I thought. Every time I had gone there someone had been seriously hurt, shot, stabbed or I had made an arrest or had to back up another officer making an arrest. I pulled into the block off of North Ave. I could see a cab in the middle of the street blocking traffic at the opposite end of the block from where I had entered. I assumed and imagined *everything.* A shooting, a cutting, child abuse, drugs, etc., all of it. After all, it was Pearlman Place!

As I exited my radio car I saw two feet facing up and protruding out of the back seat of the cab, driver's side. *Okay,* I thought, *what could this be?* It seems as though over time, this job makes one untrusting, negative, cynical, sarcastic, and callused and always thinking bad thoughts. I see two feet protruding from a cab and immediately I think it was an attempted hold up and the cabbie killed the suspect or vice versa. Not that maybe, just maybe, something innocent and nice has occurred. This line of thinking is sad and dysfunctional. Just like this job, at times, not always, but at times.

I approached the cab carefully. By now a crowd of six to eight people had gathered. I became more alert. As I peered into the back seat I saw something totally different from all my evil and bad assumptions. Nothing like I had expected. A young girl was in labor and the baby's head was sticking out slightly. The baby was crowning, a term I had learned in the academy. "Holy shit," I said aloud. I immediately requested an ambulance. This young girl was screaming in pain and yelling, "Get it out, get it out!" My thoughts briefly pulled away from the immediate problem facing me when I heard this angry, vicious outcry to, "get it out!" *This is an innocent baby, not a fucking monster, how can she be so ignorant, this bitch?* I wondered. I said to the people gathered around, "get me some towels." I knelt on the ground and placed my hand on the baby's head. *Maybe the ambulance will show up and I won't have to deliver this baby.* I thought to myself. No such luck, baby Pearlman Place was not waiting. My hands were gooey and slimy by now and so was the back seat of the cab. The smell was nasty. The young mother's water had broken in the cab. I was gagging, I was sick to my stomach. I held onto the baby's head and pulled gently but firmly. The mother was screaming, cursing and thrashing about. I wanted to choke her out to shut her mouth. Whoosh! The baby actually popped out into my waiting stinking hands. I was definitely grossed out and unprepared for delivering my very first baby.

The baby was charcoal in color and quiet. The umbilical cord was disgusting looking also, resembling a deformed snake. I placed the baby on the mother's stomach, placed towels on both of them and got up off my knees from the ground. The mother had finally settled down and was assisting me.

I looked around and saw the paramedic approaching. I must have looked green, pale or in bad shape for the paramedic asked if I was going to pass out. "No," I replied, and vomited on the street. The baby was doing better than I was, everyone there, was doing better than I was.

I got back into my radio car and went directly back to the station gagging and choking all the way there. *What had happened?* I wondered. *I had actually delivered my first baby! Yeah me!* My shirt smelled like something I have trouble describing, was covered in a watered down type of bloody fluid and was slimy. I threw it in the trashcan at the station and washed up in the bathroom for over ten minutes. I was under the impression that delivering a baby, regardless of race, was supposed to be a wonderful, uplifting, pure moment in life. Not for me. Bringing a newborn child into this world and the wonder and exhilaration of witnessing one of God's miracles was an incident that was disgusting, smelly, and slimy and not something I would want to experience again.

As luck would have it, it did happen again. I cannot recall the details as I can on Pearlman Place but I remember it occurred on Dallas Street. I delivered another baby but this time it must have been uneventful or the traumatic experience I had earlier had jaded me. I was disgusted with this bitch for screaming for me to, "Get it out," and it was my first baby delivery. I guess the second delivery couldn't compare in my memory and I cannot recall the scenario on Dallas Street. However, I won't forget baby Pearlman Place, the stench, the screaming and the hurt that the *1900 block of Pearlman Place* had dealt to me, once again.

SONYA

After working the east side of Baltimore city for nearly three years I learned the ways of the street. I had seen enough violence and disregard for personal life to last me a lifetime. I thought I had seen it all. Every now and then a situation arises that still makes a police officer shake his head in disbelief and disgust. Something touches your inner core, the right and wrong that you've lived all your life is suddenly questioned. How could this be? How could some one do this to another person?

The call came out for, "investigate the problem," and see Ms. Duncan. I arrived at the call with an, "I don't care," attitude. One of those days when a police officer is numb to his surroundings and just doesn't give a good shit about what he is supposed to be doing or what calls he handles. A routine no frills mundane type of day, do eight hours and then go home.

I met Ms. Duncan at 1100 N. Patterson Park Ave. As I walked into the house she was at the door waiting for me. She explained to me that her thirteen-year old daughter had been beaten and raped by her "live-in" boyfriend. The boyfriend had held her and her daughter against their will the day before by standing them against a wall in the kitchen with a loaded double barreled shot gun pointed at the both of them for six hours while he drank alcohol and verbally abused them. This was done because the mother had become aware of the rape/beating and confronted him about his actions. He made them both promise at gunpoint, not to call the police. However, the mother had a chance to call this day because He had gone out for several hours. I had received the call.

I was to find out more information from the daughter directly afterward talking to Ms. Duncan. The boyfriend had been raping this thirteen-year old innocent girl for nearly a month. Not only had he raped her the day before, but he had also tied her to her bed with an electrical cord, beaten her on the back and the back of her legs with a 2 x 4 board and the electrical cord.

But most disturbing, disgusting and for her, what must have been the most petrifying, horrifying and degrading act, was that of the boyfriend pulling out pubic hairs from her pubic area with a pair of pliers! After tying this little girl to a bed the sadistic bastard would continually rape her, force her to perform oral sex on him, perform oral sex on her, and beat her at random with a board and electrical cord. Then if the pain, suffering, degradation and humiliation weren't killing this little thirteen year old girl's fragile mental and psychological state, the sick fuck would then utilize pliers to forcibly remove patches of pubic hair from this girl's, tender pubic area. I closed my eyes when I was hearing what this thirty-seven year old man had done and was doing. I could picture the rape and beatings along with the pubic hairs being pulled out in patches by a pair of pliers. The scene was very vivid in my mind. Sonya's pain and agony must have been excruciating and nearly unbearable.

The thought of someone doing this to a thirteen-year-old girl caused me to question this suspect's very existence. *Why would someone do this? What could possibly possess a man to pull out pubic hairs with a pair of pliers,* I wondered. I became flushed and a hot flash raced through my body. Sweat formed on my forehead and upper lip. I was furious, but not in a violent way, more of a get even, pay back, I will put this animal in jail type of ferocity. *I will put my heart and soul into this investigation and I will go over and above to convict him. I will pool all my skills and knowledge to do exactly what the criminal justice system mandates to properly arrest and convict this beast.* I thought. I was incensed. I was on a mission from God to right this atrocity. I had a renewed sense of worth, a burst of energy and righteousness.

I called the crime lab and a female police officer to the scene to process the house and rape victim. As Sonya was leaving I could see the fear in her eyes and the lack of any self respect or self esteem. I put my hand on her frail shoulder, looked her in the eyes and said, "I promise I will put him in jail for a very long time". She just looked at me in a blank stare, our eyes locked for a short time and she just turned away and walked out of the house with the female officer. *Why?* I asked myself, *why?* After gathering all the facts I stayed with Ms. Duncan for one-half an hour. The boyfriend still had not shown up. I instructed her to go to the hospital with her daughter, Sonya.

A fellow officer, Ron Drake, and I waited for the suspect. I had explained to Ron what had transpired and what I wanted to accomplish. I had Ron wait up the block in the radio car and I stood behind the front door. I stood there for two hours. I didn't care; I just wanted him to come through the door. I observed him coming up the steps. He was wearing exactly what Ms. Duncan had described. He came through the door and I stuck my gun right into his ear and shoved him against the wall. "If you don't put your fucking hands behind your fucking head, I'm going to BLOW your fucking head off" I said loudly. "DO YOU HEAR ME ASSHOLE?" I called for Ron, he replied, "on the way Dan". I knew I had only a very short time to let this piece of shit know I was furious over what he had done to this young girl. I took my knee and forced it into his back. I shoved his head into the wall several times. I was twisting the handcuffs so hard that my hands hurt. He was screaming for me to stop. "FUCK YOU" is all I could say. *I had to stop what I was doing, it wasn't right! So what, he deserved this Danny,* is what I said to myself. I had waited for two hours and all that time I was replaying and planning how I was going to beat this beast to unconsciousness, beat him to a pulp or even to death! The scenario changed and each time I imagined myself doing more and more to inflict pain and even death. Now that I actually had him in my grasp I knew I couldn't kill him and I didn't inflict nearly the amount of pain I had imagined poor Sonya had experienced. But he was in pain, I was somewhat satisfied, but Sonya's pain was worse and deeper than either of ours.

I wondered if I was gong too far with gathering evidence in this crime. I questioned myself quietly but quickly dispelled those thoughts when I found the pliers. I told the crime lab tech whom I had known for nearly six years, (ever since I was a Cadet), that this case had sickened me and asked him to do all he could to help me in my quest to convict this bastard! He assured me that he would do this and also felt my energy. Together we took and labeled every bit of evidence we could find, and then some. We took the board she had been beaten with and matched it with the marks on Sonya's back and legs. We did the same with the electrical cord matching it to her back and wrists. Pictures couldn't lie, they would tell this horrifying tale to the judge and jury. At this point I discovered he had beaten her with the cord also, perfect matches. The sheets and pillowcases were taken along with the covers of the couch seats, for he had raped her there too. They gave us a perfect match we found out later, his semen, sperm and her vaginal fluids, that were taken from her at the hospital. We took the pliers that somehow still had two pubic hairs on the jaws. I asked the crime lab tech to take a close up picture of the pliers with the hairs very visible in case they were later disturbed. No questions as to what they were. No item of evidence was overlooked. I even called the female officer by phone and told her to stand by for me at the hospital. With pliers and pubic hair in hand, in a sealed evidence bag I went to the hospital and stood by as the doctor clipped pubic hairs off of the victim's body. They were also placed in a sealed evidence bag and I personally took them to the evidence control unit so there was no question as to the chain of custody or to the authenticity of the pubic hairs.

I spoke with Sonya quietly and gently in person and asked her if the crime lab tech could take pictures of the bare patches on her pubis if she was covered properly and this was done with discretion. She looked at me again as she did at the crime scene, but this time she seemed as if she knew what I was doing and why. She nodded yes and I winked at her. She smiled a very small smile, or did I just want to see that? I wasn't certain. In my mind it was a real smile and I left it at that.

I had done all that I knew how to, all I was trained to do and used all my learned abilities to make this case the one case in my short career, that there was no question as to the guilt and that this rapist/pervert and aberration would be found guilty beyond a reasonable doubt and incarcerated. I had, to that date, not lost a case in court. I would make certain with all my heart and soul that I would win this case hands down.

The case came to trial nearly one year later. I was ready. I stayed up half the night reviewing it. My notes, my reports, and the evidence. I walked into the courtroom confident and sure. Not long after my testimony the jury went in for deliberation. One hour later this rapist received a guilty verdict and was to receive a twenty-year sentence. The jury, as well as the judge, was sickened and appalled. I felt wonderful, rejuvenated, satisfied and had that great feeling of accomplishment you get when all goes well because you went the distance.

I was to feel even more of a rush when the judge called me into his chambers and he along with the Assistant State's Attorney congratulated me on my testimony and with the gathering of evidence. "Rarely do I see such dedication and perfection Officer Shanahan" the judge said. I told him that this particular case had touched me so deeply that I did all I could make that known. "You did," was his reply, and I left.

I never saw Sonya again, but she kept looking at me in criminal court as I testified. She was quiet and meek during the entire trial. When the verdict was read, she did or said nothing. I could only hope that she knew that many extra steps were taken to find this man guilty of this horrible crime and it was done just for *her*, or, was it for *me*?

THE GOOD COP

PALM GROVE LIQUORS

A mid summer's night, 1978. I was on routine patrol on my post. It was an uneventful day, things were quiet. Suddenly the calm was broken by the dispatcher,"336, assist the firefighters at Milton and Biddle Sts., at The Palm Grove Liquor store." Firefighters and police have a special unspoken bond, as we do with nurses. We seem to get along quite well. A lot of police officers and firefighters marry nurses. I'm sure it's due to the essence of our job duties. All of us work shift work, deal with death, destruction, sadness, injury and evil, nearly everyday. We have a lot in common. We understand one another; it makes for a solid relationship. There is always something to talk about and to discuss when you are a police officer, firefighter, or nurse.

I arrived quickly at the Palm Grove. I was confused as I parked my car, something was amiss. The firefighters were coming down the ladders in a hurry, not climbing up, as they should, *what was wrong?* I wondered. I learned why very quickly! Gunshots rang out and I then realized why everyone was coming down, not going up. After making my way to the cover of the fire engine I discovered what was taking place. Apparently there was a suspect on the second floor firing out the windows at the citizens and firefighters. *What to do?* I puzzled. My heart was racing, my palms were sweating, and I was excited but confident in my abilities. *I've been in firefights before, I'm okay. Just think Dan, think.* I was reassuring myself; I was pumping myself with adrenaline, adrenaline to handle the situation like a man, like the police officer I was sworn to be. PROTECT! I had my gun drawn but could not get a clear shot at the suspect, he was standing to far back in the room.

Pat Henley arrived and made his way next to the fire engine with me. Pat and I worked a two-man car often and were very adept at working together. We knew each other's next move, we acted and reacted alike. "What's going on Dan?" He asked. "Got an asshole up there that set the bar on fire and then when the firefighters tried to put the fire out this jerk off starting firing at them." They think he's on flakes; they make you feel like Superman. We have to go get him Pat" "Yeah I know!" The firefighter overheard us and pulled two breathing apparatus's out of the side compartment of the fire engine and two air tanks. "Put these on boys and see if you can breathe." He gave us a quick class on how to breathe in the mask and what to do and not to do. He simply said, "Breathe".

Pat and I were excited and scared. We wanted inside, we wanted to kill this drugged out asshole. It's a rush that begins at your feet and continues up your body to your head. The feeling of invincibility and vulnerability mixed together with doing what has to be done, and doing what is right and justified.

This is where being sworn to protect and do your job is put to the test. We knew we could wind up shot or dead, but we also had that desire for intrigue and danger. Danger that sends chills up and down your spine and causes your hair to stand up on your body. I absolutely loved it! I was well trained, had been in firefights before and had the confidence of a young police officer. "Let's go Pat!" I yelled. We looked at each other, shook hands and ran directly into the line of fire to the back door of the bar.

I cannot explain completely what goes thru your mind at a time like this. Your body shakes but not uncontrollably. The urge to make this bad guy disappear and the surge of energy that is needed to run into a burning building that is nearly engulfed with flames and contains a drugged out psycho firing down upon you, is for some reason overwhelming, exhilarating, and very exciting! There is no equivalent to this feeling and to the experience of bringing a shooter out of a burning building, the odds that someone is going to die is quite high and you are well aware of that fact. What a rush of excitement, danger, and adrenaline.

Pat went up the stairs first. I followed closely. As we climbed the stairs my face became very hot from the growing flames, my glass face shield began to fog up. I thought that my contacts were melting from the intense heat! My hand came up to brush my hair out of my face and I indirectly touched the facemask. It wiped a spot clean. Good, the fire is fogging the mask; my contacts weren't melting, *silly*. I cleared the fog and began to slither across the floor after reaching the top of the steps, the landing. I was holding onto Pat's pant leg. The smoke and heat were horrible, the visibility was very bad and I needed to keep close to my partner. We were to keep each other alive. As we crawled close to the first door on the left the suspect suddenly came bolting out of that room, the bathroom, and began firing his handgun at us. At that moment gunfire erupted from my right. I got to my knees to fire but as I pulled the trigger Pat stood up! "Shit Pat, get down!" I yelled. "I nearly shot you in the back of the fucking head!"

Suddenly and simultaneously gunshots came at us from my right, bang, bang! The suspect was firing from my left, bang, bang, bang. Pat was firing directly in front of me, pop, pop. The fire was getting extremely hot and dangerous. As the shooting continued all the windows in the room began to break and the glass and cool water was hitting us. *What the fuck is happening? Why is the glass breaking in on us and not out? Who is firing at us from my right and where did the suspect go that was to my left?*

My mind was whirring, my thoughts abounding with decisions and questions. There was so much going on so many threats of danger, life-threatening danger. I waited to be shot, or burned, or cut by breaking glass. I stayed low to the floor and held onto Pat. "You okay Pat?" "Yeah Dan, who is over there to the right!" "I don't know but I'm going over to find out!" I yelled. "Police Officer." "There is a police officer over here" I heard. "I think the suspect is down!" "Pat, can you see him?" I yelled. "No, but I've got a leg and it's quivering, I think this fucker's pumping out and dying, we better get him out of here!"

Pat pulled the suspect towards him, everyone holstered their weapons. It was quiet except for the crackling and hissing of the fire as it engulfed the building. All I could hear was the flow of oxygen into my mask. The heat was unbearable. I would suck air in, there would be a click, and then I would exhale. That's all I heard in this eerie burning terrifying quiet. Swoosh, click, swoosh, swoosh, click, swoosh, I was receiving life giving cool fresh air.

I was able to grab the suspect's leg. Pat and I dragged the dying suspect towards the top of the steps, the landing. The fire was intense. I lost sight of the other officer, *where did he go? Shit, how did he get in ahead of us?* I wondered. Suddenly I could hear again. I could hear officers shouting on the radio, "are you okay in there, 335, 336? What's your situation?

Apparently the officers outside heard the shooting, watched the firefighters break the glass in to give us some air and to release the heat. But we were so engrossed with our present firefight our tunnel vision and ear muffling kept us from hearing the other officers, just as Pat and I had no idea where the other officer came from the officers outside had no idea whether Pat and I were alive or dead.

The suspect began to struggle as we dragged him to the steps. He was on his back and I had his left leg. I tried to break his leg around the banister, I have no idea why, but I was insistent on breaking this guy's leg. I couldn't. Pat and I dragged the suspect down the steps out into the fresh air. Plop, plop, plop, we heard his head hit every step. We didn't care. This fucker tried to kill firefighters and more importantly, Pat and myself! I removed my air mask as we got out of the building. Pat and I dragged the suspect out to the middle of the street and dropped him right on top of a manhole cover. He wasn't moving. I was sitting on the ground next to him. Pat was standing next to me with his hand on my shoulder. We both were quivering but only we two were aware of it. I looked at Pat and he looked back at me, "Damn!" Is all we could say to each other. That was so very intense and also a great rush, especially since we were not injured!

One of the firefighters that fitted us for our air tanks came over to assist us. He turned off the oxygen and took our masks. "Most firefighters have to take lessons to breath in these things, you guys did great!" He said. I walked over to the suspect, "What's your name shithead?" I asked. "Fuck you!" he replied. He was having trouble speaking in full sentences. He was pumping out, or bleeding to death.

"That's okay anyway you fucking asshole, you're going to die Then I'll find out your fucking name from your prints and your fucking toe tag! Punk!" I called for a paramedic. There were four on the scene, two for each ambulance that responded. All four were tending to a firefighter that had *sprained* his ankle. "Hey guys, I think this guy's dying," I yelled. "Fuck him, we have a firefighter with a sprained ankle, we'll get to him when were done!" He yelled back. *Jesus Christ, this muvafucker has four gunshot wounds in him, they know he's dying, he's pumping out and they are fixing a sprained ankle. Shit! Hey Fuck It! DAMN!* I thought.

The suspect began to shake violently, he stopped, he began taking very short breaths and then I heard that old familiar gurgle. That death gurgle, it lasted for a few seconds and then the victim expired. He died, threw a 7, as we called it, crapped out, right in front of Pat and I. I looked at Pat, "Shit

Pat I was just kidding. I didn't mean for him to die now." "Too late Dan, you killed him." Said Pat. "Fuck you, you killed him!" I felt no remorse and was actually angry at this asshole for trying to kill me.

The paramedics picked up the dead guy to get him off the street. It reminded me of Popeye when the car crashes and the ambulance only takes the crashed car and leaves the victim lying on the street. I had to laugh to myself. However, dead guy on the manhole cover wasn't laughing, he was just dead.

We cleared the area and all of us left the corner of Milton and Biddle, all of us except for the soul of the guy we had shot. He had a bullet hole in each arm and in each leg including one that severed his femoral artery, which killed him very quickly. He bled to death. The other officer was Officer Ike. He was a SWAT team member and went in ahead of us also with an air tank on. No one knew this. Which is improper procedure? Pat or I could very well have shot him.

His bullets were found to be the ones that actually killed the suspect. Ike wasn't supposed to be in that building. I lied to his supervisor and told him we went in together, that Pat and I asked him to back us up. Evidently, Ike had shot and killed four separate suspects over a two-year period, and his supervisor's wanted him to lay back and stop *killing people*. I lied, but I saved his job. He probably saved Pat's and my life. Definitely a fair exchange.

The suspect's toxicology report came back as him having a high level of alcohol in his blood and a very high level of flakes, or PCP. Superman wasn't very *super* that day. That day at the Palm Grove Liquors.

Chase Street

I received my Third Bronze Star on a sultry summer night. I was searching for a robbery suspect that had just robbed a cabby at gunpoint and was fleeing north on Chase Street toward Chester Street. I was riding with a trainee that evening, Paul Raines, I was trying to show him how cool and exciting being a cop in the crime ridden Eastern District really was. Paul had only been on the street one week. This was the first time he would ride shotgun with me. I would find out later, that it would be the last time he would ever ride with me.

The description was broadcast as "two black males, 16 to 20 years of age, dark skinned, tall and possibly armed with an automatic handgun, heading north on Chester Street." The holdup had only occurred four blocks away from where Paul and I were. "Let's find them Paul," I said. "Okay Dan" was his reply. We turned west onto Chase Street from Milton Avenue, I drove very slowly. As we approached the intersection of Chase and Chester Streets I saw two black males. One with a black coat on and the other had on a red sweatshirt. "336, give me that cab holdup description again" I asked. The description was repeated; only this time the dispatcher advised one suspect had on a black coat.

I pulled up very slowly to the corner where these two suspects were standing. I was getting no eye contact from either suspect. Usually the citizens on the streets, good or bad, would look or glance at me and there would be some type of eye contact. Sometimes citizens would look directly at me and spit on the ground. I would learn that this is their way of being disrespectful. Neither of these suspects would dare look in the direction of the radio car. They were trying to act as inconspicuous as possible but they had no idea that their actions were very abnormal and obvious. I got that gut feeling that these were the hold up men. "Paul" I said, "these are the two suspects, I'll take the one in the black coat, he's supposed to be armed, you grab the one in red. Ready, go!" I slammed on the brakes, screeching the tires, shoved the car in the park position and we jumped out of the radio car, engine running and keys left in the ignition, the foot chase began, the chase was on!

I saw Paul running after the older and taller suspect with the red sweatshirt. I then directed my attention to my suspect, a black male, 5'6", dark skinned and looking very young. We went running at top speed, east on Chase Street. I yelled into the radio, "336 I'm in foot pursuit of one of the cab holdup suspects and my partner was last seen in pursuit north on Chester Street after the other one". *I'm chasing this guy east on Chase Street, I liked that, chasing a suspect on Chase Street.* I thought. Why would that thought enter my mind as I was running after an armed hold up suspect? Anyway, we ran two blocks. It was then I realized that I was gaining on the suspect. *How could this be?* I thought. *He's younger and must be in better shape than my twenty-six year old fat ass.* As I was gaining on this guy I noticed his right hand in his right coat pocket. *He was doing something, but what?* I thought. *The gun Dan, he's trying to get the gun out!* I unsnapped my holster carrying my .38 cal. revolver and continued to run the suspect down. I got approximately three feet away and was ready to grab this kid when he suddenly and abruptly stopped. From that moment on, all was in slow motion. *I've been here before,* I thought. I noticed his right hand come up and I heard three quick clicks. Click, click, click, I heard coming from his automatic weapon, as he fired directly at my face. I lost contact with reality, those three clicks were thundering loud and were occurring in slow motion also. Each click seemed louder than the last. The barrel of the gun was jerking up and down each time he pulled the trigger, again, in slow motion. Everything I was experiencing was happening so slowly and clearly, it was deliberate. My ears were closed and my eyes were in complete tunnel vision. I couldn't hear anything or see anything other than the gun being fired in my face. *Where was the pop? Am I shot? Should I shoot? This kid looks so young.* I questioned myself over and over. The questions kept coming but were not being answered. *Where's the blood? Am I shot?* I kept subconsciously asking myself these same questions as I watched the gun. *No pops, no pain, no blood, I guess I'm not shot.* I raised my gun, I just couldn't fire. *He looked so young,* I thought, *why was I questioning myself?* I thought, again.

Earlier that day at roll call, we were cautioned by our shift commander to use extreme caution when firing our weapons. "You can't stop that bullet once it leaves your gun men". He said. The words kept coming to the forefront of my immediate thoughts. The shift commander was trying to protect his men when in actuality he had caused me to stop and questions my designs. It could have cost me my life!

Earlier that week an off duty police officer, Scotty McGowan, had walked into a sub shop and ordered a sub. As he was waiting for his order a suspect, Jawan Mcgee, entered and attempted to hold up the sub shop. The officer identified himself and pulled his gun pointing it at the suspect. The suspect quickly and deliberately reached into his coat pocket and pulled out a black and silver object. He pointed it at Detective McGowan. Detective McGowan fired a shot at the alleged hold up suspect. It would be discovered later that the black and silver object was not a gun but a cigarette lighter. The suspect was paralyzed from the waist down. This incident came to be the top news story for days to follow. Police officers throughout the state were questioning their procedures. Administrators were ordered to reexamine the police department procedures on firing a weapon. This action at role call could have caused me to be thinking twice before acting or firing, most likely costing me my life. Administrators were trying to protect their officers but it was backfiring. Had the gun of the suspect I was chasing fired, I would be dead.

I began to beat the armed suspect in the head with my revolver. Thud, thud, thud, it was still happening in slow motion. I still couldn't hear anything or see anything but blood squirting out of this punk's head and face. I kept hitting and hitting and hitting. I was momentarily incoherent. Suddenly, I was grabbed and pulled off the suspect from behind. Just then the world came back to me, or I came back to the world. I could hear again and I could see radio cars and cops. I had just returned from "that place". The place a person likely goes to when their adrenaline surges and the senses get so acutely tuned to the immediate time of serious fright, and thoughts of dying appear. I had just returned. "Danny are you okay? It's Lee, stop swinging your gun, its okay now, and he's down." My senses returned and I was functioning normally again. I was breathing heavily, my heart was pounding and I was covered with blood, but not mine. I looked on the ground and saw blood running everywhere. The suspect's gun lay on the ground five feet from the suspect. He was moaning and screaming in pain, as he lay there handcuffed.

I looked directly into the suspect's eyes, "You fucking piece of shit!" I said

loudly! I kicked him in the stomach with my boots. I then holstered my blood

covered .38 caliber revolver and stepped back so the ambulance could patch

up this *handgun toting, asshole kid.*

Lee told me later that he had seen the kid pull the gun out. He also saw

something I didn't. The clip containing 10 rounds of 9mm ammo had fallen

out of the suspect's pocket and onto the ground. The suspect had, in his

haste to kill me, forgotten he already had a round in the chamber and he had

racked the round that was already in the barrel, out of the gun. Since the clip

had fallen out there were no rounds to replace the one ejected, the suspect

was firing an empty 9mm. We found that round on the ground. The suspect

couldn't get the clip into the gun quick enough and rack a new round into

the barrel. Lee said he thought I was going to fire and he was hoping I would.

Instead I withdrew. He told me I just kept hitting him in the head over and

over again. I had also evidently fallen to the ground with the suspect and

continued to beat him. Lee was calling out for me to stop, being only five

few away from me, but I didn't respond. So he grabbed me and that's when

I came back to reality. Back from, *that place,* and stopped hitting the suspect.

Where is *that place*? It is a strange but soothing place and I had been there

before. I was also going to find out before my career ended, that I would

return to *that place* a few more times. What a place, *that place.*

The suspect I arrested needed over one hundred stitches to close the

gashes in his head. Paul Raines had lost the suspect he was chasing but he

would be captured later. Within a month, Paul Raines resigned from the department. He, like Lee, was with me but too late to help. I don't think he could have handled this life, this dysfunctional life.

As I have learned, a cop has to become dysfunctional to become functional as a police officer. I truly believe this. I was definitely dysfunctional throughout my career and ever since I lost my career as a police officer.

The suspect's parents were called into the station due to the fact we thought the kid was fifteen or sixteen years old, a juvenile. If he was a juvenile he couldn't be charged as an adult and must be released into his parent's custody. Both his parents adamantly claimed he was sixteen. I had gone to the front desk to tell the sergeant when the suspect's record came up on the computer. He was twenty years old!! I was happy; this asshole could receive true justice for attempting to kill me and for armed robbery of the cabbie. He was charged as an adult and taken to city jail. Then I arrested his parents for lying or making a false statement to a police officer. They continually complained that I was brutal by beating their son. My sergeant refused to take their complaint; I said to the both of them in disgust, "Shut the fuck up, I should have shot your punk son between the fucking eyes!" They never complained any further.

As I drove home that night I wondered why his parents would lie to me knowing that their son could very well have gunned me down, murdered me. I felt a queasy feeling in my stomach. I went home and put my favorite record on the stereo, The Carpenters softly sang, "Bless the Beast and the Children". I placed the headphones over my ears, drank some beers and shook, shivered, smiled and wept softly, as I replayed the night's near deadly experience in my mind I stared at the wall, tears slowly fell from my eyes.

It was a quick fix; I was healing mentally, emotionally and psychiatrically. I attempted to make things right in my head so that I could go to work the next day, do my job, stay alive, and be functional. Or is it *dysfunctional?*

Maggots

I was to find out very early in my career that a police officer remembers streets by the incidents that occur there and personally touch them. At least *I* remembered streets by what I had experienced at those locations. For instance, each time I rode by the 1800 block of East Lafayette Ave. I remembered that Officer Frank Whitby was killed there, the 900 block of North Duncan Street was where, "Tiny" lived, the 2500 block of East Eager Street, was where I had my ass kicked up and down the street and was in big trouble until back up arrived. As I rode by certain streets, such as the 1700 block of North Castle Street, I could recall at least three different incidents that had etched themselves into my mind, memory, on that street. This area was a violent, colorful area. I know that other police officers correlate streets with the incidents that occurred on those streets, they have shared this with me. After being sheltered most of my life in a middle class white neighborhood, incidents mar my memory because they are so horrific, stunning, hilarious or exceptional. A police officer comes in contact with such bizarre people and situations that they seem to all melt together at some time or another. However, certain incidents cannot be forgotten simply due to the strangeness of that episode and can be singled out and recalled simply by driving by that block.

An elderly black lady stopped me in the summer of 1978 in the 1700 block of North Castle Street. She was sitting on the second step of her white marble steps that Baltimore is so famous for. Saturdays were usually set aside for scrubbing the white steps to a clean white sheen. It was a Baltimore tradition. Her right leg was in a white plaster cast that extended from her ankle to her knee. I looked at her as I slowly patrolled by. She motioned me to come to her, I did. "Officer, my leg was broke and it really hurts now, I can't get to the hospital alone," she said dejectedly. I felt sorry for her but wasn't sure what my options were. *Can I take her to the hospital in my radio car, or do I call for an ambulance,* I wondered and questioned myself trying to recall my duties, training and responsibilities. "Take me to the fucking hospital," she yelled in a raucous loud voice. I was startled because she was so meek only moments ago and now, now she's yelling at me. "Wait a minute lady," I said sternly. I was pissed. I paused. *Fuck it,* I thought, *let this experienced, cocky, thinks he knows it all and has seen it all cop look at it, I've been on the streets for two years now, I can do it all!* I said to myself in an attempt to handle the situation. I felt I had seen it all by now, not much unraveled or unnerved me anymore.

I stooped down to look at the cast, it had a small window cut into the cast about four inches by four inches, directly in the front for easy access, I guessed. I had no idea why the cast had a hole cut in it or what the holes' function was. I had several casts on my body before but never with a square cut into the cast with the cut out piece put back into place. *Why had she done this,* I wondered. *She's not supposed to do that to her cast,* I said to myself. Suddenly she screamed, "It hurts, it hurts, look at this!" She removed the little cut out and what I saw seemed to make my eyes pop out of my head and I gasped for air out of horror! I was wide eyed horrified! *Jesus Christ!* I said loudly. I could see all the way to the bone, the white creamy bone was exposed! Plus, there were MAGGOTS all around the bone and I could hear them munching and crunching as they moved around inside this woman's leg It sounded as if they were eating chips! All these small white disgusting maggots were eating away at the inner parts of the leg and bone. I couldn't move. My stomach churned and I put my hand up to my mouth in an attempt to avoid puking on her. I was heaving. *Shit! She has neglected to take care of her leg properly and with all the dirt and filth, flies had nested in the wound and maggots had gotten into the wound! My God I have to save her leg!* I thought frantically.

I picked her up bodily and placed her into the back seat of my radio car. I then rushed to the Hopkins Hospital Emergency Room. I didn't use my lights and siren; I just stopped at each red light and proceeded thru. The entire time I was driving I was appalled to think that this woman had been living in such filth and squalor that the maggots had gotten into her leg and were eating the bone due to her living conditions and lack of cleanliness. *How can these people live like this, a white person would never be this stupid and ignorant about matters of health such as this, she wasn't even aware that maggots come from flies, flies eat shit and FUCKING maggots don't belong in your FUCKING leg! Is this the seventies or am I living in the caveman era.* I was yelling this to myself in my head, I was flabbergasted, and I just couldn't believe this . . .

I reached the emergency room quickly, after all, this *was* an emergency, and she was being eaten alive by maggots. I picked this lady up from the back seat of the radio car and rushed into the emergency room. Two nurses that were close friends of mine, Lisa and Ann met me at the door. They knew I only would have acted this way if I thought there was an extreme emergency or a serious accident. Why else would Danny be rushing this lady into the ER, with such a serious and horrified look on his face? "Maggots, she's got maggots eating up her leg," I yelled frantically. Suddenly all the people that were rushing towards me stopped and just stared at me. It was as if someone hit freeze frame, everything and everyone just stopped and was staring at me. I was confused. *Why did they stop? Chris sakes, she's going to lose her leg from maggot infestation! What is wrong with you!* Suddenly the quiet was broken, "It's okay Danny, it's alright, the doctor put the maggots in there!" She exclaimed. "Why in the hell would he do that Ann, they're maggots! I said questioningly. "We put the maggots into the wound to eat away the infection, it's a normal standard practice". She said. "We replace them every three days, its okay Dan, put her down". Ann began laughing loudly, typical Irish girl. I must have looked like a total asshole standing there all serious and professional, holding this poor old lady. I was extremely embarrassed. I grinned, blushed, turned slowly and walked out as fast as possible with my tail between my legs like a scared and scolded animal. I was definitely embarrassed and it showed. I was ignorant to this medical process, maybe just as ignorant as I thought this black woman looked to me earlier.

I left the lady there as Lisa had instructed. As I drove back to my post it hit me. I was so very quick to judge that black woman, by thinking she was stupid and ignorant as to her condition, but I was the stupid one that was not only ignorant about medical procedures but even more ignorant as a person, narrow minded and prejudiced enough to think that just because this lady lived in an all black, low income area, she wouldn't know what was going on with her own leg. She was right all along. It was the way it was supposed to be. *I* was the ignorant low life racist that was only seeing things in black and white, not human being to human being. *I* was the shit-eating maggot for thinking as I had. Where were my morals? How badly had racism infected me? Why was I like this?

Where had my unconditional love for human beings gone, that my parents taught me? I had this caring attitude at one time in my life, before becoming a cop in this city. *Shame on me!* I felt terrible the rest of my day. *Can this wrong way of thinking be righted?* Racism and prejudice lived and thrived in this district. *How can I make any type of difference in this shitty world? How can I change these awful beliefs about blacks and their neighborhoods?* Maybe I didn't want to, NOT MY PROBLEM.

Lies of Revenge

4 p.m. to 12 p.m. shift, Pat Henley and I were working the same unit. 335 car. It was a familiar location that the call was broadcast to. "335, 1035 N. Patterson Park Ave. for a disorderly subject." Pat immediately said, "That's the asshole that stands in his doorway and yells shit at us Dan." "Yeah I know Pat". I said in disgust. "He stands in his doorway and calls us crackers, pigs and says he's going to do shit to our mothers." I then said. "Just once Pat, just once, I'd like for this asshole to come down off his steps. We've been putting up with his shit for weeks. We can't lock him up unless he comes off those steps. I hate that law, it's not fair." "No shit." Said Pat, also in disgust.

I had a hatred for this guy. At times a police officer has to be seen as a person, not an unfeeling, uncaring machine sent to do a job. Not a soldier fighting a war on crime who's numb and oblivious to his surroundings, but a thinking, feeling, normal human being that makes mistakes and experiences different emotions performing the job of being a police officer.

We had to handle the emotions that at times, attempted to take over our normal thoughts and overpower our legal knowledge and morals. Overpower our sense of righteousness. It was, at times, extremely difficult holding back the emotions and holding back the urges to be brutal and violent with a person that committed a crime of brutality and violence. We had sworn an oath but that oath sometimes took a back seat to emotions. This wasn't proper conduct but it was indeed human conduct. We are human.

The asshole at 1035 N. Patterson Park Ave. had been taunting and belittling Pat and I for some time, we had contact with this man at least five times in a months passing. I was totally pissed and Pat was in the same frame of mind. We had been partners for nearly six months and were very comfortable with working together. Pat was larger than I and was very athletic. He feared very little on the streets and like myself was excited about being a police officer and liked the violence and experiences of the Eastern District.

Together we had handled many violent calls, had been in many battles with bad guys and were considered the tough guys in our sector along with Harold and Lee. Our entire sector had a reputation for being the wild bunch or bad boys of the district. We were always in fights and foot pursuits and if it were a slow shift we would find crime and violence. We weren't pacified with quiet and calm, we wanted excitement, after all, we had the rep. Internal Affairs Division normally had an investigation of some sort that was ongoing that involved one or several of sector three's officers. Internal Affairs investigated alleged complaints of brutality and police misconduct.

Pat and I performed well together. Each of us knew what the other one was going to do and when it would be done. We functioned as one, a team. We had developed a camaraderie, were close friends and we enjoyed working with each other. Usually there was only one, two man car, in the sector, and it was the shotgun car. The only car in that sector with a 12-gauge Remington pump shotgun in the trunk. The shotgun was an intimidating weapon. The sound of a shell being racked into the chamber reverberated off the buildings and closely situated homes.

The row homes were merely eight to ten feet apart. The sounds echoed off the buildings, especially on quiet evenings, and especially the sound of a shotgun racking a shell into its chamber, that sound could not be mistaken. People would flee when we pulled the shotgun out and racked the pump action. It definitely produced an adrenaline rush and was absolutely macho. We rolled on most calls, especially the hot calls. Harold and Lee were referred to, as Batman and Robin and Pat and I were the Boy Wonders.

Harold and Lee were our teachers as well as the other officers in our sector. Eventually it came to be known that Pat and I were little Batman and Robins. We were just as brave and just as violent. Harold and Lee had been officers for over ten years and were seasoned, experienced, and were excellent teachers. We loved being cops. Gung ho, kick ass, young cops.

Pat and I arrived at the location on Patterson Park Ave. "Fuuuuuccckk you whitey! I had yo mama last night! Come in here I'll kick your cracker asses!" The insults continued. This shithead wouldn't let up and most assuredly knew Pat and I were working that night, why else would he call. He was waiting to see us and to stand just inside his doorway or yell at us from the second floor window so Pat and I couldn't get our hands on his smart ass. He was aware of the law. A citizen cannot disturb the peace of a police officer.

A citizen must cause other citizens to become disturbed by their actions to violate that law, same as disorderly conduct. More than one person must be present to become disorderly. Not police officers, citizens. A crowd must gather or traffic flow interrupted to fulfill the disorderly statute. None of this can be done while standing inside your own house. He knew this, so did we, and we were pissed.

I've had enough of this piece of shit. It's time. I thought. "Pat, why don't you go around back, I think this asshole wants to see you, when he comes out I'll be right behind him and we can beat the shit out of this loudmouth asshole" Pat looked at me puzzled. I smiled and Pat smiled back. He knew I had a plan, a plan to satisfy our craving for revenge, a plan to quench our thirst.

In order to reach the back of a row home in the Eastern District, Pat had to walk to the end of the street to the alley, then walk down the alley approximately fifty feet, then turn back up the alley to the desired home. This home was basically in the middle of the block and it took some time for Pat to walk the distance. This allowed me time to set up my plan. The loudmouth and his taunting would be silenced. "Call me when he comes out!" I yelled to Pat as he walked away. He didn't answer. He didn't have to. We functioned as one.

The past three calls we had at this location, before the dirt bag came down to the front door to yell obscenities at Pat and I, he would lean out the second floor window and shake a piece of pipe at us. The pipe was thin and only three feet long. It resembled a rifle barrel. Although it *resembled* a rifle barrel, and I *knew* it was a piece of pipe, this pipe would *become* a rifle barrel and it would allow me to enter the house for my much needed, but illegal revenge, a lie of revenge.

On cue, as I yelled out from the front sidewalk, "police, who called!" The subject, soon to become a suspect, leaned out the second floor window and began yelling again. "Hey copper! Eat Shit!" He was shaking the pipe out the window. Then it happened. I saw it! A rifle barrel pointed directly at me! My mind was whirring. *I can't do this.* I thought briefly. *I can't do this! It's not legal.* I pondered. Suddenly he yelled again. "Up here assssssholle!" That's it. I pressed the button on my Motorola radio and did something that would upset me later but felt right at the time. I spoke, "335, we've arrived at Patterson Park Ave." My voice then rose abruptly and loudly in pitch. "Dispatcher, give me a back up! The subject on the second floor is pointing a rifle at me! Pat, I think he's got a rifle, I can see the barrel, I'm going in!"

Pat immediately knew what was transpiring but was not able to question my ethics or me, at that time. I was doing this of my own volition. I wouldn't or couldn't involve Pat. He didn't need to know the truth, or as it was, the lie, at this point in time. I heard Pat's reply. "335A, I'm going in the back door!"

I also heard the dispatcher, "335 needs a 10-16, (back up), unit at 1035 N.
Patterson Park Ave., an armed suspect with a rifle on the second floor, use
caution." Then came the responses of my comrades, my fellow officers, that
had no idea of what I was pulling off, they just knew when Pat or I called
for a 10-16, a back up, we definitely needed back up. "334, on the way, 332,
I'm three blocks away, I'm responding, 336, I'm leaving the station, I'll cover
the back with 335A."

The wheels were set in motion, the troops were coming, there was no
turning back now, and no telling the truth, and it was time for revenge! I
wanted revenge, even at the cost of losing my job. I am human. *Jesus Christ,
what am I doing?* I questioned myself. *Dan, this is not good!* I paused mentally,
briefly. *Fuck it! He's going down, to late asshole, time for revenge!*

Simultaneously, Pat and I kicked in the front and back doors. We reached
the first set of steps leading to the second floor, together. Just then the subject,
who was still on the second floor, now turned *suspect*, started to run down
the first two steps. He saw us, stopped dead in his tracks, and turned around
to run back up the steps. The suspect ran back into the same front room that
he was yelling at us from. He knew we were coming for him and, *Hell was
coming with us!*

Pat and I ran to the top of the steps and stood directly in front of the
locked front bedroom door. "Ready?" "Ready!" We spoke at the same time.
We then kicked the door wide open. The suspect that had allegedly pointed
a deadly weapon at me was standing in the corner. Pat and I rushed him,
grabbed him by the throat and slammed him to the floor. I shoved big
mouth's head into the floor and Pat drove his knee into the suspect's back

so we could affect the arrest. Pat was pushing hard with his knee into the man's back. I was bouncing the suspect's head off the floor with force. Each time I pushed his head down he would pull his head back up and yell for us to stop. "Who's the white cracker now? Muvafucker! Who's mama you going to fuck now? Asshole!" I was yelling into his fucking ear. Pat yelled too. "Shut your fucking mouth shithead! You ain't so fucking tough now are you pussy?" The suspect finally wised up and realized he was being paid back for his many words of insult and degradation. He knew he had this coming and decided to cease and desist.

Suddenly I heard officers running up the steps calling for Pat and me. I had forgotten to call off the back up units. I called to the dispatcher to call the incident clear. "335, we have the suspect in custody, 10-22 the call and send us a 10-14," (disregard the call and send us a paddy wagon). By now our sergeant had arrived, we explained to him that we believed we were in grave danger of being shot with the supposed rifle.

As Pat and I dragged bigmouth down the steps and out to the street, the wagon arrived. Pat and I threw the suspect into the wagon bodily, with a thud. The doors were shut, *just as we had shut this asshole's mouth!* I thought. I explained to Sergeant Abrams that as Pat and I arrived at the location of the call dispatched, the suspect was standing in the second floor window and had yelled for us to, "come up and get me!" and that, "I've got something for you!" I observed that he was pointing, what I believed, was a rifle at Pat and me. I went on to explain that the suspect was standing back from the window a foot or two and I couldn't tell that what he was pointing at us was actually a piece of pipe resembling a rifle barrel. Pat and I were *forced* to take safety measures for the suspect had given us NO alternative. If it were *actually* a rifle, our lives would have been in danger.

Sergeant Abrams looked at Pat and I and said, "good job boys, you did all the right things, I'm glad you're okay." I secretly felt a sigh of relief. I knew what I had done was risky and illegal, but I had pulled it off, I had succeeded! I wanted revenge and was willing to lie for it.

When the case went to court, I spoke to the Assistant State's Attorney that was handling the case. I explained that it was not a rifle and maybe, just maybe, *everyone* overreacted, especially the defendant. He was given probation before judgment, which is a slap on the wrist, and was set free with no fines or penalties. That's the least I could have done for *bigmouth*.

Pat and I never received a call to that location the rest of my time in the Eastern District. Bigmouth had been silenced and began to behave. I silently swore to myself that I would never do that again, i.e. lie to get revenge. The entire situation bothered me and still does. There has to be some justice for the police officer too. Even though the justice may not be doled out properly. We cross into illegal territory at times, and return, we are human and suffer with human frailties that each of us has and must grapple with.

The human side of being a police officer can be extremely frail and fragile; I realized this as I drove into the station to charge this individual with pointing a weapon at a police officer. I was very wrong.

I had lied to get my revenge, my craving had been satisfied. However, I had lied and that was totally unacceptable and morally wrong also. *Nothing*, would be entered on this man's criminal record, he was absolved. Nothing but a lie, **a serious lie of revenge**.

Lies of Protection

One of the most embarrassing, unforgiving, and unforgettable situations a police officer can become associated with, or remembered by, is the loss, theft or surrender of their service weapon. On or off duty is irrelevant, but on duty is definitely the worst of the two scenarios. I promised, and swore to myself at the onset of my career, that I would never give up my gun to a bad guy.

Some officers feel differently. I would not give up my gun if a criminal had my partner at gunpoint and demanded that I hand over my weapon or he would shoot my partner. Other officers would comply with the demand. I feel as though I might also get shot with my own gun and being unarmed I would lessen my chances of surviving. Who is to say that the offender wouldn't shoot both of us after disarming me? I want a chance. The desperate criminal might miss me or the shot(s) might not be fatal. Giving up my gun takes away any chance I might have to survive.

While working part time on Fayette St. only blocks from police headquarters cleaning cars to make extra money, my service weapon was stolen. On this particular day, I left my .38 caliber Smith and Wesson six-inch barrel stainless steel revolver on a desk by the front garage door, which remained open during nice weather. It was a warm day and the door was open. The door is situated only feet from a heavily traveled sidewalk on a street where Baltimore's main post office is located. I covered my weapon with a dirty police shirt and a small towel so that it was somewhat hidden.

At the end of the day I began gathering my belongings to leave. I noticed that my shirt was gone and that my gun was also missing. I panicked. NO way was I going to report the loss or theft of my gun! My fellow officers would never let me live it down, not to mention the punishment from the police department, which included a letter being placed in my permanent personnel file stating I was irresponsible and negligent. The punishment would also be printed in the police memos that each police officer receives periodically. That also was unacceptable and strengthened my resolve to carry out my plan. I would have been branded the remainder of my career with the stigma of losing my weapon just as officers were branded as being placed into the, "rubber gun squad". That squad was police jargon for any officer that has his gun taken from him permanently or for any amount of time, by the department, if a mention of suicide, "eating his gun," or wanting to harm himself or his family is discovered and documented.

Any officer that earns that unwanted reputation is forever remembered in any discussions of suicide, or if their name is mentioned, it's usually followed by a remark about being in the, "rubber gun squad". It is not a reputation to be proud of and certainly was not one that I wanted associated with my name. I had to cover up my disastrous loss.

On this particular day, I had injured my right hand, my gun hand, earlier in the day when I accidentally closed it in a car door ripping the ligaments, straining my thumb and spraining my wrist. This was extremely convenient. Losing my gun left me no choice but to do what I was ready to do. I ripped my left pants pocket and my shirt, I crawled on the floor to dirty my knees and tips of my shoes, I messed my hair and was ready.

I walked around the corner to a liquor store and purchased a six-pack of beer. Then I called a signal 13, or officer needs assistance, on myself when I left. As I walked down the small alley back towards the shop I let myself fall to the ground making certain that a few of the beers came out of the bag and rolled onto the alleyway, that my right hand received an abrasion and also my knees. I was going to extremes but this was absolutely necessary.

Within moments six police cars arrived at my location, including two K-9 units. The police helicopter was circling overhead. I had called for, and received, help from arriving and responding officers, much manpower, and was utilizing a lot of police resources. As one of the officers called off the signal 13, several other officers were listening intently to my made up story of how I was assaulted, robbed, and had lost my service weapon. I had purposely and deceitfully created a very serious situation.

Anytime a police officer's gun is taken by force it creates a personal affront to other officers. The fact that a criminal would have the gall to take an officers gun, plus the fact that another gun was on the street, was totally unacceptable to most officers that worked those same streets.

I briefly told the responding officers what had taken place and gave a description of the two muggers. The description was broadcast over the police radio. The hunt for the suspects that robbed and took the gun of a police officer was on. For nearly one half hour every officer in the Southeast District and each district bordering it were searching for two fictitious black men. The area where I was cleaning cars and where this supposed offense took place was mostly a black area. The suspects had to fit into the environment.

My report read as follows: As I walked north down the alleyway between Fayette St. and Baltimore St. from the liquor store, I observed two black males standing next to a vacant parked car. As I passed by them I was watching intently because I felt uneasy. As I was watching these two males, two other black males that I was not aware of suddenly attacked me. I was grabbed from behind and I began to struggle with the suspects. I was in control of the fight until the two other suspects standing by the car jumped in. I reached into my waistband and pulled out my service revolver pointing it at the suspects and identified myself as a police officer. I was then kicked in the groin.

I had a firm grasp on my gun and was about to fire when one of the suspects grabbed the cylinder making it impossible to fire my weapon since the cylinder couldn't turn enabling my gun to fire. The suspect and I grappled with the gun and since he was larger and stronger than I, he was able to wrench my gun from my hand turning the gun sideways tearing it from my hand. In the struggle I sprained my wrist and several ligaments were torn in my right thumb.

The suspect then pointed my weapon at me. I was fearful that he would fire. I began to roll to my right in hopes that I would not get shot in the face or stomach. I looked up at the suspect and saw that all four were running east towards Baltimore St. I was able to run back to the phone and call for assistance.

I was placed into a radio car and driven around the area in hopes that I would find one or two of the suspects. After approximately twenty minutes I was transported to Saint Agnes hospital for treatment. I then went to police headquarters. This story seemed feasible to me and I was comfortable with the extensive lie. I signed my report and left headquarters.

The police helicopter and over thirty officers searched for the non existent suspects, condensing their search around a Federally-subsidized high crime, high rise, apartment complex on Albemarle St., known to be a great hiding place for criminals. Of course I was unable to identify anyone for no one fit the description in my lie and I was not going to have an innocent citizen arrested for this made up crime. My hypocrisy only goes so far and I did have some morals left.

I was a hero for not giving up my gun without a fierce struggle and for fighting so intensely so as not to let someone get my gun. A good police officer does not give up his gun, I didn't. Now, rather than being ridiculed and humiliated I was praised, took off five days for my injuries to heal, and received a new revolver. My high-risk lie had succeeded. The fact that I went to such extremes to cover up the loss of my gun still concerns me. My heart feels heavy and I feel like the liar I was. I had to, as officers say, C.Y.A., or cover your ass, in this case, cover my ass.

My handgun was found five months later in the Northern District when officers responded to a family disturbance call. When the officers arrived the wife of the man that called was yelling out the second floor window to her husband. She then threw my stolen gun out the window and onto the street and she screamed, "here's that cop's gun that you bought!" The gun was immediately recovered and the investigation began. I was notified as to the recovery and secretly I felt relieved. What if an officer had been shot or killed with my lost gun. I would have never forgiven myself. Fortunately this didn't happen.

An article appeared in the two local newspapers when I was assaulted, another article was printed when the gun was recovered and again referred to the first incident. I was uneasy for I did not want to relive the lie I had reported. I wanted it to be over.

Another incident in my life was over. No ridicule, no embarrassment, and no police action, was taken against me for conjuring up the lie to cover up my irresponsibility. I would never again lose track of my gun. I would never again put myself in the position where I had to compromise my beliefs and myself.

Unprofessional

Police officers must break the monotony and stress of performing their duties. Their actions aren't always honorable and professional, however they do, at times, have fun. Whether the acts are a little on the illegal side, or not as they are expected to be, by the public and the administration. The tensions must subside now and then.

334 post encompassed N. Broadway. Broadway was two lanes in each direction and was separated by a twelve-foot grass median. Lots of activity occurred on Broadway. Benny worked 334 post and was shopping the district for much needed supplies for his new home. I was dozing behind the Super

Pride store on Patterson Park Ave. at 2 a.m. Benny called for me to meet him. "334 have 336 10-11 me at Broadway and Lanvale St." I acknowledged and pulled my car alongside Benny's radio car. "What's up pal?" I asked. "Need your help, follow me." I followed Benny to the end of E. Biddle St. near The Continental Can Co. The can company was shutting down areas of the company. As I pulled onto the vacant parking lot I saw that the paddy wagon was also there as well as another officer in my squad. *What does he need? Why is the wagon here?* I wondered.

I was instructed to walk to the end of a sixty-foot chain link fence and hold the pole tightly. We all trusted each other so I complied. I stood there holding the pole as I watched Benny with surprise in my eyes. Benny had a large pair of wire cutters and bolt cutters and was snipping the metal rings that held the chain link fencing to the pole. The wagon man and Martin began rolling the fence into a tight roll.

I watched as they all worked so diligently, I looked at the open doors to the paddy wagon, looked back at the officers working, and back to the wagon. Finally I realized what was taking place here. We were *stealing* a sixty-foot section of new fencing from Continental Can Co. to put around Benny's new home!

I was thrilled! They trusted me this much to help pull this off. Many thoughts whirred through my mind as I performed my clandestine duty. *Isn't this illegal? Can't I lose my job for stealing? What if someone sees us? Does Benny really need this fencing THAT badly? Am I stupid, an asshole, for being here? Naah, this is pretty cool and I'm tickled.*

We spent about an hour taking the fencing down and pulling the poles out of their newly dug holes. After we were done we all pitched in, *as a good, tight, and working as one, squad does,* and placed the fencing and poles into the rear of the paddy wagon.

I was instructed by Benny to meet him at the station, I followed him. Benny had parked his personal truck blocks from the station. I knew why. We pulled up to his truck and He and I unloaded the entire, newly *acquired* fence, into his truck. ONE NEW FENCE, LOADED AND READY TO GO, *NO CHARGE!*

At 6 a.m., the culprits met at Len's sandwich shop at Washington St. and Gay St. as earlier instructed. Benny bought breakfast and coffees for all of us. What a deal! I thought, as I ate my sandwich and smirked. What a job!

Midnight shift, 1978. I attended roll call but was not really there. I was slightly intoxicated. I was at a party earlier and didn't stop drinking in time. Pat and Lee stood close to me so I wouldn't sway. The sergeant passed by quickly and wasn't checking revolvers as he sometimes did, so I made it through roll call safely.

Outside the station I had my ass reamed out by my buddies for being in that condition, and was told to drive to the end of E. Biddle St. to Continental Can Co., and park my car. I was to, *go to sleep!* At times one of us would come in to work extremely tired and in need of sleep or maybe one of us had too much to drink. That officer was told where to go to get some sleep and the other five or six officers in the squad would cover the sleeping officer's calls and each one of us would check on the sleeping officer once per hour to insure he was safe, since we all knew his whereabouts. It was the accepted norm.

Approximately thirty minutes, to an hour, prior to changing shifts at 8 a.m., one of us would wake up the officer and make sure he was okay and ready to go into the station refreshed or in certain cases, sober. Those thirty minutes the sleeper could get himself redressed and squared away to return to the station.

The night that I had too much to drink, I slept the entire midnight shift. I parked my car at the designated spot so I was safe, and propped my feet up against the passenger's door. But, not until I took off my gun belt and hung it over the passengers headrest, put my radio microphone over the rearview mirror with the volume turned all the way up in case I was called by the dispatcher or someone called for help, took off my tie, unbuttoned my shirt, and cracked the windows so I could get a little fresh air.

If the dispatcher called for me, the other officers would wait to see if I answered. If I did it made things seem normal and they would handle the call for me. If I didn't answer, one of the officers would disguise his voice and acknowledge the call, and then it would still be handled. However, if it were a major felony I would be aroused and would have to handle the call. This didn't occur often on the late midnight shifts. But, if it did, you handled it as best you could. That was the accepted, unspoken, policy.

I'm not sure how it occurs but an experienced officer can be sleeping, talking on the phone, talking to a citizen, or even both, and he will still hear his call number over the radio. I could be in a sound sleep, or in the process of taking a serious report and I would immediately answer up if the dispatcher called for me. It's as if my ears are tuned in to hear my call number above anything else. I guess it's a learned phenomenon; most of the officers mastered this ability.

I slept thru the entire shift. At 7:50 a.m. Pat pulled up beside me to wake me. "Lets go Dan I almost forgot to wake you, don't bother to get out of the car to piss or put your shit on, you're going to be late!" Pat had urgency in his voice. It was only five minutes till the dispatcher called for the shift to change. I must get myself half dressed as I drove the ten blocks to the station. 301 was the shift lieutenant's call number, when the dispatcher called, "301, 10-18, (go to the station), that meant it was time to change shifts.

I was putting on my clip on tie and ready to step out of the car to stretch when I heard the call, "301, 10-18, 301, 10-18." Too late, I had to go. The sergeant and lieutenant didn't like stragglers coming in late because that tied them up also. I put my car in drive and drove out of my, hole, my sleeping hole.

I turned right onto Edison Hwy. From E. Biddle St. Edison Hwy., like Broadway, was a large street with a grass median separating four lanes of traffic. As I was driving the eight blocks North on Edison Hwy. I felt as though something wasn't right. I observed other drivers pointing and laughing. Some drivers just stared. I didn't understand, I was in a marked radio car, had no flat tires, my tie was on properly, my gun belt and radio were on the seat, not hanging anywhere. *What was wrong, what was so damn funny?* I wondered.

I pulled my radio car alongside the station. My entire squad was standing on the steps looking at me and other officers were milling about looking inconspicuous, but *were* looking intently. I also noticed officers looking out the windows at my radio car and me. *Okay, what the hell is going on? Why is everyone looking at me?* I began to become angry. I stepped out of my radio car and everyone, all of them were laughing hysterically! I turned and looked at my radio car. Harold, Lee, Pat and Martin had fixed me and fixed me good! As I slept they had placed a spare tire on top of my bubble gum light. In those days police cars had only one light on the roof. My Pontiac had hubcaps with small holes in them. My buddies had put branches in four of the eight holes on each hubcap. They had also put branches with lots of leaves, sticking out from my front and rear bumpers, but placed them out of my line of sight. Now I knew why Pat didn't want me to get out of the car and why he waited so late to wake me! I had driven those ten blocks in morning rush hour traffic with my car looking like a huge tree with a tire! It was no wonder citizens were pointing and laughing at me while I drove those ten blocks to the station.

I was pissed but had to laugh at my car. It really did look ridiculous and very funny. I looked around at all the staring officers, flipped them the middle finger and quickly walked into the station to the bathroom with my tail between my legs. As I passed my sergeant and lieutenant I heard them say sarcastically, "Get any sleep last night Dan? Stay up and clean your car last night Dan?" I said nothing. I was most definitely caught and most definitely embarrassed. Needless to say, I didn't sleep on the midnight shift for quite some time!

The blizzard of 1979 was definitely a time of paybacks for a lot of officers. Especially Me! For years I've had to deal with citizens making complaints against me. Some were founded but most were not. People were angry for being arrested and made up ridiculous complaints against me. Not true. Citizens would write down badge numbers and names and call the Internal Affairs Division to make complaints, false complaints.

It had snowed constantly for two days. Baltimore was covered in twenty or more inches of snow. The Mass Transit buses were stranded in the middle of the streets. Police cars were inoperable as were the police wagons and jeeps due to the depth of the snow. The only way to navigate around Baltimore was on foot. That's what the police had to do, walk foot. After I walked and hitched rides on salt trucks for nearly ten miles to get to work, I rested and was assigned to my four-man team. Four men were to walk and patrol certain areas of the Eastern District in twelve-hour shifts. I was extremely excited and somewhat apprehensive. Just four officers walking around the busiest district in the city for twelve hours catching burglars, looters, thieves, and other criminals. There would be no help from the dispatcher if we found ourselves in serious trouble. No help, just four men and a shotgun. We couldn't call for back up, we didn't have the choice of putting a suspect in a paddy wagon. We had to walk the arrestees into the station.

Myself, Pat, Martin and Mike left the district and began the fifteen-block walk into the center of the district. The area where all the looting and robberies were occurring. As we walked west on Federal St. from the district I had an eerie feeling in my stomach. It was very quiet as we walked because the snow had muffled the usual sounds and there were no automobiles. All we heard was the crunching of our feet on the freshly plowed snow. We didn't talk. I feel that all four of us were silently wondering what lay ahead of us the next half a day. It was 9 a.m. We had never experienced such isolation as police officers there was always more help than was needed but not for these twelve hours, we were alone and on our own. If a serious situation occurred like having to shoot a looter or thief or if we were jumped and beaten by a crowd of looters there was no help just us. It was scary, exciting and spooky. I was very nervous, yet confident, but still wary.

We wore our own heavy black or blue coats, not police issue, and attached our badges to the coat. NO nametags were worn. Therefore if a citizen had a complaint, no information such as name or description was available. We also wore skullcaps, not police hats with the large identifying numbers displayed on it. All of us were basically anonymous. We knew that.

I had my flashlight, nightstick, and two extra guns as well as my knife. I wasn't taking any chances of getting injured. I was ready! I also placed ten plastic flex cuffs in my skullcap. I had a sickening feeling that one set of stainless cuffs weren't going to get it out there in the cold no mans land. I would be correct in that assumption.

We walked up Federal St. to Gay St. and headed south into the belly of crime and looting. As we approached the liquor store at Washington and Gay Sts. Three looters came running out of the store. I was completely taken by surprise, as were my partners. I had no idea what to expect out there but would become educated quickly. Two scooted past me. As the third ran past me I saw that he had several fifths of liquor in his hands and that his back pockets were stuffed with pints and half pints. I hit the looter as hard as possible in both rear pockets with my nightstick and heard and saw the bottles break. The liquor made an immediate wet spot on his pants. I also saw bloodstains on his ass as he ran. *Good, he's cut too! Gotcha asshole!* I thought.

He continued past me and I threw my stick at him, missing. He escaped, but I had busted his ass and the bottles. I was sure he was headed for Hopkins Hospital sooner or later. One for ME!

My partners chased the other two suspects to no avail. It was difficult to even walk in that amount of snow let alone run. We entered the liquor store and observed that it was in shambles. Everything was gone, destroyed, or damaged, beyond repair. *These bastards are stealing from their own. They are destroying businesses that help them in their everyday lives. Why? Fuck it! I don't care; I'll catch em and do what I can.* We attempted to secure the door but it was not done properly. We had no tools.

Next the team walked down to Federal St. and Chester St. Looters came running out of the small convenience store, arms full with merchandise. I was able to grab hold of one of the looters. I cuffed him with my steel cuffs, my first arrest. My partners ran after the other suspects and caught them also. I handcuffed my looter to the stop sign located at the intersection. I would be back momentarily to take him to the station. I had more bad guys to catch. Suddenly, a call for help. I ran a block to another liquor store where my team members had several looters inside the store. My team locked up twelve suspects. The flex cuffs came in handy. I assisted in the arrests and all sixteen of us began the two-mile trek to the station. We walked up Gay St towards North Ave. As we began our walk a snowplow rolled up. Mike flagged it down. He had a great idea. Put all the looters on the salt truck and have it take us to the station. Great! We helped each looter up onto the salt truck and Mike hung off the driver's door, Martin off the passenger's door, while Pat and I sat up on the salt guarding our prisoners with the shotgun. It was a great idea and we were ecstatic about the way we looked going up the street like desert rats with our catch. *This is really cool! A salt truck full of shitheads and us four musketeers bringing them in.* I was in heaven. Macho shit!

As we approached the next intersection a young looter jumped off the truck and began to run away. *Damn! Look at him run with his hands behind his back, impressive.* I thought as I leaped from the truck to pursue the prisoner. I began to gain on him when I tripped and slid completely out of sight under the snow, Mike ran over top of me stepping on my back! *Christ Mike!* I yelled into the snow as my head was buried deeper into the snow. Mike caught the running prisoner, smacked him a few times and dragged him back to the salt truck. No names, no badge numbers, Paybacks are great, It's about time after all these years of having to be polite and cautious when making arrests, There was always a way to identify us, not now, all stops were being pulled. *This is GREAT SHIT!*

The salt truck couldn't get up Sinclair Lane. We were dropped off at Sinclair Lane and Belair Rd. Only six blocks to the station. As we were unloading the prisoner's one of us had another great idea. To avoid another escape we would flex cuff all the prisoners together, but not all facing the same way. One prisoner would be facing front, the next facing back. No one could run. Great idea! I was really enjoying this snowstorm.

We began trudging up Sinclair Lane. A few of the prisoners were becoming mouthy. "This is bullshit officer, we can't walk like this! I'm calling my attorney. Yeah fuck this!" Two more prisoners chimed in. I was getting pissed off. "Shut up assholes, you looted not us!" I said. The complaining continued. I was getting annoyed. I then had an idea. I walked up behind one of the prisoners and nonchalantly tripped him. This caused two prisoners on each side to fall also. They began yelling at each other. "Get up nigger, what you doing boy!" I waited a few more minutes and tripped another prisoner. They went down again. I was happy, they were yelling at each other and had no clue I was the asshole causing them to fall and scream at each other. I was definitely getting my Payback! The other officers were smiling at me and enjoying my antics as well, they too joined in. We were having fun the entire trip to the station.

We reached the station and proudly walked into the sergeant's desk with our catch of the day. I was in my glory, we all were. All the prisoners were placed in cells. The four of us decided to do the paperwork later. We were having too much fun to stop for bullshit paperwork. Besides, we only had four hours left.

We walked back to the area we were to patrol with a spring in our step. We were talking and joking. *This was so much fun.* All day long we could hear other officers calling in arrests, they too were enjoying the freedom and paybacks. A call for assistance came over the radio; we were only a block away. I heard three gunshots! My heart leapt! We ran to the intersection of Washington and Federal Sts. I noticed an officer sticking his head out of the second floor window of the liquor store. All was fine. Apparently the officer had heard someone looting the store and entered to investigate. The suspect ran to the second floor. The officer followed. When the officer reached the landing the suspect let his full size, 180 pound, white husky dog, loose on the officer. He was yelling for the dog to attack! The dog did. The officer fired three shots into the dog killing it instantly. I stood at the landing thinking how beautiful this animal was. The dog was pure white and had bright red blood spurting out and running onto the floor. It was a sad scene but the officer had to protect himself. No one showed up to investigate, no supervisors were called, and the situation was handled then and there. Not the usual protocol.

The suspect jumped thru the closed window, fell into the snow and escaped. Unbelievable! I just couldn't believe what I was experiencing! This was like the Wild Wild West with snow! I could see where the suspect had fallen into the snow and ran. *I'll never live thru anything this exciting and frightening again. This entire day is nearly beyond comprehension. No one will believe these stories!* I thought to myself.

It was nearing 8 p.m.; it would take us nearly an hour to return to the station. We checked on a few stores on the way in, they were either destroyed and emptied completely, or damaged and only the small-unwanted items remained. We did remove a few items for ourselves, batteries, small remaining bottles of liquor that were dropped onto the floor, and we did find three full bottles of Crown Royal Whiskey. We couldn't resist. We knew we had to sleep at the station until our next shift at 9 a.m. and we wanted to party too.

We were about six blocks from the station when a National Guard Humvee pulled alongside and offered us a ride. We jumped in and on the Hummer and continued on our way. As we reached the station I notice that someone or something had run over a stop sign. *Running over everything.* I thought to myself. Suddenly my mouth dropped open and my eyes went wide open also. *HOLY SHIT! Jesus Christ! I left that fucking looter handcuffed to the stop sign on Federal St! SHIT! He's been there for most of the day! Oh my god I can't believe I left him there. I wonder if he's okay. Is he frozen, is he dead? Oh my god!*

The guard dropped my partners off at the station. I looked at the driver and told him what I had done. Pat looked at me in disbelief. Then he laughed. "Jesus Danny, how could you do that?" "Asshole".

We arrived at Federal St. in minutes. There he was, my prisoner hand cuffed to the stop sign sitting in the snow. His ass had melted into the snow. Two clearly marked ass cheeks had melted themselves into the snow leaving two half moons indented in the snow. The looter was half frozen and was irritated. He was irate and complaining. I apologized to him over and over again. I told him, I felt so bad and that I wouldn't lock him up, he could go free. "Fuck you!" He said. "I've been here all fucking day, my ass is not being locked up, let me out of these cuffs and let me leave!" He yelled. I let the prisoner yell and scream at me. He deserved it and so did I. The poor man was gray in color and definitely cold. I uncuffed him and jumped in the Hummer. We left faster than the looter.

The National Guard Officer looked at me on the way in and just laughed, I too had to laugh. I knew the prisoner was okay, but he did sit for a long, long, time. "Poor little looting Popsicle." I said. We laughed even harder and continued on to the station.

I was the brunt of the jokes all night. I deserved it, leaving a prisoner handcuffed to a stop sign for over six hours in a major snowstorm was not very astute and professional of me. Fortunately for me, due to the snowstorm, I heard NO repercussions.

Most of the officers that worked the day shift that day gathered downstairs at the gun range. Everyone was drinking the liquor and beer they had looted, or should I say, acquired or had taken off the looters.

We drank and fired our guns at the range targets for hours. After the sergeant came down to stop the party we cleaned our weapons, had a few more drinks and slept on cots all over the station I slept on top of the counter at the range. I fell asleep thinking how wonderful a day I had and how great it felt to get a little payback. After all, this is a thankless job and people tend to complain and make complaints against officers continuously. Not this day or night, the snowstorm of 1979 had seen to that.

Blood

I had been on the streets of the Eastern District approximately five years when I experienced one of the most frightening, unnerving, and unsettling episodes in my then short career. I was sent to the location of the 1800 block of N. Regester St. to investigate a problem call. I was actually very nervous and had no idea what lie ahead of me as I walked into the row house at approximately 10 a.m. I had no idea what had transpired in this house of horror, but I was definitely aware it was gruesome, evil, and bloody. I could smell the metals and minerals contained in the blood. When enough blood is present at a crime scene or accident scene you can actually smell the metallic odor, same as you can taste it when you bite your lip. The taste and odor are unmistakable, as is the smell of a dead body that is decomposing, a one of a kind smell or taste.

As I entered the dwelling I observed that all the furniture and bedding had been turned over. The drawers to the bureau had been pulled open and emptied onto the floor. The entire front room on the first floor had been ransacked. The narrow hallway that leads to the kitchen and the rear of the house was empty except for a lone lamp table that had also been kicked or pushed onto its side. As I reached down to lift up the table to clear my way, I could definitely smell a strong odor of blood metals and they were becoming stronger. When I lifted my head to glance into the kitchen I was completely taken aback. I was in total awe by the scene in front of and all around me. BLOOD! More blood than I have ever seen at any homicide, serious traffic accident or any type of gory injury. *Holy Shit! What happened here? How could all this blood be from one person? Maybe there were two victims. Had to be, this is too much blood.*

The amount of blood was staggering. It was nearly beyond my comprehension. Actually it was beyond my comprehension. I could not grasp what I was seeing. Blood was everywhere I looked no matter where my eyes strayed or where I glanced. As my eyes danced around the kitchen they were met by nothing but more blood. Blood that was smeared, pooled, dragged down cabinets and walls. Blood that was on cabinet handles, tables, chairs, the floor, everywhere my eyes wondered the sight of red exploded into my pupils. There were handprints of thick blood that dragged down the walls in different areas of the kitchen that began thinning at the fingertips as the smear traveled further down the wall running out of blood as it continued down, caused by the victim attempting to hold himself up by using the wall as a brace but being unable to stand and eventually fell to the floor. Now more than before I felt as though there were two victims bleeding. *This amount of blood could not come from one person*, I worried. *What was I going to find upstairs? Pieces of bodies, heads, arms, legs? A hatchet or machete? What was it?*

Dark red, light red, thick, thin, smeared, and dripping blood was spread over the entire kitchen. I was seriously frightened, had no idea what caused this amount of blood to be spattered, smeared, and puddled about me and wasn't certain I wanted to continue on up the narrow stairs. It was quite obvious by the scarlet markings and blood evidence that whatever or whoever was responsible for this amazing amount of blood loss was up the blood covered walls and stairs leading to the second floor. I was trained enough to know not to disrupt the crime scene by stepping in the blood at the scene of a crime. However, I had no choice. No matter where I stepped or how carefully, I was stepping in large amounts of blood. It was senseless to attempt to follow this rule of investigation. I tread thru the blood to the first step leading upstairs.

I took a moment to look around and then gasped a deep breath before I gathered the courage to climb the stairs of blood and unexplainable markings that I was certain belonged to a seriously injured and possibly dead human being or beings.

I began talking to myself, *Shit, I really don't want to go up there. Why do I have to go? Maybe I can call the morgue and have a medical examiner come out and I won't have to see what's up there. No Dan, you have to go it's your job. Aren't you curious as to what you'll see? You like the excitement so much, pussy, go upstairs and do your job!* I bit my lip and started up the stairs. As I rounded the small, narrow turn that lead upstairs, my eyes were once again assaulted by the sight of more blood smears and bloody finger markings that dragged down the walls as the victim obviously attempted to crawl up the stairs leaving a trail of red markings.

My heart began beating in my ears. I was sweating and shaking slightly. My adrenaline was pumping at a furious rate. My eyes and ears were on full alert as was my fight or flight mode. I was ready to run, but was aware that I couldn't. Normally I would have drawn my weapon out of fear of being injured but I was certain that the person that caused this horrible scene was most likely dead and of no threat to me. That amount of blood loss was a definite indication that whoever was upstairs was surely dead. I was very scared not for my life but for what I was afraid I was going to see. My mind had conjured up the worst-case scenario. Worst of all, I had not heard a single sound or noise come from the second floor since I entered the dwelling.

I reached the second floor landing. I was safe! *Nothing had jumped out to harm me or frighten me,* I was thinking. I could see that the blood drippings were becoming less bloody and were thinning out. I was assuming that the victim or victims had finally bled out. No blood was left to drain out of the body. I turned to my left and observed that the bedroom at the front of the house had also been ransacked. All the furniture was knocked over and the bed was overturned also. I observed no signs of blood and knew that my search must end in the bathroom. There was nowhere else to go and I had spotted small drops of blood heading to the bathroom. I decided to check the front room first. I don't know if I did this to alleviate the other rooms in the house or because I was postponing the obvious.

I slowly and carefully walked towards the partially opened bathroom door. It wasn't ajar enough for me to see the entire bathroom, of course! *Why should this be any easier or less frightening than what I experienced downstairs. Why couldn't the door be completely open so I could see the horror from afar?* I thought. I moved articles of clothing and small furnishings out of my way as I approached the bathroom. I stopped to wipe the blood off the soles of my boots on a shirt using only my boots, no hands. I slowly pushed opened the door and the first thing I saw was a white sink stained with blood. I then saw a head hanging into the tub. To my relief there was a body attached and there was only ONE body!

Embedded into the skull was the round end of a ball peen hammer. The handle was lying down next to the ear. The skull was holding the hammer into place. There were three more holes or indentations in the skull also. They were deep enough that they were very visible and it was quite obvious what had caused them. They were clear and concise holes that were bleeding very little. The man must have bled out. He had no more life giving blood to obscure the wound. The holes were clean and dramatic.

The body was that of a black male but he was nowhere near the color black. He was ashen or light gray. I was sure he was dead. How could a human survive that amount of serious, deep, and deadly blows to the skull, lose such a tremendous amount of blood, and still be alive? I reached out to touch his neck to feel for a pulse. I was amazed! He was warm. I became excited and ran my bloody hand around to the front of his neck to feel for the carotid artery, the main artery that supplies blood to the brain. I knelt and was very quiet. I could feel only one thump but to me that was sufficient. My entire attitude changed. I had a live person that needed medical assistance and needed it now. "334, I need an ambulance immediately at 1818 N. Regester St. I have a man with a serious head wound and I don't think he will last much longer. I'm in the second floor bathroom" "10-4," answered the dispatcher.

As I awaited the ambulance I tried to talk to the dying man. He was unconscious and barely breathing. However he was breathing. That was a miracle in itself. My fears and nervousness had disappeared when I realized that this man needed me. The scared little boy that entered the bathroom was once again a police officer. I stayed with the man and gently talked to him telling him to, "hold on and concentrate on breathing." I dare not ask any questions as to who may have killed him for I feared that he would die with me alone in the bathroom slumped over the bathtub that was also stained with blood. I felt a sadness come over me. I was certain he would die there with me. I talked quietly and about myself and my family. I spoke of nothing in particular, for what does a dying man want to hear?

The paramedics arrived and were also amazed by the amount of blood and the protruding hammer. They worked feverishly to keep the man alive. When he was carried down the bloody steps and thru the blood soaked kitchen one of the paramedics slipped in the blood but didn't fall. He looked at me, "I don't think this guy is going to make it, you might want to contact the homicide detectives." I did.

A homicide detective contacted me by phone at the dwelling. He advised me that they were extremely busy working on actual murders and to contact them if the man died. Until then I should do the investigation. I called for the crime lab and began to sketch and write. As I was writing a younger man came to the house to see what the commotion was about. I asked who he was and was told he was the dying man's son. He seemed nervous and upset and wouldn't go into the kitchen. He talked to me in the front room, first floor only. I thought this odd but he was the victim's son.

I arrived at Johns Hopkins Hospital and inquired as to the hammer victim's condition. He made it thru surgery and was stable. I felt satisfied for several reasons. He was alive, I could find out who attacked him and charge them with attempted murder, and I felt good inside because I talked to him as I thought he was dying and he didn't.

I would discover weeks later that the son did in fact beat his father for drug money and had ruined the house to make it appear as a robbery. I arrested him at the home without incident. The investigation revealed that the son began hitting his father in the kitchen the first three blows and the final blow where the hammer stuck in his father's head was as the father was crawling up the steps to get away from his murdering son. They had struggled in the kitchen for some time. The father falling and getting back up then falling again, the entire time the dad was reaching out to hold onto anything he could to maintain and retain his balance while blood spurted out of the three holes in his cracked skull which smeared and filled the kitchen, its walls, cabinets, and its other contents with that blood.

Three months later I stood in court with the father and his son. The father had to be wheeled into the courtroom in a wheelchair and wore a plastic helmet to protect him when he had seizures and his head hit the ground. The father could talk but very slowly and sometimes his words were inaudible. He told the judge that he had forgiven his son for what he had done. The judge listened sadly then said, "That's fine. I don't! Twenty-five years city jail! Take him out of here and out of my sight!" The son wept, the father stared blankly into space and I celebrated and reveled quietly to myself. That bloody kitchen and hallway would remain with me much longer than twenty-five years.

Mistakes

Sometimes a police officer takes chances. They have to take chances. That's the nature of the job. However, these chances can become deadly mistakes. That's how a police officer learns to protect himself, by remembering his mistakes from the situations that he experiences over time. Usually the chances/mistakes aren't deadly. They get lucky, very lucky. This was the case with Officer Ron Drake and myself.

Ron had been on the street about six months prior to me being assigned to the Eastern District. He had a little more experience than I. Ron worked 333 post. Half of that area was a high crime area. The other half was occupied by older citizens and was somewhat quiet.

I received a call for a suspect armed with a knife in the 900 block of. N. Chester St. Ron received the call to be my back up unit. We arrived at the same time in front of the address. As we approached the front door, which was a screen door with glass panels, I could see no one standing in the vestibule. I opened the door and Ron and I entered. As we carefully walked into the vestibule we saw a thin black male standing at the top of the steps. He was holding a large butcher knife! He began yelling at us. "Come on up here white muvafuckers! I got something for you two fuckers!" He was swinging this large knife as he motioned us to come up the steps with his other hand. Again he screamed, "Come on pigs, I'll cut your white ass!"

Ron and I should have waited for more help to arrive. The suspect was violent, loud, abusive, and nearly out of control, besides he was waiving a butcher knife at two armed police officers. We should have waited. We took a chance by not calling for back up. We didn't even think of calling for back up. Hopefully it wouldn't be a deadly chance, a deadly mistake.

I looked at Ron; he looked back at me and we said, "fuck it!" at the same time. That was a rookie move. The suspect began backing up as we climbed each step. He was standing in the middle of the main room of this row house as we reached the landing at the top of the twenty or so steps.

The suspect was swinging the knife and yelling. I was approximately fifteen feet away, Ron about ten feet away, and to my right. Simultaneously we unholstered our revolvers and pointed them at the suspect. He didn't care. This didn't affect him. We had a problem. I didn't take my eyes off the suspect. "What do you think Ron, should we shoot him?" I was serious. He did have a butcher knife and he was violent and threatening. "We can't do that Dan." Ron said quietly. He was right.

After a minute or so of decision-making conversation, Ron and I decided to rush the suspect. We put our guns away and rushed at the suspect. He raised the knife over his head. Ron and I then grabbed for the knife. I reached his wrist first. As I pulled downward with all my strength to remove the knife, the suspect's arm came full circle and smashed into Ron's upper back twice. One stab wound was behind Ron's neck. The second was above his right shoulder blade.

I could have Shit! Ron and I wrestled the suspect to the ground, I had a death grip on his wrist, a violent struggle ensued! *This guy is so very strong, come on Danny, get him under control!* I thought as we rolled around the floor. Subduing this knife-wielding suspect was taking a tremendous amount of energy and strength. Finally we were able to cuff the suspect. We didn't have time to call for help, the struggle didn't allow for that to happen.

Ron lay on the floor. I was extremely upset. I knew he had been stabbed but I wasn't aware how seriously. He was bleeding. His blood was covering my hands. I was incensed, frantic, very nervous, and upset with myself that Ron had been stabbed. I felt it was my fault. I couldn't hold the arm still. I wasn't expecting the suspect to push down, as I pulled downward. I made a serious mistake. *We* made several serious mistakes.

Many thoughts went thru my mind as I attempted to collect myself and assess the situation. *Maybe I didn't try hard enough, was I afraid and puss out. No, just did all the wrong things. I should have shot this bastard, God he was strong. Damn Danny you fucked up big time! Ron, I hope Ron is okay. I need to call for an ambulance; I need to fuck this guy up too!* I thought nervously.

I called for an ambulance and checked on Ron. He had his vest on so the wounds didn't go in as deep as I thought. Another lucky break. Still, I was pissed. I grabbed this piece of shit and held the back of his head by the hair. I had a nice tight grip. His hair was wrapped around my fingers. My left hand was holding the cuffs and I was twisting hard. I stood the suspect up and placed him on the edge of the top step. I pulled his head back and shoved it into the doorjamb with as much force as I could muster, three times. Blood was squirting out of his face. *Good! Fuck Him!* I said to myself and aloud. I then put my right foot out and tripped the asshole down the twenty or so steps, handcuffed and helpless. He had nothing to stop his fall. He tumbled violently down the steps, bouncing off the walls on the way down. When he reached the bottom of the steps he had gathered enough momentum that when he hit the screen door the glass broke and cut the shit out of him! He had cuts on his back and legs. *Fuck him!* I thought, "Fuck you!" I yelled down the steps. "How dare you stab a police officer? I should have shot you muvafucker!"

Ron and the suspect were transported to Hopkins Hospital in separate ambulances. Ron's wounds were not serious. I was so very relieved when I heard this from the doctor. I went to the hospital with both the injured. The suspect received many stitches and was taken to the district for booking.

I would receive a bronze star for not shooting and killing this guy, and for keeping Ron from becoming more seriously injured. Ron too received a commendation. I felt as though I should have received a smack in the head or a kick in the ass! Not a medal. I had made serious mistakes in judgment.

I guess I did okay, I thought that night. *But did I have to trip the guy down the steps and bust him up like that? Yes, I did! It was the way of our squad, besides he hurt Ron. Piss on it!*

I put the Carpenter's on the stereo, put the headphones on and listened to Karen's sweet soft voice. I stared at the wall, drank six beers and made it all, RIGHT, again. The mistakes we made and chances we took weren't deadly, not this time . . .

Kill Officer Shanahan 1979

I went to work as I had done so many times before, but this shift would turn out to be different, very eventful, and scary. It was mid summer and warm. After roll call, my sergeant, Charlie Abrams, called me to his small cubicle, his office. He advised me that I could not go out on the street and perform my regular assigned duties. I was working another post. I would not be allowed to patrol my normal area of two years. I was very unhappy with this decision. *It's my post to patrol and I'm responsible for protecting it!* I thought.

I felt as though it was my personal duty to do my job. I questioned Sgt. Abrams and he explained that someone had called in a threat, a threat to kill me. This threat was called in to kill Officer Shanahan at the corner of E. Eager St. and N. Chester St., at 8:00 p.m. That was my post.

I had been aggressively patrolling my post for nearly a month or so and my arrest rate was up considerably. *I must have pissed off some of the bad guys. So, they have me murdered, or scare me off, or intimidate me. They do this so they can continue breaking the law and continue their criminal activities? Bullshit!* I thought. *I will not be intimidated by, The Element. How dare they think that they can scare me away from doing my job!*

I was not going to stay away from my post because someone threatened to kill me at 8:00 p.m. I had been on the street for nearly four years and was street smart, cocky, confident, and I felt I could handle any situation that would arise. I felt comfortable in my surroundings. The ugliness, crime, hate, squalor, death and sheer fact that I was in the district with the highest crime and homicide rate, not only allowed me to feel its pulse and its life force, but also gave me a sort of attachment to this monster. It was my driving force, my way of life, and my lifeblood. No one was going to take this from me. I felt a personal affront by this threat. This was personally unacceptable to me.

I was comfortable in those surroundings and in that atmosphere. After I left the department I would ride my Harley around the district and my old post at midnight and later. I felt that no one would look down on me there; no one would pass judgment on me in that shithole. I was at home.

The other officers on my shift heard of the threat. I would not be labeled a *pussy*, a *coward*. I would not run scared. I went upstairs to my locker and retrieved two additional handguns and my boot knife. I also grabbed twenty more rounds of ammunition and put them in my pocket.

While I was there I did something that few of us, at that time, rarely did. I put on my Kevlar bulletproof vest. I very seldom wore my vest, except in the colder months to keep my chest warm. Any other time I found the vest to be to confining, hot, and restricting. Few of us wore them. No one seemed to care who wore their vest and who did not.

All the officers in the Eastern District had been issued a Kevlar, bulletproof vest, and were instructed to use it. We wore the vest at roll call so the supervisor could see and touch it, then we went to our radio cars, removed the vest and placed it in our brief case or in the trunk. It really didn't seem to matter who did or did not wear this lifesaving device. No one cared. One day a fellow officer would wear his vest and the next four he wouldn't. I was the same way, If I came to work feeling nervous or apprehensive by my surroundings, I'd put my vest on, if not, it went in the trunk or back in my locker. I did, however, wear my vest religiously on the first night of the midnight shift. This came after the day shift, which included lots of sun and daylight. The midnight shift had all the darkness and boogiemen. But, after that first night, all was well, no vest.

It was 7:45 p.m., *only fifteen more minutes to live*! I thought jokingly. "Yeah Right!" I said aloud as I walked to my radio car. "No one is going to chase me off my post and keep me from being a cop!" I was talking aloud to myself as I sat in my car. Then I became defiant and felt indestructible. A sense of machismo came over me and I felt like the all time, *BAD ASS!* I pulled onto Edison Hwy. And again I said aloud, "Come and get me assholes! I'm right here!"

I drove directly to the corner of E. Eager St. and N. Chester St. I slammed the door closed and slowly walked to the corner, standing on the sidewalk. I began to twirl my nightstick and whistle a song. I thought about getting shot in the back. *This is definitely not acceptable,* I thought. I backed myself up against the wall and waited. Once or twice I called out, "I'm here! It's me Shanahan! Come and get it!" I was taunting the bad guys. But I was ready. My six inch .38 caliber Smith and Wesson service revolver was on my hip, my two inch .38 caliber Smith and Wesson revolver was in my left pocket, my .22 caliber automatic was in my waistband. I also had my nine-inch boot knife in my left army boot. I was definitely armed and dangerous, not to mention, scared.

I also double-checked my Motorola radio to make certain it was functioning properly, *just in case,* I thought. There I was, defiant, pissed off, a smart ass petrified police officer, standing with my back to the wall on one of the most recognized corners in the Eastern District. Recognized for its reputation of danger, drugs, shootings, stabbings and death, awaiting my fate.

As I stood there I began seeing the scenario unfolding in my mind. Two cars, six bad guys, shotguns, Uzi's, hand grenades, flame throwers, anything imaginable was in this make believe car, with make believe bad guys. I shook my head and laughed quietly. *I'm a sick asshole,* I thought. *Am I being smart here?* I wondered. Just then Sgt. Abrams pulled up to the corner. It was now 8:15 p.m. "You Asshole!" He yelled. "I told you to stay off your post and here you are on the exact same corner I told you to stay away from! Get your dumb ass in that radio car and get the fuck out of here!" He bellowed.

At that instant I realized how stupid and foolish I was and how I should not tempt my fate like this. I should not be here. I walked to my radio car and slowly got in. I was in deep thought as to my actions. I quietly and sheepishly drove away. Suddenly I stopped and yelled, "Fuck you assholes, I'll never leave!" I yelled this to some imaginary bad guy or to someone who was watching me, maybe a *real* bad guy.

A week later I was called into the district and instructed to go downtown to see Colonel Guerrasio. He was Chief of Patrol and was responsible for all patrol officers. I entered his office, "Sit down Shanahan." He instructed. "You have another threat on your life again, it was my second, I'm not comfortable with this situation, so where do you want to be transferred to?" My heart sank, "Don't take me away from my post and my district, they're a part of me, an intricate part of me sir." "I'm aware of that Shanahan, how about the motorcycle division?" He asked. My heart *really* jumped! "Okay!"

I said loudly! *I could miss the Eastern District to be in motorcycles*! I was sure

he was joking; no one with only four years on the street gets transferred to

the motorcycle division, other then Officer Tony Petralia who was in fact the

youngest officer in the traffic division. That was considered an elite squad

like the mounted division. Most officers waited ten to fifteen years to get

into one of those divisions. Escort dignitaries, the President of The United

States, funerals for V.I.P.'s, it was an honor to be a motorcycle police officer!

It was also, macho, sexy, cool, and just plain, ALL THAT! I was transferred

there one week later. The bad guys had to wait.

THE MOTORMAN, THE RITUALS

Most police officers I worked alongside of and knew, dressed neatly. A few officers didn't look very nice in their uniforms. Some had wrinkled shirts and pants, some dirty shirts that they didn't keep tucked in, and others, just didn't care what they looked like, and it showed. They looked messy. Others, like me took great pride in the way we looked and the manner we presented ourselves to the public. I felt that a police officer should not only *be* professional but should also *look* professional. I wanted to look sharp, professional, neat and clean. I would have it no other way.

I seemed to have a renewed attitude, a good attitude, upon being transferred to the Traffic Division I was away from the everyday violence I had been experiencing in the Eastern District and it seemed as though the move to the Traffic Division soothed and minimized my feelings of despair and hopelessness of not being able to make a difference in the world of death and destruction that the East side of Baltimore City was dishing out to me. I did miss the men I had worked alongside of for four and a half years, they were good men and terrific police officers. We had formed a bond, a, camaraderie. We had survived many a trial and tribulation and still managed to keep a sense of humor. I feel strongly that humor and making light of some incidents that we are subject to as police officers allows us to continue on doing our jobs with enthusiasm

There was no room for compromise in the area of appearing neat and professional, and no compromising when it came to maintaining my weapon. My .38 caliber Smith and Wesson revolver was my lifeline. It had to work no matter what the conditions and could never fail me. No bad guy was going to take my life due to me not maintaining my equipment. Even my handcuffs were well oiled and were checked each day to ensure that the cuffs were in proper working condition and would easily latch onto a suspect if a violent struggle ensued during an arrest. I firmly believed that I was the good guy, the guy that wore the white hat. The officer that would, make a difference, in this world.

Thursday nights I would watch Hill Street Blues, a police show that was the rave at the time amongst many of the police officers, especially the young officers, such as me. I watched the show, drank beer, spit-shined my shoes or boots with cotton balls and melted shoe polish, and enjoyed every minute of the show and routine. I never missed an episode. I ate, drank, lived, and breathed, cop.

While working the Eastern District, shiny shoes were not a must, but my combat boots fitted with the extra thick tire tread soles were at least clean and had a satin black sheen. It was futile to shine boots that were constantly running down suspects thru dirty streets, running thru trash laden alleys, stepping in dog shit and walking thru roach infested dwellings, trying to do a job. Clean up a dirty district.

However, when I was transferred to the motorcycle unit, this changed. I prided myself on having and maintaining the shiniest pair of black leather boots. There was only one motorman whose boots were shinier than mine *all* of the time. He was a Sergeant Major in the Marine Corps. That was acceptable, *only* because he was a Marine. This ritual or routine of keeping clean and professional looking was very important to me. This ritual became even more intense when I was transferred to the elite, highly coveted, motorcycle unit. I wanted to appear shiny and bright just like my new black leather boots.

I purchased new blue tinted lenses for my new eyeglasses and was issued a new stainless steel .38 caliber Smith and Wesson revolver, upon my assignment to the motorcycle unit. Most officers had the blue steel revolver that looked dull and boring. Some still carried the Colt 38 that was issued in the 1950's or earlier, and looked its age. Most officers didn't have the newest style shiny stainless which was much more professional looking, silver, shiny, and new, not unlike me. Plus it was the newest model weapon the department had issued. Only the older officers that wanted a new weapon had the new stainless revolvers or the officers in specialized units such as the mounted division or the honor guard. All of these were high visibility units, and of course, the highly prestigious, motorcycle unit would get new shiny, stainless revolvers, including *me!*

I also purchased new knee high black motorcycle boots and had two small pen compartments specially sewn on the outside right boot. The department issued spats, which were covers for your black shoes that came up to your knees. These were very unprofessional in appearance and no one else I worked with wore them. They were outdated and looked very unbecoming.

The custom sewn pen pocket was also black leather to match the boots and was sewn on the outside of the boot so the silver pens would be readily noticed. I also had heavy duty stainless zippers put on the inside of the boots to make them easier to put on and take off, plus it was more metal to look good in. Image was everything. These pen compartments contained two engraved silver, Cross-pens, with my name engraved nicely in them in script lettering. Daniel J. Shanahan. These pens were slipped neatly inside the specially sewn pocket.

I had metal cleats attached to the bottom of the heels so to protect the heel from wearing out so fast from riding the dressed out, extra chromed, 1200cc Harley Davidson Police Motorcycle. Also, the cleats were perfect for making a neat clicking sound as I walked, especially in the halls of the courts. Everyone heard a motorcycle cop coming before they actually saw him, due to the cleats. These cleats were also instrumental for other reasons.

At night, when riding my Harley Davidson Police Motorcycle at higher speeds with other officers, we would press hard down on the cleats against the pavement, making sparks fly from the boots. This was extremely cool and looked even more cool when the sparks trailed five to seven feet back from the bottom of your boots and from the back of the motorcycle at sixty mph, or faster. Of course, the next day we all had to go to the boot man to replace our cleats! We didn't care. The thrill was worth it.

There were many thrills as a motorcycle officer including racing our motorcycles on the Jones Falls Expressway early on Sunday mornings. Four or more officers would meet and we would race up to, and over, one hundred mph to see which officer had the fastest Harley. The losers pitched in money and treated whichever officer won, to breakfast. It was thrilling to escort a funeral of a dignitary, V.I.P., or unfortunately, a fallen police officer or firefighter. Ten or more motormen would begin leading the funeral procession. Then, as we reached the first intersection the lead motorman would signal and the last row of officers would downshift, crack the throttle on this powerful 1200cc Harley Davidson Police Motorcycle, and speed past the other motor officers to reach the first intersection to stop all traffic flow so as to allow the funeral procession to continue uninterrupted. The procession must not have to stop. It would continue on at all costs. Once the first two officers's agreed that the intersection was safe, and as the procession was going thru that completely stopped intersection, the first of the two officers would again speed away. The thrilling part of this escort was speeding away from that intersection, shifting gears and roaring past the entire funeral procession to reach the front of the procession or the very next intersection. It was a constant leap frog concept, once your intersection was clear you leapfrog to the very next which could be blocks and blocks away. Therefore speeding past all those cars in the procession was extremely cool. Fast starts, loud pipes, and high speeds were acceptable. If there were many cars as there usually were in escorts such as politicians or fallen police officers, the distance from the back of the funeral to the very front and beyond was large. Speeding past all the cars while shifting gears was loud, impressive, an adrenaline rush, and great fun. I always volunteered for escorts. It was a chance to show off my uniform, motorcycle, motorcycle skills and it was very macho and good for my hungry ego which seemed at times insatiable.

There were more rituals. They may have been rituals, traditions or maybe just pranks that motormen played on each other. Many times my motorcycle helmet or ticket book, "went to the beach". This occurred only twice until I realized I had to be very much aware of where my helmet and ticket book were placed during roll call. Ten or more motormen were seated randomly in three rows in the roll call room. Sometimes an officer was seated behind me. My helmet and ticket book were placed innocently on the floor next to me while attending roll call and receiving assignments. The officer seated behind me would nonchalantly and unknowingly slide my helmet away from me with his boot. The helmet would mysteriously be placed into the sand filled cigarette butt can located in the rear of the room. Somehow the helmet would be filled with this sand and cigarette butt mixture. Many roll calls were riddled with angry screams of, "who sent my helmet to the beach"! It took much time to remove all the sand from the helmet so as not to be sandy the remainder of the day.

If this prank couldn't be pulled off properly, the black shoe polish around the inside rim of the helmet or on the chinstrap, satisfied the pranksters needs. Once, only once, did I remove my helmet after leaving the headquarters building after morning roll call, to issue a ticket.

Sometimes I removed my helmet and hung it on the handlebar as I performed my duty of enforcing traffic laws and spoke to the motorist. This unknowing motorist took one look at me and burst out laughing. I had no idea why until I was invited by the older female motorist to see my reflection in her make up mirror that she removed from her purse. There I stood in all my splendor thinking I was looking professional, neat and clean, only to have a black shoe polish mark across my entire forehead and all over my lower chin. I must have looked like a total clown. I most definitely did not issue this lady a citation, I laughed along with her, tucked my black shoe polished head between my ass and quickly walked away completely embarrassed, and bent on revenge. Some unsuspecting motorman would suffer thru this same ordeal as soon as I was able to get my revenge.

Motorcycle officers are trained to ride in pairs and to ride and look professional at all times. When two motorcycle officers ride together they must act as one. This takes much training, much nerve, and can be unnerving at times. Two experienced officers can ride side by side with only six to eight inches between the two motorcycle handlebars. We rode closer in distance at speeds up to eighty mph than when we parked our bikes side by side. This is the way it would be, anything less was unacceptable. Perfection and professionalism were the only rules of the day.

There also were times when a motorman had to ride extremely slow. We were trained by having slow races. This exercise was just that, a slow race that had to be completed without placing a foot on the ground. This was accomplished by using the throttle, the clutch and the back brake in unison. This allowed the bike to remain, virtually, standing still. I mastered this slow race. It was a very necessary tool in police escorts. Escorted dignitaries aren't driven fast. Police Motorcycle Officers don't put their feet down every time they come to a near stop. It wasn't acceptable. We were a high visibility unit.

We were trained by the best of the best training officers. Norman, Hal, and Sgt. Erick Anders, were the three outstanding trainers that had patience, knowledge and most importantly a good attitude and a good sense of humor. "Boss Hog," as we referred to Sgt. Anders, was nothing like the little pudgy sheriff on Dukes of Hazard. My sergeant was well over six feet two inches tall, and weighed two hundred and fifty pounds. He was a big man and looked impressive and mean on his 1200cc Harley. There was absolutely no resemblance to The Dukes, "Boss Hog". He liked the nickname.

Years after he retired, he became aware of the name's background, I still think he liked it no matter the origin, he had that all important, sense of humor. "Boss Hog," was fair and taught the new men exactly what was necessary to remain in this elite and desirable unit and how to survive riding a motor at high speeds during chases or responding to emergency calls. He was smart, fair, and exuded professional leadership qualities that assisted us in becoming and remaining top notch motorcycle riders.

We escorted the Pope, the President of the United States; we met and escorted the Vice-President from Chopper One to his destinations. We escorted many senators and congressman and various dignitaries that visited our city for many political reasons and functions. A motorman, as well as a mounted officer, must look and perform to perfection every day and for every escort. I liked that. I was proud to be a motorcycle officer and I was happy.

Every now and then, after the Sunday morning races, I would ride out the Jones Falls Expressway into Baltimore County, where I was not supposed to be, for it was out of the city limits. I would ride east on I-695 to my parent's home in Parkville. Once there I would park my motor in the rear of their house to avoid being noticed as I ate Sunday morning breakfast with my mom and dad, where I didn't belong, and in violation of police department general orders. I didn't care, after all, I was one of the elite, and I was special. This was not a part of my normal Sunday routine but sporadically I would take the short ride to see my parents. I always listened to my police radio in case I was needed for I would not be charged with dereliction of duty and I was merely one mile from the city line. Even though I took certain liberties because I had so much freedom of movement, I didn't abuse my liberties. When working as a patrolman in a district an officer worked a small confined area and had to be accounted for at all times. In motors we worked half the city or three to four districts at a time since we were few in number. There were only thirty-five or so motorcycle officers to cover the entire city performing traffic enforcement duties, funeral escorts, wide load escorts and other traffic related duties. Motorcycle traffic enforcement officers worked only two shifts, the districts worked three.

The motorcycle unit consisted of many fine officers that performed their jobs properly and professionally we were seasoned officers that had worked in patrol for over five years or more and performed our duties properly while still having a little fun and enjoyment. We knew what we could and couldn't get away with; we had been around the block.

As I rode to my mom and dad's house, sporadically, on these spring and summer Sunday mornings, I could only look down at my shiny boots, my shiny motorcycle, and my shiny revolver and would revel in the exhilaration of doing the two things I loved, being a police officer and riding a police issued Harley Davidson 1200cc motorcycle. On top of all that, I was getting paid to do what I loved! I looked forward to going to work and really didn't care to have off the two days out of every eight I worked. I believe I was one of the few individuals in America that didn't want to take a vacation from their employment. What a job!

Since I wanted to look my very best and to fit in with other motormen, I also purchased a Sam Brown black leather belt. This is the type that crosses the chest and connects onto the gun belt. This was also a standard item for the motorcycle officer. Just before I was forced to resign, the motorcycle unit was issued black leather jackets. These made a motorman look exceptionally macho.

Looking at myself in the mirror I resembled a WWII German Officer, spit shined to perfection, polished and intimidating. Macho and egotistical were two words that epitomize a motorcycle cop and rookie cops as well. Just being a cop was macho enough but the ego boost of being a rookie police officer or a motorcycle cop was unmatched by anything I had experienced.

Looking at the back of my shiny boots, my girlfriend's grandfather's Iron Claw was noticeable. It was neatly tucked inside my right boot. This tool opened and closed like a bear claw and was made to grab and hold a suspect. It was against regulations to carry, but I wore it anyway. The Claw was different looking, a conversation piece. It was cool and had a history, it was carried in the very early years of the police department when police officers had no radios, had to walk a beat due to the lack of radio cars, and had to go to a telephone call box once an hour to check in with the desk sergeant in order to receive an assignment, call or to let the sergeant know his whereabouts. In those days if an officer needed help he would strike his nightstick against the pavement in rapid succession causing an unmistakable sound. A sound recognized by other officers', which alerted them that a fellow officer was in need of help. Those were the days my grandfather, Sgt. John T. Shanahan, was a motorcycle sergeant patrolling these same streets. These same streets I was patrolling over fifty years later. My engraved three-inch boot knife with the initials, D.J.S., protruded from the back of the left boot and looked intimidating. That along with the antique Iron Claw put the finishing touches on my look of perfection as a motorman. Perfect looking yet functional.

All these fun toys and the black leather boots along with the black leather motorcycle jacket produced an image of professionalism as well as a stunning look for a police officer. Add my three bronze star medals and the coveted silver star medal with the black leather background of my motorcycle jacket along with the chrome name plate and chrome whistle with the silver loop chain hanging below my beautifully designed silver, blue and yellow

Baltimore Police badge, and a picture of perfection, machismo, and love for my job emanated. It was extremely obvious that I was very much into being a Baltimore City Police Motorcycle Officer.

I even had a macho and intimidating routine that I utilized when pulling over a citizen for any reason. After I activated my lights and siren to pull a violator to the curb or side of the street, I would wait until the driver looked into his rear view mirror. At that point I would turn the siren off and quickly kick out the kickstand in an angry manner. Quick and snappy! Then I would reach up and quickly unzip my Velcro fastened chinstrap on my helmet. Next, I would reach to the front of the bike where the windshield was, which was holding my ticket book. I had my shiny motorcycle boot up on the foot peg so as to allow the frightened, usually nervous motorist, to see the boots and the full package as I reached to the outside of the right boot to retrieve my silver Cross pen, my engraved, silver Cross pen. After that I placed the ticket book, which was enclosed in a black leather cover with my name also engraved on it, under my arm. I would approach the driver's side of the vehicle, stating in a low professional no nonsense tone, "License and registration please."

At times, after requesting the driver's license and registration, the driver would hand me the papers and their hand would be shaking slightly, or they would stutter. Especially, women, and young drivers. I liked that, I knew I had intimidated them and to me that meant something. I could be the unforgiving typical motorcycle cop or the nice guy, my choice.

Motorcycle officers had a reputation for being harsh and unforgiving when stopping a motorist and had a reputation for always issuing a ticket, no exceptions. I didn't fit that mold; I gave breaks and was polite and professional unless the driver had a bad attitude. If this was the case I quickly fit into that nasty image people had of a motorcycle cop with no problem. I was playing a role and I was giving the performances of my life.

Not only were there rituals followed when becoming and being a motorcycle officer, the first and foremost ritual and my most favorite, was getting dressed. Getting dressed and making the transformation from being a mere person to becoming a welldressed Baltimore City Police Officer, a Blue Knight, as author Joseph Wambaugh wrote, a shiny Blue Knight.

The dressing ritual began with a full uniform placed neatly on my bed. Each item of clothing would be inspected for cleanliness and must be wrinkle free. First I would put on my skintight motorcycle pants and secure the foot straps under my feet, which held the flared seated pants taut. The pant legs were form fitting to my calves while the thigh and seat portions were baggy to allow for comfortable riding. The tight pant legs looked nice inside the shiny leather boots. The next step of this ritual was to put on my undershirt, which had to be clean and neat. I would sit down on my bed and very carefully put my polished motorcycle boots on. Always being careful not to scuff the toe of the boot, the shiniest part, the Hill Street Blues shine. I'd pull on the boot and zip up the stainless zipper located on the inside of the boot. I would then double check to see that my Cross pens were still in the custom sewn in pocket. Then my boot knife and Iron Claw were put into their proper places.

It was now time for my white shirt. My perfectly ironed and lightly starched white shirt. My mother ironed my shirts by hand before I got married and moved out of the house I grew up in. She would say a prayer, a Hail Mary, each time she ironed one of my police shirts. The collar pins on the shirt were placed exactly as the instructions had advised. One inch from the front of the collar and one inch from the bottom of the collar. I utilized a small piece of cardboard exactly one inch by one inch to achieve perfection. The next step was *almost* my favorite step. I would place my medals of commendation on this perfectly ironed white shirt. The three Bronze Stars were centered above the empty area the badge would eventually occupy, and above those, the coveted Silver Star was proudly placed in just the right spot. Just the right spot to be noticed by all, for I was extremely proud to have received this medal. That was from the shooting incident at B.J. and The Bear nightclub where I had saved seven peoples lives. It meant so very much to me. Bravery, courage, steadfastness, and most of all, luck! I was proud.

Next in this dressing ritual would come my nametag. I wouldn't hear of wearing the black plastic name tag issued by the department that showed just my first two initials and my last name, D.J. Shanahan, Noooo, it was to boring, unnoticeable, and nondescript. I had a specially made chrome nameplate that was emblazoned with my full first name, my middle initial and my last name in black, which was inset and recessed in to the chrome, Daniel J. Shanahan.

Now for my badge! Now for my favorite part of getting dressed! Badge number 296 was wiped off with a soft rag after breathing a hot breath onto it allowing for a clean wipe. My badge was beautiful! Even though it was exactly like the other thirty five hundred badges worn by Baltimore Police Officers, *my* badge was different. It belonged to me and I worshipped it. I felt honored and special to be wearing it. The Baltimore City Police badge was colored with red, yellow and blue. These colors blended well with the chrome and the royal blue letters of, "Baltimore Police." This badge looked and felt special, extremely special to me. I placed the badge into the holes provided it on my shirt. I often thought of all the officers that were injured or killed wearing this badge. This badge that represented good, honor, honesty, fairness, valor, heroism, pride and professionalism. And, above all, a feeling of making a difference. Many times I thought of my brother Mike and how he got shit on and was forced to quit this department. How much he must miss this job. This job that is so special, so intense, so different and satisfying, at times. This badge that fought and conquered evil. I likened my badge to my Catholic medal I wore around my neck. The Saint Michael Medal that is worded, "Saint Michael Protect Us." Saint Michael the Archangel that God sent to cast Lucifer and his band of bad angels, out of heaven and into hell! I *was* Michael the Archangel, or at least I *thought* I was.

I would be sickened later in my career for what I would do to this badge of goodness and glory. I would severely disappoint myself and let myself down. I would disgrace myself, my family, and would not forgive myself for my actions, the actions that tarnished and dulled this beautiful, shiny, badge, and tarnished me forever.

As I put my shirt on and buttoned the buttons from the bottom up, I would stand in front of my full-length mirror. As I watched my reflection it seemed I grew an inch or two. It seemed I was taller, braver, smarter and better than the average person. I felt as though I honestly and truthfully stood for something. I had a definite purpose in this world. To do good and to fight evil! I tucked in my shirt and put on my black leather gun belt. Four black loops attached the gun belt to the belt around my waist. They are called, "keepers." They keep the gun belt attached to the belt holding the pants up to keep everything in line and neat.

I picked up my shiny, stainless steel .38 caliber Smith and Wesson six shot revolver from the nightstand. I pushed in the lever that released the cylinder and flipped the gun to the left causing the cylinder to snap open exposing the bottom of the six S&W .38 caliber rounds that filled the cylinder. These were pulled out, wiped off and inspected. I had also cut an "X" into the tip of the leaded bullet.

By doing this, the semi-wad cutter bullets would expand quicker upon impact and give the bullet additional knock down power, I was told. Before I closed the empty cylinder and snapped the cylinder closed. I pulled the trigger to make certain that the firing pin hit the round by holding my thumb against the inside of the guns back strap feeling the floating firing pin strike my thumb. This insured me that the firing pin would strike the bullet and it was sure to fire. It was, and would be, my lifeline.

I loaded the six rotated bullets into my revolver. I rotated bullets from my gun belt into my gun each week. This ensured that each round would fire and not fail me due to continually setting in the same place collecting rain or moisture as they stayed around my gun belt. I spun the cylinder and it would spin with ease and precision. As the cylinder was spinning I snapped the empty cylinder into place causing a much liked metallic sound. After a quick glance to assure myself that the cylinder completely closed I placed the gun into my Wild West type holster. The holster had nothing but a thin strap holding the gun into place. Not like the snug fitting, hard to remove gun from holsters of today. Today's holsters are much safer. Today a suspect must struggle to remove an officer's gun. My holster was unsafe but functional.

Some days as I prepared for work, I would stand in front of this floor length mirror and draw my gun. I would draw down on myself. I would occasionally twirl my gun, or point it directly at the mirror with the barrel pointing directly at my head and face. I wanted to see and feel what looking down the barrel of a gun was like. What it might be like if someone pulled a gun on me and pointed it at my head and face. Even though I had experienced this on Chase Street, at B.J. and The Bear Nightclub, and on other occasions, I had no idea what it felt like with no fear or violence involved, where time and life weren't an issue. I don't know why I performed this crazy act. Typical badass, full of himself, cocky, confident, cop. I was Wyatt Earp, John Wayne, and Errol Flynn, all rolled up in one persona. I was a cop that loved all he was and all he was doing.

Now, I was complete, the rituals were completed also. I wasn't Dan Shanahan, a normal citizen. I was Baltimore Police Motorcycle Officer, Daniel J. Shanahan! I was, "the man!" I was, "The Police." I was, Five-0!" as in McGarret from Hawaii Five-0. I was too cool!

I loved my job profusely. I was so very content and happy. I felt comfortable on the streets and confident in my abilities to handle any situation that may arise while patrolling the streets of Baltimore City. I was seasoned, hardened, and callused. I was the epitome of what a police officer should be. I looked, as well as acted the part, with enthusiasm and vigor. I will never again have a job that could make my blood rush, my skin crawl, and allow me to experience things that very few people ever will. A job which allowed me to be so close to death and violence so many times, yet survive, as being a Baltimore Police Officer, a Baltimore City Motorcycle Police Officer. What a job! What a wonderful and exciting job!

Speed Thermometer

As a motorcycle officer for nearly five years, I've heard many excuses and reasons for speeding or breaking the traffic laws. One particular excuse always comes to mind and it is a classic that I will never forget.

I was shooting radar and clocking vehicle speeds on the Jones Falls Expressway. I had written six speeding tickets and was about to leave when my radar gun began to make the high-pitched sound that indicates a speeding vehicle approaching. At fifty-five mph, a radar gun makes a noise at a set level. As I used the gun over and over, I could recognize a speeder by the higher than normal sound of fifty-five mph. At speeds of seventy five to eighty mph, the gun seems as though it's screaming. It's very easy to know a speeder is approaching by the high-pitched sound emitted by the radar gun. The higher, the faster.

I pulled this driver over about a mile after he passed thru the radar trap. I asked for his license and registration. "Why did you stop me Mr. Officer?" said the elderly black man. "I stopped you for speeding sir, I clocked you at seventy-five mph in a fifty-five mph zone". Usually I allowed twenty mph over the posted speed limit before I wrote a ticket, I thought this was more than fair. A lot of officers wrote at ten mph over the posted limit, I felt this unfair and inappropriate. My feelings were, if a citizen is driving seventy-five mph in a fifty-five mph zone they must know that they are exceeding the limit. I knew when I was driving if I was traveling twenty mph above the limit, I was speeding. If not, they should know.

I tried to be as fair and easygoing as possible as a police officer. I usually gave the driver the benefit of the doubt and allowed twenty mph over the limit before I wrote, I also had, at times, taken citizens home if they smelled of alcohol but weren't, "falling down drunk." I would, at times, lock their cars, put the keys inside the vehicle, and order them to walk home. I never locked someone up for drunk driving unless there was an accident involved or they were blatantly drunk, running over curbs and parking meters. After all, I drove drunk quite frequently. Why be a hypocrite? It all depended on the driver's attitude. If I stopped a driver and the attitude was ignorant and combative, i.e. "Why are you stopping me, don't you have a real criminal you can bother?" or, "Why are you wasting my time, I wasn't speeding?" That driver was getting a ticket for something; I would make up a charge. Conversely, if a driver had broken the law and they had a good excuse, an excuse I hadn't heard yet, or an excellent attitude, I would either drop the speed or infraction to a lesser degree or let that driver go on without a ticket.

I liked having the power to take away someone's freedom or to write tickets, but I also enjoyed the power to let someone go. Absolute power does corrupt, absolutely. A lot of officers abuse that absolute power, some don't at all. I did, at times, abuse my powers.

"Officer, my speed thermometer said I was going sixty mph, you must be wrong," the old man stated. *What in the hell is he talking about, speed thermometer?* I wondered. The man pointed at his speedometer needle and said, "You know, my speed thermometer!" I then realized what the man was saying. I should have known when he called me, *Mr. Officer.* I smiled to myself but still wrote the man a speeding ticket but for driving only ten miles over the limit, not twenty. This accomplished two things. I had a ticket written, for there *are* quotas to fill each month, and I had dropped the fine from fifty dollars to twenty-five dollars and dropped points placed on his driving record from two to one. Everyone was appeased and content. I then made a note on my copy of the ticket reading, speed thermometer, so I would recall that incident when testifying in traffic court. I made these notes for my own recollections. If the driver was rude and ignorant I would write two initials on the ticket. A.H., this let me know that this driver was an *asshole*, when I pulled them over. I could testify with more conviction and attitude and this would let the judge know that the driver was nasty. A police officer can testify in a manner that the Assistant State's Attorney or the judge would instantly know that this person was rude and abusive to the officer. An officer can also testify in a different manner if he wanted the powers to be to become aware that this person was kind and polite. It's all in the manner a police officer testifies, his tone of voice and mannerisms. It's a given among the judges, attorneys, and police officers.

Judge Gerstung was probably one of the most colorful, fun and fair judges I have stood before and testified in front of. I always felt he liked me but he didn't show it. That would be unprofessional. Judge Gerstung was extremely professional and ran his courtroom with a stern fist but with a fairness that I enjoyed. He had no problem telling an officer that he or she was wrong by locking up a citizen and taking away their freedom, but also he was very harsh on someone that insulted or assaulted one of *his officers*. I liked and admired that. He always referred to us as *his officers*. He disliked anyone disrespecting a police officer; he was especially harsh on someone that physically attacked one of us. Judge Motsay was another judge that I admired and respected; He also was lighthearted and fair. Judge Resnik was extremely professional but had a dry sense of humor, or none at all, but he too was well respected. One day I was able to get Judge Gertsung to admit his fondness of me.

I was in traffic court and Judge Gerstung was the presiding judge. I enjoyed his court demeanor; he was quite funny and entertaining. On this particular morning I was the last officer to present his traffic cases to Judge Gertsung for adjudication. I had to testify about the old man and his *speed thermometer*. I thought I would have some fun. Hopefully I wouldn't anger the judge with my antics. "Your honor, I stopped Mr. Washington on the Jones Falls Expressway at the 4.3 marker for exceeding the posted limit of fifty-five mph by traveling sixty-five mph. I am a certified and qualified radar operator and my radar unit was checked for proper calibration thirty minutes prior to the issuance of this citation".

This was normal testimony for each speeding ticket. Judge Gertsung looked at Mr. Washington and asked for his side of the story and inquired as to his plea. Mr. Washington began his plea. *"Mister Judge, Your Honor,* Officer Shanahan says that I was *proceeding* the speed limit by ten mph, but as I passed Officer Shanahan my *speed thermometer* said I was only going sixty mph. Now I knows that my *speed thermometer* don't lie, it's *acrit."* I was biting my upper lip in an attempt to keep from laughing out loud. I glanced at Judge Gertsung and he too was trying to control and hold back his laughter. It was quite obvious to me and the rest of the people in the courtroom. All of us collected ourselves and then it happened! I couldn't resist, I had to do this. Judge Gertsung, noticeably wanting to laugh aloud, said, "Well Officer Shanahan, tell me about this discrepancy in testimony". I began, "Mister Judge, Your Honor, I am absolutely positive that when I clocked Mr. Washington's speed that my radar gun showed him driving sixty-five *degrees* in a fifty-five *degree* zone. I do know my temperatures Mister Judge, Your Honor. Mr. Washington's *speed thermometer* may have told him different but my radar gun doesn't lie to me, it was cold that day Mr. Judge Your Honor, but my speed thermometer doesn't lie, I'm certain of that". That did it! Judge Gerstung let out a burst of laughter; he couldn't contain himself any longer. I too began laughing aloud. The courtroom visitors joined the judge and me and the entire courtroom was in hysterics. The only person *not* laughing was poor Mr. Washington.

Judge Gerstung couldn't collect himself, he couldn't stop laughing. He did manage to stand up, recess the court for ten minutes and in his attempt to catch his breath, he paused and said, "Shanahan, in my chambers NOW!"

"Yes sir, Judge Your Honor Sir," I replied. "Is your temperature rising sir?" I could see his back moving up and down while he was walking away from me attempting to stop laughing but to no avail.

As I entered into his chambers Judge Gerstung's head was down on his desk and in his hands. He had stopped laughing. He looked up at me and I again began laughing, he started up again. We laughed uncontrollably for minutes. He finally stopped, looked up at me and said, "Shanahan you ass, I tried so hard not to laugh and lose control of my courtroom, but when you did the bit about the sixty-five degrees in the fifty-five degree zone I was no good. I always liked you Dan and I must say I will tell this story until my dying days." He continued on saying," In all my years I have never had to excuse myself from the bench, which was great! *Speed thermometer! Geez!*

We took a few minutes to gather ourselves and went back into the courtroom together. Judge Gerstung told Mr. Washington that he would find him not guilty and told him that he could leave right away. Judge Gerstung would not look up at Mr. Washington; he probably couldn't without laughing again. Mr. Washington was still unaware of the fun we had at his expense and just looked at me with a quizzical expression. I smiled a very large smile but dared not begin laughing again. Mr. Washington left the courtroom.

This was one of the funniest moments in my career. Judge Gerstung and I became much friendlier after that incident, each smiling at one another upon meeting up now and then. We both knew that the episode was unique and it made us smile inside. Judge Gerstung has since died; I won't soon forget him, that morning, our laughing together and, Mr. Washington with his talking *speed thermometer.*

DIE BITCH DIE!

It was 1981. I was a hot-shot experienced police officer, not just a police officer, I was a *motorcycle officer*. Confident, cocky, well dressed, and quite comfortable working, existing, and surviving in one of the nation's highest crime ridden and rated one of the most violent cities, Baltimore.

I was driving westbound on E. Monument St. in my radio car, a large Ford LTD. I always kept it clean, waxed, maintained, and looking nice. Just like me!

I glanced ahead a block or so as I patrolled the East Side of the city and noticed and smelled smoke. Not a car fire, not a brush fire. *Shit the entire house is on fire, it's engulfed! Christ!* I thought. I sped up and reached the burning house. I quickly pulled to a stop. I threw the car keys onto the floor and ran to the front of this small single dwelling, nothing like the row houses in the area, this sat alone. Unusual for that area of the city. I could see no one, hear no one, either inside or outside of the dwelling. It seemed odd. Odd, in a swiftly fleeting police officer's thoughts way of thinking. The house looked occupied or as if it had been inhabited but something was amiss, something didn't fit.

I yelled into the partially opened front door. "Anyone there?" No answer. Again, "Anyone in there, Police!" Again no answer, *Good, no problem, all safe.* I thought to myself. I called into the dispatcher and requested a fire company to respond to a fully involved dwelling fire at the 2300 block of E. Monument St.

I stood there all alone watching this home burn. *No big deal Dan, right?* I thought uncaringly.

Suddenly I saw a young black female flailing her hands in the air and yelling something, something I could neither hear nor understand. She was pointing at the dwelling. I ran to her as quickly as I could. As I reached her she yelled, "There's a baby in the house!" "Where?" I asked nervously. "The baby's upstairs, in the house, baby upstairs!" She repeated. I believed her. Her face showed signs of sincerity and real concern.

This changed the entire complexion of the situation. My mind whirled. I had a situation. I had an innocent life that needed my help, not just any innocent life, a baby, a child, not only will I cast off any regard for my personal safety, I'll do it even faster, It's a child.

A baby, not black, not white, not Hispanic, or Asian, etc., a baby. There are no differences and no prejudices when it comes to young children, babies, or the elderly. They are the helpless. They can't control the fact that they were born black, Hispanic, white, etc. That did not count in my prejudiced police officer mind, the baby counted.

I had no time to tell the dispatcher that I was going inside this burning dwelling, this hellfire. I'm going to be a hero. I thought. But what if I get burned or die? Tough shit, my mind is made up, it's a baby! For Chris sakes Danny, GO! My mind raced.

I ran inside and was immediately assaulted by heavy smoke and intense heat.

I began to cough, my eyes burned. This is like Palm Grove liquors. I thought to myself. But this time I had no air tank or mask and no partner. I was alone.

I noticed a six to ten inch space on the floor that was clear of smoke. *That's right! I remember! Heat and smoke rise, air is at the bottom of a fire.* I felt better.

The ceiling was on fire so were the walls. It was very dark in the back of the dwelling but light shone thru the front windows. *Why? Why was it so dark back there? What was it?* I fell to the floor and gasped for a few deep breaths of cleaner air. I ran up the stairs. It was so hot! My eyes burned even more.

I searched all three top floor rooms, nothing. I yelled and screamed. No answer. *It was quiet, a scary quiet,* I thought. The noise of the fire was wondrous yet petrifying to me. Crackling, snapping, and popping. *Not like the Palm Grove fire. I was all alone, just me, this savage fire, and yes, the baby, YES THE BABY!* I worried. I put my handkerchief to my mouth and nose. I inhaled a small amount of smoke and hot air, and choked. *So what!* I thought. I fell to my knees and got another chest full of smoke free air. *Where's the baby! I must go downstairs! No I can't yet!* I checked the rooms again then ran downstairs. *Why so damn dark, Why? No baby! I must get out.* My heart was sinking, I was so disappointed. *I must get out, NOW Danny!* I mostly fell down the only set of steps in the dwelling that I could locate. Half tripping, half running, and mostly falling and stumbling, merely attempting to get air and to get outside.

Please God; don't let me have missed this child, please! I tried, I tried. I reassured myself. I stumbled, tripped and fell out the open front door. I gasped, choked, and gasped for clean fresh air once again. I could hear the sirens. I was doubled over trying to get as much air as possible, or was it because I had a pain in my guts, a pain because I didn't find the baby, because I failed.

As I stood there rubbing my burning eyes I smelled and realized that I was on fire! SHIITTT! I yelled as I patted the little smoldering holes that the embers from the fire falling on my back had caused. The embers had burned thru my shirt and were now burning my Kevlar bullet-proof vest. The vest had kept the embers from reaching my skin.

I was a mess. The hair on my arms was singed, my head too. There were little hairballs on the tops of my hands and knuckles where once there was hair. My eyebrows and eyelashes were also burnt. I could not slow my heartbeat. I could not catch my breath. I was in a panic. *Oh God where was the baby? Why was it so dark in the back of the house, so light in the front? Had I failed?* I worried. A horrid sense of sadness fell over me. It was a horrible sensation, empty and dark. I felt sick to my stomach.

As I slowly looked up towards the sirens, I saw her again. The expression of fear and anxiety that had assured me in my head, with all my experience and street smarts, that there was a baby in that house, had disappeared from her face. She was expressionless, but she almost looked mad. She was yelling but I couldn't hear her this time due to the approaching sirens. The sirens were overtaking her words. It was then that the mad look seemed to change into an evil smirk, a look of Satan. She looked at me and began to laugh. She pointed at me and again began to laugh. *Why was she pointing and laughing at me?* I wondered curiously.

The sirens stopped, I suddenly heard it, heard her. "DIE BITCH, DIE MUVAFUCKER!" She said it in that black slang slurred tone I had heard so many times in my earlier years in the Eastern District and had somehow learned to understand and decipher.

"It's a vacant house officer, it's boarded up in the back." Came the loud confident voice of a firefighter approaching me. "Holy shit! You burned!" He asked. "I don't think so." I was barely able to reply. "What the fuck you doin going into a vacant dwelling fire. Didn't you see that all the windows in the back and sides were boarded shut?" He asked. "I didn't have time to look." I replied. I stood up and pointed to the black female Satan that sent me in the burning house for the fictitious fucking baby. She again said loudly. "DIE BITCH, DIE, WHITE MUVAFUCKER!"

It suddenly dawned on me what had been amiss, wrong, out of place. The back was so dark because those windows had been boarded shut along with the side windows. Most cities board up the windows in vacant dwellings so that the occupants of the neighborhood don't bust out the windows and to prevent anyone from entering that vacant house. I wasn't able to observe that the windows had been shut from my angle of sight as I pulled up to the burning house. I was in too much of a hurry also. Now it all fits! Like a sick puzzle with the pieces slowly being fitted together. The black bitch had set me up! Set me up to die or to become seriously injured. *Why! FUCK ME! Why! You know why asshole.* I said to myself. *You're WHITE. She's BLACK! It's her way of getting revenge!*

I stood up again in defiance, looked at the firefighter who now had realized and understood what had occurred, for he was also white, and I shrieked as loud as I could, "You fucking nigger! You fucking NIGGER BITCH!" With all the hatred and anger I had welled up inside me. I had to contain myself and keep myself from pulling my gun out and blowing her fucking nigger head off her fucking shoulders.

She ran! She disappeared around a corner. I'm certain she could hear the anger, despair, and hatred in my voice. The firefighter patted me on the back, "You're okay pal, you're okay, fucking niggers." He slowly walked away from me.

I reached my radio car my fingers slowly searched the floor for my car keys. I could smell the putrid smell of burnt hair. I rubbed my hands together to remove all the small burnt hairballs that were once hairs. I started the car and turned all four air conditioner vents towards my face and turned the air conditioner on high. The cold air felt great! It was exhilarating! I sat back in the seat and the back of my head gently hit the headrest as I let it flop back letting it go wherever. I inhaled cool fresh air deeply into my lungs.

My God, what had just happened to me, what? I wondered. I was at a loss, my thoughts empty, and my thoughts vacant. Just like the burning house, the house with NO baby in it.

BJ and the Bear

I received the coveted and much respected Silver Star my ninth year on the street, 29 May 1982, as a motorcycle policeman. The three bronze stars, for Chase and Biddle Street, Palm Grove Liquors and 800 N. Chester St. were all awarded while an officer in the Eastern District.

When I walked across the stage at Police Headquarters to accept my Silver Star in front of all the new graduating recruits, the upper echelon of the police dept., including the Police Commissioner, Frank Battaglia, and of course my family, I was so very proud. A proud human being and more importantly, a proud Baltimore City Police Officer. I was in my motorcycle uniform and I looked great and felt capitol!

That day, many officers received letters of commendation or Bronze Stars for performing exceptional acts of heroism or for performing their duties above and beyond the call of duty. However, I was the only officer to be awarded the *Silver Star.* That made the ceremonies more special to me and mine. The only medal awarded over the Silver Star was given only if an officer was shot or killed in the line of duty. The Silver Star was highly respected and coveted. Any officer wearing that star was looked up to and admired. I knew that, and, *I had it!* How I was to be awarded this prized possession, and exceptional ribbon, was bizarre and peculiar.

This particular night, my partner in the motor unit that night was Officer Norm Stamp. Norman was in the motorcycle unit since 1968 making him the one officer in the entire United States that remained in a motorcycle unit for that amount of time. He was a legend. Norm and I were very much alike, always involved in situations that most officers shy away from, fair and just, and always looking the part of a sharp dressed motorcycle officer. We both enjoyed our jobs tremendously.

Norm stopped a speeding vehicle at approximately 1:30 a.m. on Pulaski Hwy. Near the city county line. The driver was arrested for drunk driving and I heard Norm call for a tow truck to impound the vehicle. I responded in my radio car to assist.

The Federal government allots monies for overtime to Baltimore City officers to work from 11:00 p.m. to 2:00 a.m. Thursdays thru Saturdays in order to target drunk drivers and speeders. This was called the *Drunk Squad.* We liked it because we used to kid and tease that only the drunks were allowed to work this overtime, insinuating that the only officers to work this detail were drinkers, *we were.*

One particular evening after Norm and I worked the Italian Festival all day, and drank all day with our attorney, Bob Donadio, on his boat at the Inner Harbor where the festival was held, we worked the drunk squad detail. It was 11:30 p.m., We were shooting radar under the Eastern Ave. underpass. Norm couldn't see the numbers on the radar unit and I was so impaired I had to lean against my motorcycle to keep from falling over. A vehicle sped by. Norm looked at me and said, "Well, go get him!" I looked back at Norm and laughed. "I can't, I'm too fucked up asshole, so are you." Norm agreed and we packed up, mounted our motorcycles and raced into headquarters with our lights and sirens blaring. We slept on the benches in the locker room hiding from our sergeant until 2:00 a.m. Of course we had no tickets written and there was no way we could have arrested *anyone* for drunk driving because we were more drunk than our targets!

As Norman arrested the youth for DWI, I arrived to assist in the towing. As I drove up to the scene I observed a young male in handcuffs standing next to Norm. Three young females were standing on the grass away from the arrest. The girls were noticeably scared and nervous. I awaited the tow truck, impounded the vehicle, and questioned the young girls. They had no way home and no money. They lived in Baltimore County, which was out of my jurisdiction. I called in to the dispatcher advising that I was transporting three females into Balto. County and gave the time and mileage. This is standing operating procedure to protect the officer from any sexual complaints. The mileage and time can be checked to assure and insure that all is as it should be, no detours were taken, and no improper actions took place on anyone's part.

I had to get these girls home. I contacted their parents and set up a meeting further out Pulaski Hwy. At the Pacific Inn restaurant. I couldn't leave them at the scene; it was a dimly lit industrial area. I drove the two miles into the county and dropped off my passengers.

After a short discussion with one of the girl's parents exonerating the girls from any wrongdoing I turned my radio car around and headed back to the city, back to familiar terrain.

It was now after 2:00 a.m., I had only a half-mile to go to reach the city/county line. Also, I was near an off ramp, which exited Interstate 95, which also included the Harbor Tunnel and the Maryland Transportation Police as well as Maryland State Troopers. They all patrolled this area. As I looked around I noticed a white van driving in the lane to my right. I barely noticed the vehicle due to the darkness of the area and the fact that the van had no taillights, running lights, or tag light. It was completely unlit and I was only twenty-feet away before I noticed it. This was a dangerous situation at this time of night. *I have to stop this vehicle before someone gets hurt, I can hardly see it.* I thought.

I activated my blue lights and stopped the van about fifty-feet from the entrance and parking lot of a bar called B.J. and The Bear. I did this just to advise the driver of his precarious situation and to help if necessary. I was out of the city and had no power to write a ticket, and didn't want to call a County Officer to meet me.

It was now approximately 2:15 a.m., I approached the van and was greeted by a polite and courteous older driver and also a younger man in the passenger's seat, which was later, found to be the driver's nephew. The driver told me that all the lights, including the instrument panel lights, had gone out suddenly five-minutes earlier. "It must be a short or blown fuse officer," Advised the driver. I learned that the driver lived close and nearby and decided to release him after I ran a check on his license. He was polite and cooperative I had no reason to detain him, besides I wanted out of the county.

As I turned away from the van I heard a loud noise, a banging noise came from the bar door. The steel door that was used to enter BJ and The Bear Lounge had been flung open forcefully striking the brick wall causing a loud bang. This caught my attention. I observed a man shouting at another man and also shaking his fist at him. I could not hear the words. I watched intently as the first man out the door ran across the small parking lot in front of a parked large step van and jump into the driver's side open sliding door.

It was after 2:00 a.m., *most bars are closing,* I thought. I observed four to five cars parked facing the front wall of the bar and I also observed that the step van was parked parallel to Pulaski Hwy., a main route. The step van was closer to the street than the other cars and it was in a position closer to the street so that it could drive away quickly if necessary. My eyes shifted quickly back and forth. First to the open bar door then to the driver's side of the step van, to the door and back to the step van. I watched nervously and with apprehension.

I began to think with my cop mentality and distrust. *The door was violently thrust open, two men arguing, after closing time, step van not parked as other patrons cars are, vehicle poised for an easy getaway, this could very well be a holdup!!* I dropped the license and began running towards the rear of the suspicious step van. I was about twenty-five feet away when I realized I should slow down and also pull out my .38 caliber revolver. I did both. As I reached the back of this large truck I heard that unmistakable sound of a round being racked into a shotgun or an ammo clip is being pressed into a weapon. *Oh Christ, Oh shit!* I murmured aloud. *This guy has a shotgun and all I have is this fucking peashooter! I'm really fucked now!*

I stopped dead at the left rear of the truck. *I can't see in there, how can I make a decision, how can I get a look?* I said to myself. I may have said it aloud, at that point I didn't know what to do or think. The fear of the unknown is terrifying and unsettling. I didn't have to wonder long. Suddenly and unexpectedly a man jumped out of the driver's open door, I couldn't believe my eyes! I yelled in my head the only words an officer speaks when he is realizes that he is in serious trouble or if he is about to become involved in a car accident. *AH SHIIIITTTT!* I was surprised and astonished the gunman didn't hear me.

There he stood with his back to me unaware that I was even present. He stood very still with his back to me wearing army boots laced to the top, fatigue pants flared at the boot tops, a green army belt with the shiny buckle, and a green multi colored army camouflage tee shirt. I also noticed the scariest of all, a rifle sling draped across his back. I had no idea what he was holding, what was in front out of my view. *What is he carrying, what have I gotten into? Shit Danny.* I worried.

The suspect was holding an AR-15 automatic rifle with an extra large banana clip protruding from the bottom of the rifle and a sling that went across and over his shoulders.

My mouth dropped open. I had never seen such an intimidating and fearsome looking weapon in my life. It even had a bayonet attached to the barrel. A wave of fear came over me, a numbness that began at my toes, traveled up my back and to the base of my skull. It overtook my entire body. I felt hollow inside, like a crab shell or a large empty drainpipe. I was very very scared. I knew I was going to die on this parking lot. I would bleed to death face down on the asphalt, it would be horrible. My mind played out the scenario.

I would shoot the suspect, he would pull the trigger on this automatic weapon one time and spray me and the parking lot with a shit load of bullets, my body would jerk several times and I would die. I was about to die, I had no doubts. *I must be careful* I thought, *be cool Dan, watch yourself; you have to think Dan, what should I do? Oh God help me.* I talked to myself over and over. Suddenly I knew. *Shoot the bastard, yeah shoot this asshole Danny.* This all transpired in seconds. He still knew nothing of my presence.

I yelled loudly and in fear! I could hear the words resonating in my head. "Police Officer!" "Don't turn around or I'll blow your fucking head off!" The adrenaline rush was incredible, exhilarating, and caused a phenomenal sensation to race thru my body. My whole being was on high alert, my mind, muscles, eyes and emotions. I was *tuned up*. I was mentally in high gear, high-speed. I was aware of his every movement. I was searching for any slight indication that this gunman would turn and fire a volley of bullets at me. *I must shoot if he turns, I must shoot.* I worried. I worried with confidence. A confidence I had unfortunately learned thru other frightening incidents.

He turned, ignoring my command. He turned in one rapid movement. I attempted to scream, STOP, but nothing came out of my mouth. I fired one shot at his torso. I fired as he simultaneously raised the AR-15 to fire at me. I waited, just as I had waited on Chase St. near Biddle St. with the cab hold up suspect. I waited to hear the gunfire, feel the bullets tearing at me, waited to hear the rapid explosions of an automatic weapon. I could see in my mind my body jumping uncontrollably as each bullet slammed into me. Where were the bullets? I quickly dismissed these thoughts it wasn't happening. I hit the ground. I heard a loud screeching scream come from the suspect. I didn't know why he screamed. I rolled and rolled. My hat fell off as I rolled behind the tire of a parked car twenty feet from the truck. I recall reading the tire, GOODYEAR. I realized that a rubber tire could not stop these bullets. *I'm going to get shot yet*. I thought.

All motion stopped at this point. All was quiet. *Why?* I suddenly pictured the Three Stooges when Curly drank a glass of water after Moe ran him thru with several swords during a basket trick. *Why am I thinking this shit at a time like this!* I wondered. Why would I think of this when I was certain I was about to be shot to death? I have no idea, no clue.

The screams continued, the gunman was on the ground thrashing about holding his hand. I then observed that the weapon was five feet from his reach, five feet from the front of the truck and close to the bar door. I jumped up and ran from around the car, gun in hand. As I closed in on the suspect, another man came racing out of the bar and picked up the rifle, points it at me and begins to walk towards me very slowly. *What is he doing? Jesus!* I worried excitably. "Drop the rifle! Drop the rifle!" I yelled. He continued walking to me. I aimed my revolver at him, slowly applying pressure to the trigger. I could see the hammer come back slightly; suddenly the patron threw the weapon to the ground, evidently, realizing he was about to be shot.

I stopped squeezing the trigger and heard a gentle click as the firing pin hit the next round. The gun did not fire. I had not applied enough pressure to cause the pin to strike the primer hard enough for the revolver to fire, not enough pressure.

I was to discover later that the second man that picked up the rifle was the bar manager and was bringing the rifle to me. He was not at all a threat, or so he thought. He had *no idea* how close he came to being dead. No idea how high and intense my emotions were directly following firing the shot that hit the first gun wielding suspect. I was extremely scared and nervous when the manager pointed that weapon at me. It worked out.

As I ran over and picked up the rifle I half-assed called the dispatcher. My voice was loud and probably inaudible due to the fear factor."1336 I've just shot a suspect on Pulaski Hwy. At BJ and the Bear bar! I need an ambulance! He's shot!"

The police dispatcher thought I said that *I* was shot and broadcasted the call that all police officers dread hearing. "Signal 13! Officer down! Signal 13 at BJ and the Bear located on Pulaski Hwy. in Baltimore County." That is the one call that sends chills up a police officer's spine and makes him quiver. I feel as though a police officer thinks for a very short period of time that it could be them that are down, they that are shot. Any officer in the immediate area responds to this call for help from a comrade.

I did not hear the dispatcher for I had walked cautiously over to the suspect and he was screaming as I called in. The suspect continued to scream and rolled slightly to his left. I saw a bayonet at his side. Just then he attempted to swing the bayonet at my legs. I became incensed. This guy had the balls to attempt to murder me after I told him I was a police officer and ordered him to drop his weapon, then, he tries to injure me with a bayonet. I had forgotten about the oversized knife.

I became even more angered as these thoughts passed. A rush of anger overwhelmed me. I kicked the suspect in the head and again in the face. He dropped the bayonet and I then kicked that out of his reach. I can remember how my anger began to subside as I kicked and injured this asshole. The more blood I saw the less anger.

Blood was covering his head and face. His hand was a mangled clump of flesh. I could see no fingers. *Good,* I thought, *asshole can't use that hand again.* "Fuck you!" I yelled at him, "Shut the fuck up asshole!" Evidently, as he raised his weapon to fire my bullet ripped thru his knuckles destroying his hand and taking off his thumb.

I felt no remorse or guilt, just satisfaction. *Street justice, merely street justice,* I thought angrily.

After the police dispatcher put out the officer down call, he also called Baltimore County Police, Maryland State Police and the Maryland Transportation Police. Four agencies were headed towards me thinking I was shot.

I heard sirens in the distance and when I looked up I was totally and completely in awe. There were approximately twenty or more radio cars coming towards me from all directions. I was amazed at the amount of flashing lights, nothing flashing in sequence all random. Twenty or more police cars lined up and down Pulaski Hwy. It was like a Christmas tree. I stood next to the suspect with my foot on his back because I couldn't handcuff him due to his injuries. I felt like a king! All this manpower and all this commotion just for me, Dan Shanahan! I was flattered. I was proud to be a part of this team, the camaraderie was overwhelming and awe inspiring. I was able to grasp the feeling that at this scary, upsetting, and even thankful moment in my life that I was surely a blessed individual. I was blessed.

A Baltimore County Police Officer came running towards me and asked if I was okay. "Yes was my reply. Why?" "Are you shot he asked, are you hit?" "No." Was my reply. He relayed this to the dispatcher and clarified that I was not shot but in fact, the suspect was.

I was still somewhat dazed. The officers on the scene shackled the suspect's feet for me. I felt satisfaction and comfort with the amount of officers around me. I felt safe. I was not shot, no holes in me to leak water, and I was in one piece. I was relieved and knew I was okay once again. Thank you God . . .

I walked into the bar and saw seven patrons that were visibly shaken. "Give me a double shot of Jack Daniels and a coke." I said to the bartender. I walked outside and leaned against the wall of the bar and sipped my drink. I was shaking noticeably; I had a reason to shake. "It's okay Dan." Said the Homicide detective I knew. "Drink up, you're very lucky Shanahan, your soldier had armor piercing ammo in his rifle and clip. Had he fired nothing would have stopped those rounds."

I took a deep breath, another drink, and wondered why God loved me so much to keep me safe so many times and what He had in store for me. I hoped I had something good to accomplish. I continued to shake and continued to finish my drink.

I was to learn later that the suspect was a disturbed Vietnam Veteran named Mad Dog. His girlfriend was a dancer at BJ and the Bear. He was in the bar drinking and became involved in an argument with his girlfriend, Peaches. Mad Dog punched Peaches. Several patrons observed this and three of them grabbed Mad Dog in an attempt to stop him. "I'll fix all of you!" He yelled angrily as he stormed out the door thrusting it open into the wall, and entering the parking lot.

The same parking lot I was fifty feet away from with a car stop. His intent was to kill all the patrons, the manager, bartender, and Peaches. He would use the AR-15 with the banana clip containing seventeen rounds of armor piercing ammo. I interrupted, saving seven lives, SILVER STAR.

That was the peculiar portion of this story; the bizarre part picks up six months later as I waited outside the courtroom waiting to speak to the Assistant State's Attorney handling the Mad Dog case.

The witness list consisted of me, Peaches, the elderly man driving the van I had stopped, and his nephew seated in the passengers seat that night. They had stayed in the van and witnessed the entire event, all of it. The others were on call in case the State needed them. They did not need to attend court that day.

I walked into court, introduced myself to the Assistant State's Attorney and inquired as to where the witnesses were seated. What he told me was nearly unbelievable. It was bizarre. All three witnesses had died! I had no witnesses, just Mad Dog and myself.

The Attorney had three newspaper articles and three obituaries in his hand. He handed them to me and said, "Peaches committed suicide in March, The driver of the van had a heart attack and died in May, and the nephew drowned in an Essex river in August!" I was completely astonished and taken aback. "No way!" I muttered. "It's true." Came his reply.

The judge listened to my testimony and that of no others. He found Mad Dog guilty and asked me what I would prefer him to do with Mad Dog for attempting to kill me. I told the judge that I had learned that the suspect was a disturbed Vietnam Vet and that I had an admiration for all Vietnam Veterans. If the judge could get this man help I would be satisfied.

Mad Dog was sentenced to six years in a mental hospital with intense therapy. I was glad for him. I sat in my police car after court that day and murmured words to myself. I don't recall what I murmured but I knew that this was a bizarre case and very much unbelievable. I left the parking lot of the courthouse and went back to work.

Take out

A police officer is trained to know when to use the siren and emergency lights provided to him on his radio car/motorcycle. After several years on the street use of this emergency equipment can turn into *misuse* of emergency equipment.

I stopped at Milton and Hoffman Sts. At Jimmy's Chinese food store to pick up Chinese food to go. I told my wife, Nancy, that I would sneak home for a half hour and have Chinese dinner with her. Jimmy's Chinese food was the best in the Eastern District plus he never charged me. Sometimes near payday, I'd leave $10.00 on the counter as I left. It was very much appreciated on both sides.

I picked up my order and headed the twenty minutes to my apartment off of Eastern Ave. to meet my wife. As I was leaving Jimmy's I received a call to check out a malfunctioning traffic light. I proceeded to East Baltimore St., At Patterson Park Ave., to observe the traffic light. It was short timing North on Patterson Park Ave. I called in to the dispatcher to notify Traffic and Transit of the problem. I then realized that my Chinese dinner was getting cold. And that I should head home immediately. I wasn't about to eat cold Chinese food; after all I had emergency lights and a siren.

I made a right turn onto Baltimore St., and put on my high beams. It was just beginning to get dark. I also activated my grill lights and my overhead blue lights. As I was reaching for the siren I noticed a figure run out from between two parked cars on the right side of the street. I was traveling approximately forty miles per hour. I swerved quickly to my right and barely missed the pedestrian, but had. She had made it to the double yellow line located in the center of the street. I took a quick deep breath of relief. Suddenly, like a scared rabbit she darted back across the front of my radio car in an attempt to reach her original spot between the cars. No such luck! I nailed her with the right front of my 1979 Pontiac Lemans, causing her body to fly approximately twenty-five feet into the air and caused her body to wedge itself under the tire of a parked car that was sitting at the right curb.

I slammed the car into park and jumped out of my car."1336!" I called to the dispatcher, "1336, I have a personal injury accident and I'm involved. Send assistance to Baltimore St and Lakewood Ave., I also need an ambulance!" I knew she was seriously injured, I hit her hard and she went quite a distance. I ran up to her seemingly lifeless body and knelt on the ground partially under the parked car. What I saw horrified me! I couldn't see her head! "Oh my God, Oh my God! Dispatcher please send help I can't find her head! I can't find her head" I was panicking, I was out of it, I was confused and dazed.

In my head I knew what I had done was wrong, She didn't attack or hurt me, She just made a mistake by running in front of my radio car. *I may have killed her to get my Chinese food home still hot!* I felt horrible, sick to my stomach.

A priest came out from across the street, he had witnessed the accident. "Calm down my son." He said. "Father I killed her, I CAN'T FIND HER HEAD!" She was wearing a black leather jacket. Where the collar was and where the neck should be there was no neck or head. The bottom of the coat was at her waist. "Where's her head father! Where's her head!" I was nearly hysterical! Just then the priest grabbed the limp body and slid her out from under the car tire, I saw her head just pop out!

She was wearing a 3/4 length leather coat; it had risen up and over her head when she hit the street. When it rose up and covered her head it appeared to be just a waist length jacket and that her head was gone!

I have never been so happy to see anyone's head! I was so relieved! She had not lost her head. I had lost *my* head as well as my cool and I most definitely panicked. I was disappointed in myself.

The priest anointed her head, for she did have one now, and said a prayer. Five or seven minutes had passed since the accident and she was still unconscious. The ambulance arrived and they placed her body, complete with her head, into the ambulance. As I helped to close the door my eyes were tearing up. *What had I just done?* I thought. *Oh shit!* I must have collected myself, for I ran to the radio car and put all the Chinese food and the *six beers* into the trunk, took the trunk key off the ring and placed it into my boot. I didn't want anyone to think that I was in a hurry to get home to eat.

Officer Earl Boram, a friend of my family and mine arrived to handle the accident. Any time an officer is involved in any type of auto accident, The Traffic Investigation Unit must handle the call. Here is my official account of what occurred;

After handling the malfunctioning traffic light at Baltimore St., and Patterson Park Ave., I was stopped on the east side curb finishing paperwork. Suddenly I heard a car engine kick into overdrive. I looked up in time to observe a black Chevy, Maryland partial tag _____729, proceed directly thru a dead red light at a high rate of speed. I activated my emergency lights, high beams, and spot light, to pursue the violator. I was certain he would injure someone. I turned to proceed East on Baltimore St. As I approached Lakewood Ave. I saw a figure run out from between two parked cars and directly in front of my radio car. I swerved to my right to avoid the pedestrian still in total control of my vehicle at all times. The pedestrian panicked and doubled back into the path of my vehicle once again. The right front fender of my 1979 Pontiac Lemans impacted the pedestrian causing her to be thrown several feet east of the point of impact, wedging her under a parked car tire. The vehicle was legally parked against the south curb. I called for assistance and administered first aid until the ambulance arrived.

The pedestrian had in fact been drinking and ran in front of my police car in an attempt to reach the bus stop located on the opposite side of Baltimore St. The pedestrian did panic and did run into my radio car.

The official outcome; pedestrian at fault. No police officer error. I had lucked out, or lied myself out, of another serious situation that could have cost me my job. I was to discover later that I had crushed this thirty three year old woman's pelvis, broke both of her legs, cracked several ribs and injured her back. I really damaged this person. But, I made it okay in my mind, *she fucked up by being drunk and running in front of my vehicle, she should have seen the emergency lights and high beams, she was drunk, not me.*

As cavalier and uncaring as I made myself feel, deep down I was crushed and disappointed in myself for the serious injuries I had inflicted just to get my, *take out,* Chinese food home warm, and six beers home cold, ten minutes earlier. That's life in the big city—Baltimore city.

I found out later, after shooting and killing Booker Lancaster, that this woman, this woman at fault for the accident, would receive a $25,000.00 settlement because the publicity from the killing would have caused a jury, most likely, all black jury, to rule in her favor and the jury would, as I was told by the police department attorney's representing me in this accident, give her the entire courthouse and the steps, because they would have learned of my killing Lancaster. And because this woman was also black.

So, She was *wrong and drunk,* but to avoid any unnecessary confrontations she and the city settled! $25,000.00 for her and an indictment for ME! BULLSHIT!!

BOOKER LEE
LANCASTER

JULY 13, 1983
THE DEATH OF BOOKER LEE LANCASTER

J uly 13, 1983 at 9:00 am I left my apartment to pick up a car to wax on

my day off. I waxed police officers personal cars on my day off to make

extra money. I worked in the basement of the Eastern District. I picked

up supplies on Harford Road at Broadway. This was the district I worked

and I felt comfortable in this area even though the area was dangerous.

As I drove a block from my apartment I realized that I didn't have my

off duty gun with me. *No big deal*, I thought. I drove another block. *Should*

I go back? Nah.

I drove to the end of my street and something told me to go back and get my gun. After all, it was police policy to have your gun on your person when in the city limits. I went into my apartment and grabbed my .38 caliber Smith and Wesson revolver with a 2" barrel. I stuck the gun and holster next to my car seat along side the center console. This was to save my life, going back for my gun.

I drove south on Harford Road. As I passed 25th Street I heard a loud screech of tires, then a short screech. As I looked up, the car in front of me was coming to a quick stop. I hit my brakes and stopped suddenly. I couldn't see what had caused all this commotion and I really didn't care. I had things to do. I looked down the right side of the street and saw no cars. I pulled into the curb lane and drove past four stopped vehicles that were occupied and to my left. As I cleared the front of the fourth car I saw a large black male sitting on a blue motorcycle dressed in a black leather vest, black leather cap and jeans. He and his motorcycle were facing north in the southbound lane. This was not only illegal but it was not acceptable to me. As I steered my car back into the proper lane I passed by this motorcyclist and thought, *who does this asshole think he is?* I heard him say, "white muvafucker," as I went past him. I had turned down my stereo and could hear his words very clearly. I looked directly at him and replied, "Fuck you asshole".

During my first trial the newly appointed state attorney would ask me if I had said anything to Mr. Lancaster as I drove by. "No" was my reply. "What if I had witnesses say that you said something to Mr. Lancaster as you drove by him?" He asked again. "That would be a lie I replied". What if I told you that witnesses saw your mouth move as you passed him, would this be true?" "No" I said. I had lied to this newly appointed, first ever; black State Attorney, Kurt L. Schmoke. I had lied. My attorney, Jim White, had instructed me to leave this out of my testimony. I did as he had told me. I merely left this out of my testimony. I didn't want the jurors or attorneys to think I instigated any of this deadly confrontation. Also I was white and felt that would pose a problem. It would, and it did?

I recall saying to several white officers after Mr. Schmoke was elected state attorney for Baltimore City, "I feel sorry for the first white officer that shoots a black person in Baltimore City while he's State's Attorney". Unfortunately, it was to be me.

Kurt Schmoke was the predecessor of William Swisher, a white state attorney that was pro police and pro white. Schmoke was the first black states attorney in the history of Baltimore City. He was hailed the, "fair haired boy," by many Baltimore politicians.

I drove past Lancaster and traveled approximately four blocks. I pulled over to the curb and stopped the car in front of Gail Industries, the store I purchased my car waxing materials from. I put the car in park but hadn't turned the engine off yet. Suddenly I heard the loud roar of Lancaster's motorcycle. I looked to my left and saw Lancaster pull in front of my left front fender and somewhat to the left. "You cut me off! You white muvafucker!" he shouted at me. He had a rough gravelly voice and was angry. He was very large, six foot-four inches, 250 pounds and sitting on a Harley Davidson he looked intimidating. To an average citizen he would have been extremely intimidating and frightening. He was the "bully on the block"; I was to find out later. I even had a few blacks approach me and quietly thank me for ridding their neighborhood of this over towering menace.

Booker Lee Lancaster was wearing a black leather vest, a tee shirt, black baseball cap on backwards which was covering a black leather skin tight cap, a black leather belt with a large buckle, an eleven inch hunting knife in a sheath, a black leather wallet with an eight inch chain connecting it to his blue jeans and black leather boots with the pant legs tucked inside. He was every bit a biker, plus he was large, loud, and pissed off. The hunting knife was threatening looking on its own and even more so when put in the hands of this very large, leather clad, motorcycle rider that was seriously angry and looking for revenge. The knife had a four-inch handle and a seven-inch blade.

I looked directly at this gorilla of a man and said back to him, "fuck you shithead!" He began to dismount off the left side of the motorcycle. As he was coming around the front of the bike he continued staring at me and said, "I'm going to kick you little white ass." I motioned for him to come to me with my left hand, pulling all four of my fingers towards me several times saying, "Let's go muvafucker."

I knew as a police officer that I was supposed to be respectful to citizens and not to use foul language or trigger words like punk or nigger, these words could trigger a violent response and were not acceptable but used frequently by white officers including myself. I could be charged with misconduct. Therefore these words are known as trigger words.

Lancaster came over to my car, a low to the ground 1969 White Firebird. Sitting in this car looking up at Lancaster, he seemed even larger, he loomed over me. I was not scared or intimidated at this point. I felt confident and sure of myself. I was a cop in this very area for over twelve years and was not easily intimidated by blacks, bullies, wise guys or smart asses with attitudes. Most white non police officers would be scared or intimidated when in an all black or mostly black neighborhood, any normal citizen would.

Lancaster reached into my car window and smacked me in the face. I became angered. Not because he had punched me like a man but because he *bitch slapped me*. His second blow hit my left jaw and the third blow, my left shoulder due to the fact that I was leaning to my right in an attempt to lessen the blows and pull away from him. He now had his head inside my car.

I punched him in the face and he removed his head from the inside of my car. I tried to open my car door and quickly realized that when he had leaned into the car his chest had pushed the lock down. I couldn't get the door open, once he realized I was trying to get out and couldn't, due to him holding down the lock button, he purposely held the lock down with his hand. I was trapped in my car and was concerned about this.

I was able to pull his very large hand slightly off of the lock, just enough to get to the lock. I quickly pulled up on the lock and flung the door open as hard as possible, striking his legs and pushing him away from the car. I jumped out of the car, grabbing my gun.

As Lancaster regained his balance I noticed him reach back with his hand and unsnap the sheath that held his large looking hunting knife. All I could see was a large handle. I knew it had to be the big knife. I thought at this point that I had problems but still was not scared. I was apprehensive and on guard, but not scared. I had been in violent situations before. *I can handle this*, I thought.

As I exited my car, I pulled out my gun and pointed the shiny .38 caliber Stainless at him. It was glistening in the morning sun; this struck me odd, briefly. "I am a police officer," I shouted. "You're under arrest for assault". I said this loud and clear. "Fuck you" was his reply. At this point he began to move to my left, as if dodging my gun barrel. I too moved, but to my right and close to the spot where he had just stood. We had turned in a circle. *What's he doing?* I thought. *Just don't take your eyes off him and watch the knife,* I told myself.

I was now more concerned of my situation but still felt confident in my abilities. My heart was beating fast now. Again I said, "I am a Baltimore City Police Officer and you are under arrest". "Fuck you". He replied again. I was becoming worried. I had to think; *I've told him twice now that I'm a police officer. I have my gun pointed at him; he has a large knife on his side unsnapped. He is pissed, large and not listening. Think Danny think, he should be listening, but he's not. I'll cock my gun, no don't, that takes away any last action and last resort I might have and he might get the best of me. I don't want my gun cocked. Why isn't he listening? Okay, one more time.*

Lancaster has now moved to the driver's side rear quarter panel of my car. I am out in the middle of the street approximately fifteen feet away, we have nearly switched positions. My gun was pointed at his chest, "put your fucking hands on the car or I'll shoot asshole". I yelled. "I told you two times I'm a police officer and you are under arrest, put your hands up and don't touch the knife". I was now seriously concerned. This situation had heightened. *I'm in trouble,* I thought.

Lancaster did not reply to my last order. He just stood there looking at me. Neither of us moved. Me and my gun, he and his knife. I began to tense. I had a bad feeling. I was thinking, *either he is going to put his hands on the car and give up or he is going to come at me with that knife.* I was nervously watching his eyes and at the same time his left hand. The knife was on his left side. It was as if I could see it all, I could. My senses were peaking.

Suddenly he lunged off the car at me. I don't know if I moved or not. I was very scared, past apprehension. I was extremely scared and beginning to fear for my safety. *Danny you're in deep shit,* I began talking to myself as I reacted. *Shoot Dan, shoot this fucker!* I had a perfect shot at his chest. *It's not time to kill him Dan, just stop him. The knife is coming out of the sheath Dan, it's going in your stomach! Just stop him Dan!*

BANG! I didn't hear the gunshot; my ears had somehow closed or seemed to have closed. Everything was muffled. But, I saw the bullet go into his arm. I actually saw the skin part, and the bullet enter his arm. *Where am I?* I thought? Wow, I saw his skin part. *Why am I able to see this?* I asked myself. The events were happening quickly, but to me so very, very slowly. I saw the tip of the knife. *"Oh shit! Here it comes right into my gut".* I have never before in my life been so scared.

With all the violent situations I have been in throughout my career this is the most scared, petrified, uncertain and fearful of dying I had been. I could picture, imagine, Lancaster sticking this very large knife in me and twisting it. Again I started talking to myself. *This situation is out of control. I'm going to die.* Lancaster came closer and I saw the tip of the knife. It was a knife like I had never seen before. The blade was more curved than usual and it scared the hell out of me.

I was now definitely not in control, definitely intimidated and definitely in fear for my life. He grabbed my collar with his right hand. He was extremely strong. It was at this instant, this 1/100 of a second that I knew, beyond question and with certainty that this man must die and I must be the one to kill him. Bang! A second shot!

I was amazed at myself. All the close calls with death that I had experienced, not once did I feel so certain that it was time to kill. An uncertainty but an awareness, and also a gut feeling, that if I did not kill this person at this very instant, that I would definitely die, not be seriously injured, but die. All doubts had disappeared, been lifted.

Doubts do appear. Your mind goes thru procedures and weighs the right and wrong of the situation. It's these moments of hesitation, these split seconds that can cost an officer his life. I had placed my gun against Lancaster's lower left stomach and fired again. *I know I shot him this time, but when is he going to give up and die,* I wondered. *He has two bullets in him now, when is the threat going to subside?* He was still trying to stab me. I had my gun held out to my right side, out of his reach.

The barrel was still smoking. I had a death grip on his left wrist using my left hand. He was still attempting to stab at me. His wrist kept coming at me and pulling back. He would thrust the knife forward and I would resist and push it back towards him in a stabbing motion. Back and forth, the knife went, back and forth. *I cannot let him stab me.* I worried. The thrusts continued.

So much was going on all at one time. The two shots, the knife in his hand, watching the hole open in his arm, him grabbing me, the continuing thrusts of the knife, trying to keep my gun out of his reach. The physical struggle and my mind racing to save my life, and to protect myself, were overwhelming me. *Die you fuck, die!* I kept thinking, *die and get away from me!* We dropped to the ground.

This entire scenario, from Lancaster lunging off the car to the second shot must have taken fifteen to twenty seconds. It seemed an eternity to me. All slow and deliberate, no haziness, everything clear, concise and slow. It's as if I was above us, watching this life and death struggle, filming it in slow motion. Watching every move, but not seeing every move, not taking it in.

Suddenly I felt Lancaster's thrusting motions stop. He became easier to manage, weaker. I recall hoping that he was dying. He was leaning against my right leg which was half bent as if, bending in church at one knee. His body weight was lying against me. His right hand was on the ground and his upper torso was against mine. His back was up against me, twelve inches from my face. His body jumped, his eyes were half open. Again his body jumped and our eyes locked once again.

I felt as though Lancaster was dying. I felt a relief but at the same time a slight sadness due to what I knew I had done. I had a human being in my arms, it was quite clear to me he was dying and I was solely responsible, no one else, just me. I breathed deeply. Just then something I never expected happened. I expected him to just fade away in my arms, just like the movies or television. Just slowly die and fade. Not this man. Two bullets in his body, one ripped through the heart, the other blasted thru his liver, spleen, right testicle, and thru his leg. He knows he is dying, he must know.

Suddenly his eye lids flew open, his eyes were very wide and looking directly at me. Time came to a standstill once again. I expected to hear a soft quivering, dying, sorrowful voice. I was mistaken. This twice shot dying individual said, "you shot me, you shot me you white muvafucker"! I was in awe! I was totally taken back by this statement. This man is dying and still in his last breath, he calls me a white muvafucker.

For him to make this incident racial was beyond my comprehension at that time. I instantly went from numb and somewhat sad, to anger, disgust and disbelief. *How could this be?* I was not at all expecting this. I stood up and Lancaster fell from my knees and he slammed to the ground, face first. I knelt over him. My mind whirled in disbelief! *How dare he attack me, pull a knife, attempt to stab me, force me to shoot him in an attempt to save my own precious life, continue to attempt to violently stab me, force me to shoot a second bullet into his body slowly but definitely taking the life out of him and still, and still say that? Fuck him!*

I told the state attorney that I had no idea how he came to have an abrasion on his face, but I did know. I knew damn right well how it got there. I did it. When he said, "You shot me, you shot me you white muvafucker!" I stood up and let his body slam to the ground in disgust. I actually pushed him to the ground! I would have shot him three more times if I had the chance and I was that type of individual. I was so angry! I was incensed!

Booker Lee Lancaster took his last breath and died. His body jumped and twitched slightly and his fingers quivered. He was gray in color now, not black. I heard that familiar death gurgle that I had heard so many times before. But this one, this one was louder or did it just seem that way? I don't know. Things got a little fuzzy when I stood up. I was looking down on this lifeless body wondering what started all this. I questioned myself, *am I right here? Did I have cause to shoot and kill this guy? Did I follow all the Police Department rules of procedure and general orders? Am I right? God I hope I am. Dear Lord please let me have been justified in taking this man's life, Dear Lord, please smile down upon me.*

This is the account, true account that I told in court. However, there are those, such as then, Assistant State's Attorney, Cliff Gordy, that say it happened differently. There are those that say it happened like this;

I was driving south on Harford Rd. and was forced to slow quickly and stop, just past 25th St., due to Booker Lancaster blocking traffic with his motorcycle. He was facing the wrong way. He was facing North in the South bound lane. I had no idea what had caused traffic to stop and I drove along the right curb to pass. As I neared Lancaster and began to go past him, he became angry and said something to me. I then leaned out the window and said, "Fuck you!" to him as I drove past.

I drove another two blocks and pulled to the curb in front of Gail Industries where I buy car-waxing materials. As I stopped, Lancaster pulled up next to my car and again words were exchanged. Supposedly, Lancaster said to me, "white muvafucker, you cut me off!" I then replied, "I didn't cut you off, you were blocking traffic!" At this point Lancaster said, "I'm going to fuck you up white boy!" I then replied, "Bring it on asshole!" Lancaster then got off of his motorcycle and approached my vehicle, a 1969 Firebird, which sat low to the ground. With Lancaster standing at six feet five inches tall and weighing two hundred and sixty pounds, he was towering over the car.

Lancaster reached into my car and slapped me several times. Lancaster then reached back and unsnapped a hunting knife sheath that contained an eleven inch hunting knife. I became angry and forced opened the car door pushing Lancaster to the double yellow line in the middle of the street. I then exited my car and pulled out my .38 caliber, two-inch barrel, Smith and Wesson revolver, pointing it at Lancaster. I advised Lancaster that I was a police officer. His reply, "fuck you white boy!"

Lancaster had his left hand on the knife. I continued pointing my gun at Lancaster and again advised him that I was a police officer. He began to move to his right in a semi circle. I moved to my left at the same time. This continued until Lancaster was now leaning against my car and I was standing at the yellow line. We actually switched positions. Everything stopped at this point. Lancaster wasn't moving and I still had my gun pointed at him. At this point I said to Lancaster a third time, "I am a police officer, you are under arrest for assault and if you touch that knife I'll shoot your black ass!"

Lancaster again said, "Fuck you white boy!" and lunged off the car at me. I panicked and fired a shot hitting Lancaster in the right arm. This didn't affect Lancaster and he grabbed me by the collar. I again fired a second shot into Lancaster's abdomen. Shortly after, Lancaster's body became limp. He slumped against me. I was holding him, keeping him from falling to the ground. Then, Lancaster mustered enough energy and strength to say before dying, "You shot me you white muvafucker!" I replied, "fuck you nigger!" and pushed his body to the ground, causing facial abrasions.

After Lancaster fell to the ground, I reached under his body, made sure the knife was unsnapped and slid the knife out, leaving it under Lancaster's body to make the shooting appeared justified. Just then police officers arrived and the scene was secured. The officers that arrived spoke to me briefly, and then made sure that the knife was out and pulled it out from under the body so it was in plain sight, next to the body.

Gordy went to great lengths to show the jury how Lancaster's body could have lined up perfectly had the scenario played out in that fashion. My attorney, Jim White, showed the jury how the bullet paths would have lined up properly if the scene were played out using my account. The jury seemed confused. However, the six blacks voted guilty and the six whites voted NOT guilty, hence, a hung jury.

Four people know what actually occurred on July 13, 1983 at 9:23 a.m. Two, a drunk and a black woman standing at the bus stop twenty-five feet away, left the scene in a hurry. The third is Booker Lee Lancaster, who is dead, and the fourth is ME! Cliff Gordy was confused or was tainted by his desire to find me guilty. I explained the scenario to two juries, as my attorney instructed me, and I was acquitted.

Lancaster; Moments After

As Lancaster's face hit the ground I slowly stood up and looked around in all directions. I noticed an old drunk on the opposite side of my car standing on the sidewalk. Our eyes met and just as quickly as they met, he turned away and walked slowly down Harford Rd. towards 25th St. I never saw him again, but he had seen the entire episode, *all* of it, he was fifteen feet away. I looked around again and noticed a black female approximately twenty-five feet away standing at the bus stop. She and the drunk were the *only* two witnesses that know exactly what occurred in those thirty to sixty seconds. I would not see her again either. Only four people know the entire truth of what took place at 9:23 a.m. July 13, 1983, at Harford Rd. and Broadway. However, one is not talking and the other two have disappeared.

When I went on trial in November of 1983, there were thirty-seven witnesses in court to testify against me. Thirty-Seven! Where did they come from? You *cannot* find thirty-seven people on a city corner at 9:23 a.m., anywhere! It was overkill. There were thirty-seven different stories also. I firmly believe that had Kurt Schmoke had only a handful of witnesses, I would have been found guilty. All those witnesses not only confused the jurors, but also *me,* and I was there!

I was suddenly startled by a rookie police officer, Tim Snow. He knew me and me him. "Are you okay Danny?" He asked." I was still dazed, but answered, "He pulled a knife on me, and I *had* to shoot him!" I don't know how Tim reached me so quickly, my gun was still smoking. He had to have seen the last few seconds unfold. Just then I realized that another officer was present and that people were gathering on the corners. I felt relieved, my fellow officers were here, *and I was okay. My police family surrounded me, I was secure.* I thought.

A lot of activity was going on around me. I was still slightly out of it. I was still dazed and not certain of what just took place. Officer David Brenner, my field-training officer, friend, and buddy, approached me; it was good to see him. We instinctively shook hands. This would be later misconstrued by the State Attorney to be a congratulatory handshake, i.e., Good work, way to go, etc. That was definitely not the case and I was infuriated that it would have been thought to be a handshake of congratulations.

This was not like television, when you take a life it's not to be glorified, I didn't want any congratulations, I wanted to be comforted and assured that I was okay and that things were as they should be, that I was not harmed and I acted and reacted properly.

My eyes and mind were searching for someone to say to me, "You are 100% righteous here Dan, you did it by the book and it's okay." I never heard that, I felt alone and nervous, my heart was still pumping quickly, my mind was blurred. I heard and saw what was taking place around me but couldn't focus in on the entire picture. All I could see was his lifeless, dead body. I couldn't take my eyes off of his dead body. I continually played back the actual shooting in my mind, *was I right, was I right? God please help me.*

Someone ordered David to place me in the radio car. I was put in the back seat, behind David. We talked, "David, I shot him, he had a knife, I shot him twice, am I right, am I okay?" "It's okay Dan, relax, and settle down." That's not what I wanted to hear.

I glanced over my right shoulder and took one last look at Lancaster's lifeless body sprawled over the street. He was on his stomach with his hands neatly tucked under his body. He was somewhat turned sideways. The ambulance was backed up to his body and people were standing around him in a semi circle. I would not see Lancaster's body again until I saw the picture from the morgue, prior to his autopsy. I recall vividly that his feet stuck out off the table about a foot. The jury took notice of this also.

I still can't believe that I killed him, I was thinking as we pulled away from the crime scene, his body just faded away from sight as David drove further and further away. Lancaster may have faded from sight, but he will never fade from my memory. He will never go away. His death will be etched in my memory forever. The shooting and all thirty to sixty seconds will forever replay itself in my mind. The nightmares still come, not as frequent as time passes, but they remain. The gunshots still ring in my ears, as do Lancaster's last three words, and that death gurgle will keep its unbelievably strong hold on me until I take my last breath and die.

David pulled into the convenience store located at 25th St. and Harford Rd. I had asked him to pull over and let me in the front seat. I told him I felt like a criminal and wanted to sit up front with him. I don't know why it was such a big deal for me, but I was in desperate need of comforting and gentle words of encouragement. I was not a tough, macho, cocky cop at that moment. I was humble, derailed, meek and mild like a child. My confidence had temporarily vanished.

David bought me a soda and let me sit up front where I was comfortable and where I felt I belonged. I slowly drank my soda as we drove to the sixth floor of headquarters building, to the homicide division. I cannot begin to express or write what was going thru my mind as we drove the fifteen minutes to headquarters. I was a scared little boy, not a confident, stand up decorated police officer that I should have been. Lancaster had taken that from me, just for now.

I had someone call my girlfriend, Officer JoAnne Stump. She worked the Eastern District. I wanted her to bring me my badge and ID. I wanted desperately to have it on me, I don't know why. I had stated that I had identified myself as a police officer three times, but I wanted my badge. I felt relieved when JoAnne handed me my badge an ID.

She and David stayed with me as I sat in the small homicide office. I was sitting at a small desk located away from the entrance to the unit. Everyone was sympathetic, and continued to tell me to, "hang in there," and that, "everything would be all right." I was feeling nervous but at the same time protected and safe since I had JoAnne, David, and other officers around me.

I sat for nearly an hour. I had said nothing on record yet and no one had asked me my side of the story. Someone in the homicide unit was evidently looking out for me as the Fraternal Order of Police Attorney arrived. He had a brief discussion with one of the investigators. We went into another smaller room that is used for suspects and witnesses. The F.O.P. Attorney looked at me and said. "Dan, do you want to talk?" I replied, "Yes I do." He then inquired as to whether I could remember, and was confident enough, to accurately recall all that had occurred that morning, leaving nothing out. I wanted so badly to say YES, but I was still confused and upset. I told the attorney this, his reply, "Don't say a word Danny."

This was relayed to the detectives and they all seemed to be in agreement. I was released and sent home. I don't recall how I got home or who took me.

Unknown to me, the police department spokesman, Dennis Hill had arrived on the shooting scene and was told that the shooting was," a good police shooting." That meant I was justified in what I had done. He was also given some not so correct information by someone on the scene and before verifying these facts, went on television and not only gave a statement that was incorrect, but inexcusable.

This false information was broadcast on all three news channels at noon. Hill had stated that this was, "proper police procedure and that there were no unanswered questions." Not the case. There was the question of the knife. By the 5:00 p.m. newscast, the Shanahan/Lancaster shooting incident had become a racially charged incident with political overtones. Very bad for me.

I was sitting home watching the news when I heard Dennis Hill change his statement from that which he had issued at noon, saying that there were questions about a knife, the location of the knife and whose knife it was. By changing this statement and not getting the proper information earlier, Dennis Hill had caused major problems for this case and me. There was suddenly a scream from the black community of a police cover up, what was the correct story? POLICE COVER UP!

After Dennis Hill made his statement of errors, then City Councilman, Billy Murphy, an advocate for the black community, appeared on television and stated, "This is a police cover up and the black community cannot let these white police officers kill our black citizens in our black communities!"

Instantly, at that moment, due to that statement, a *black* Billy Murphy who was running for Mayor of Baltimore, against the *white* incumbent, Mayor William Donald Schaffer, my case not only became racially motivated, but also had severe political ramifications.

Murphy would use this shooting and my unfortunate dilemma to attempt to become Mayor of Baltimore. He had no regard for what I was going thru and I'm certain didn't care.

I sat watching and listening as Dennis Hill stumbled on his words, and attempted to clear his erroneous earlier statements to no avail. He was making an ass of himself at my expense.

I heard Murphy's sharp words and I felt a deep sense of loneliness and hopelessness. Although I was feeling uneasy about what I thought was a good police shooting, it was as though Lancaster had somehow managed to stab me in the gut on Harford Rd. that morning. Maybe it was Murphy and Hill who was stabbing me in the gut, or was it in, THE BACK!

Appease The Black Community

August 1983, not very long after the July 13th shooting of Booker Lee, I was indicted by a Grand Jury. I was indicted for the manslaughter of Lancaster and for possession of a handgun in the commission of a felony. As I pondered the charges brought against me I wondered, *How in the hell can I be charged with possession of a handgun in the commission of a felony when police department guidelines and general orders dictate that I must carry my gun when I am within the city limits? I was mandated to carry the damn gun!* It was at this point that I had a bad feeling that the State Attorney, Kurt Schmoke, and his office, were doing what was necessary to find me guilty of killing Lancaster. They were doing this to make them look good and not necessarily looking for the truth.

The Shanahan Case was riddled with racial overtones. It was a political motivator and stepping-stone for many. For example; Kurt Schmoke, Billy Murphy, Cliff Gordy, Stuart Simms and Phil Dantes.

I was invited by the Grand Jury to testify. Jim White, my attorney, explained to me that a person that may very well be indicted was *invited* to testify. He went on to explain that a person *invited* by the Grand Jury didn't have to accept this invitation. However, it did make a difference to the Grand Jury if you declined. It would cast serious doubt and dispersions upon the individual under indictment. *Invited?* I thought. *Bullshit! They weren't inviting me! They just wanted to see if I would accept!*

I wanted to tell the truth. Jim White agreed and it was decided that I would tell my side of the story. I wasn't aware that I had to appear alone, no counsel, no help, and no support. However, I could stop the proceedings and go outside to ask my attorney questions. This didn't work very well for me. I wanted to seem sure of my testimony and myself. I only went out to talk to Jim one time.

After approximately two hours of testimony and answering questions directed to me from a mostly black grand Jury, that was definitely hostile towards me, I was sick. I was mentally exhausted and was sick to my stomach. *This is not going well.* I thought.

I was extremely upset at the jurors and their combative and antagonistic attitude towards me. The jurors asked me why I didn't run away from Lancaster when he confronted me, if he was so big? "Run away!" I answered. "I wasn't trained to run away! I was a police officer, I was trained to stay and handle a situation." *Did they want me to run away if they had called me and I responded to their house, then, ran away because the suspect that robbed or assaulted or stabbed them was a big guy? No way!* I thought as I stood there in front of this kangaroo court. "If your shooting scores were so good at the firing range since 1976 then you *must* have known that the bullet would ricochet off of Lancaster's arm and pierce his heart! That must have been the second shot and you placed that shot to cover up the manslaughter!" "That's ridiculous!" I said in a nasty tone of voice.

It was quite obvious to me that Kurt Schmoke had swayed this jury. This was his first big newsworthy case since his election and it showed. He did have days prior to my appearance, and plenty of *his* witnesses testifying ahead of me to set the tone, to sway the jurors in his favor. The air in that Grand Jury room was that of, "we must indict if he's white!" They did, in fact, indict me.

I felt very, very, uneasy after testifying, as I left that room. I worried, *where will this lead?* The Shanahan case was receiving a very large amount of publicity and press. The case was reported daily in the *Baltimore Sun* and the *News American*. The story was also covered nationwide in the *USA Today* and in the Associated Press wire. Friends of mine across the country were reading about the Shanahan case and calling me. *Was all this necessary?* I wondered. I thought not. I certainly wasn't comfortable or prepared, emotionally or mentally, for all this press and publicity. I liked the notoriety but it was being overdone due to politics and that, "racial thing."

A day or so following the indictment being handed down, I was ordered to appear at the police department headquarters building. I was to see Colonel Harwood Burritt in his office, he was Chief of Patrol. He oversaw all of the patrol division. I liked him and he was fond of me. I was well aware of what was about to transpire. I would have to wait two days and the pressure was mounting.

The two days dragged by. On this particular, unforgettable morning, I exited the elevator and walked up to the colonel's office door. "Good morning sir." I said. As I was speaking to Colonel Burritt he motioned for me to come in and at the same time told me to close the door. I was standing directly in front of his desk;

I was perplexed as to why he didn't ask me to sit. "How are you holding up Shanahan?" He asked. "Okay colonel, a little nervous." I replied. Colonel Burritt then explained to me that he must suspend me from the department until the outcome of the trial was decided and also because I had recently been indicted for manslaughter and possession of a handgun in the commission of a felony. "I thought this might happen colonel." I said quietly.

I had been carrying my police identification and badge for nearly twelve years. I didn't want to give them up. They were a part of me. I cherished my badge, it stood for all that was good and just, it was a shining star to me, a shine that should never be tarnished or dimmed. I liked putting it on my shirt and wearing it near my heart for all to see. My badge was my soul.

"Do I work inside now sir or am I to be off while I'm suspended? I'm sure it's with pay." I said nonchalantly. Colonel Burritt looked past me to the doorway and directly at his aide. "Close the door and leave us." He instructed his aide. Then Colonel Burritt said the one single sentence that I feel ruined my career, me and almost my entire life. "I'm suspending you without pay Dan, and I need your badge, gun and I.D." He said cautiously. I simply

stared at him, no movement, no words, just stared. "I have no choice Dan."
He added. I was numb. I was speechless. I mustered the words to ask, "why
without pay? I've done nothing wrong, I have done or been nothing but a
police cadet and a police officer since I was eighteen years old! That's almost
twelve years! This is bullshit colonel, bullshit!" I said angrily. I continued
staring, waiting for an answer, No answer came. "What do I do? I have no
other means of support, can't you suspend me with pay?" At this Colonel
Burritt uttered words that angered me to the bone, to my inner core. Words
that filled me with animosity towards the same people I had been protecting
and putting my life on the line for over eleven years. "I have to appease the
blacks Shanahan, I have to appease the black community. They want you
suspended without pay. They want you to bleed." "Fuck them colonel!" I
said bluntly. My anger was intensifying with each passing moment. He said
nothing, just looked at me and waited. "Fuck the blacks, the black community,
the grand jury, and Kurt Schmoke! I yelled. "All I did was to save my life!"
I tossed my gun onto his desk, pulled out my wallet and badge and tossed
them onto the desk also. "Here it is! My life, my world, me." "You have no
police powers at all Shanahan." He said gently. "Also you cannot take any
police action." I glared at him in disgust and wanted to call him a fucking
coward and a puppet. But I was so devastated I couldn't. I slammed the
door closed behind me. Later I would realize that Colonel Burritt was only
doing as ordered. Suspending me without pay wasn't his decision, it was the
administration's decision, the top administrators. The colonel was a good
man; a good cop. Politics dictated his actions, not his heart. For his heart was
with mine, on the desk.

As I went down the elevator my stomach seemed to sink to the basement of the police department building just as the elevator was. I exited thru the basement and walked East on Fayette Street to my car. As I reached the car I turned back towards the headquarters building, held up both of my middle fingers and screamed as loudly as I could, "FUUUCCK YOU AND FUCK THE BLACK COMMUNITY!"

My hostility, animosity and hatred towards the police department and blacks were strong. The animosity would later ruin my career; the hostility and hatred would ruin my heart. For at that moment I was broken hearted, saddened, and in disbelief. *What do I do now? What am I now? Who am I now? I am no longer a cop, who the hell am I?"*

I don't remember driving home that morning, but I do remember the feeling of emptiness. The feelings of betrayal, deceit, and prejudice that was tearing my inner core apart and slowly devouring any good thoughts that I had been trying to hold on to about the blacks, the black community, Kurt Schmoke, Billy Murphy and strangely enough; Booker Lee Lancaster.

The Warehouse

Just prior to the start of my manslaughter trial for killing Booker Lancaster and in the midst of a jury selection, I received a short phone call to my apartment by a middle age sounding male stating, "We need to meet with you." I drove out 695 to the Woodlawn exit and proceeded down the road to the warehouse. I pulled onto the parking lot and noticed only a few vehicles.

I walked thru a small door leading to a large somewhat empty warehouse. No one was in sight. I called out, but received no response. The hair on my neck began to stand up and I had a strange feeling in my stomach. My heart was beating faster than normal. I had no idea what waited for me. I did not like the precarious spot I was in, but I had to follow thru with this. I was curious and interested, *who wanted to see me*, I wondered. This was similar to something I had seen in a mafia movie. I had the hammer on Norm's PPK pulled back, ready to fire, and stuffed in my waistband, I was uneasy and on edge. As I walked to the center of the warehouse, I noticed a pallet full of drywall or lumber and headed for it. I heard a voice. I turned to see a middle aged white male approximately 5'5" to 5'6" tall, weighing about 165 pounds. He was well dressed with balding hair. He was just standing there, looking at me saying nothing. Slowly he began to speak, "You have friends that want to help you, but you have to tell me the truth about what happened with Lancaster."

I felt uncomfortable with this entire situation; *no one is going to believe me, who is this guy? Mafia, KKK, The FBI or maybe someone from the State Attorneys office, maybe Kurt Schmoke set this up?* My mind was buzzing with real or imagined culprits or was it comrades? I did tell the truth and that's what I'm sticking with, thank you anyway, I said cautiously. He looked directly in my eyes with a cold stare and said, suit yourself Shanahan, we can't help you, it's been offered. He disappeared as quickly as he had appeared. I turned and walked toward the same door I had entered. I kept glancing over my shoulder thinking I might be shot in the back. My hand was on the PPK.

What the hell just happened here I thought as I opened my car door, Who was

THAT and who was WE? I quickly sat in my car and locked the door. Upon

arriving at the warehouse I had backed into the parking space against the wall

on purpose so no one could come from behind my car without me noticing, I

guess I was taking precautions, necessary precautions, I thought. As I drove

back home, I couldn't help but to critique this strange encounter. *This can't*

be happening, is this shooting that big a deal, that important to someone or some

group that a person is sent to me in that manner? What am I going to do? Whom am

I going to tell? The meeting took all of five minutes; this man said his piece,

made his offer, received his answer in less than five minutes and was gone. I

decided to ride around and look for his car. Maybe I could get a tag number

and discover something about my, *warehouse visitor.* I had no idea which car

was his; no cars had come or gone during my brief meeting. I decided to

leave as quickly as he did. I was uneasy and felt sick to my stomach.

I told Jim White, my attorney, what had transpired and he nearly ignored

me and was half listening. It was as if he knew something I didn't, maybe he

did, I will never know about this strange encounter at the warehouse.

Look Good to DIE

It was during the time immediately following my suspension without

pay from the police department that I was severely depressed and had a

feeling of loneliness and of having no purpose. I had my first thoughts of

suicide, unfortunately and unbeknownst to me, several would follow. My family and friends were supporting me both financially and emotionally, as were the police officers, but the administration was playing the political and racial game and I was the pawn. This wasn't fair, this wasn't just, and it wasn't right.

I was separated from my wife, Nancy, after a happy marriage and long friendship that stretched back to high school days. I couldn't see my daughter Jacquelyn Suzanne and I was awaiting my first trial for the death of Booker Lee Lancaster. I was apprehensive, uncertain of my future, and myself and I was very sad. The confident, cocky and emotionally stable police officer was crumbling and becoming unglued. I had no police powers and felt that most of what I cared for and loved was no longer within reach.

I had a prescription for Valium from my doctor. He was very sympathetic as were many friends and acquaintances and I was given special treatment and given liberties that I normally wouldn't be given. Many people were sympathetic, and I felt special at times. Before, during and especially after the first trial I rarely paid for a beer, food or much of anything. I was a celebrity and I liked it. However, this was taking its toll on me. I was constantly driving home intoxicated, I was pulled over several times and either taken home or let go because I was Danny Shanahan, a fellow police officer that was being railroaded or a white guy caught up in a racial and political chess game. People were feeling sorry for me, and doing there best to make my life easier.

I was taking five to ten Valium per day of 10 milligrams each. The large amounts of barbiturates helped me escape my depression and pain and helped me relax. I was also drinking beer heavily, including orange juice and vodka. I wasn't aware that I was plunging deeper into depression and sadness as each pill and each drink was consumed. I also wasn't aware that I was breaking the law. As my doctor prescribed my Valiums I would add a number one to the prescription with a stolen pen that matched my doctor's pen, making the amount of pills prescribed, one hundred and fifty, not the fifty originally prescribed. I thought that the pharmacist would catch this. All he said was, "I'll have to break this up into two containers of seventy-five each. I did this many times. This is called prescription fraud. I had no idea. I would abuse Valiums and alcohol all thru my trials and tribulations.

On this particular evening I came home to my small apartment located in Northeast Baltimore City on Juneway near Erdman Ave. I opened my door and climbed the steps to the second floor apartment. I had been drinking but was not intoxicated. I opened the door but did not enter. I sat down on the top step. It was very quiet and my good friend, Ann Beauchamp, was not home downstairs. She was one of the top triage nurses at Johns Hopkins Hospital emergency room. I felt comfortable with her living there. She was helping me thru this horrible time in my life. She too was separated. Her husband was a police officer in the motorcycle unit with me, I had also worked with him in the Eastern District, and we were very close friends at one time. I began thinking about going to trial, losing my badge and gun, missing my wife, little girl, and my job, that meant so very much to me. I began to weep. I was feeling so very low and alone. *I wish Ann were home,* I thought. Even though my mom and dad, five brothers, new girlfriend JoAnne, and others, cared so much for me, I was still feeling hopeless, helpless and sad. I then began to cry out loud, tears were streaming down my face and falling on the wooden steps I watched them fall and splatter on the porous wood between my knees. I cried for nearly five minutes. I was hoping Ann would come home, hear my cries and come to comfort me and stop my crying. She wasn't home and would not come home. I wiped my tears away from my face and ran my shoe over the small puddle of tears still visible on the step slowly watching them disappear as my shoe passed over, I twisted my foot smearing and forcing the tears deeper into the grain of the wooden step. I suddenly realized that this was exactly how I was feeling, stepped on, crushed and slowly being smeared into oblivion.

It was at this precise moment that I decided that I wanted to end this pain and sorrow and die. I had plenty of Valium's and a full bottle of vodka. *I would do this, I'll show them!* I thought. *They won't have me to take to trial, find guilty, and put into the city jail for manslaughter! Here, have my dead body!* I took two or three Valiums and made a large vodka and orange juice drink. I decided to clean my apartment so everyone that showed up and saw my dead body would know I kept a clean home. Why was that important at this time before my planned death? I don't know. *I would shave and wash and brush my hair so I looked good in the crime lab pictures that I knew would be taken when finding my dead body.* I thought again. I finished shaving, brushed my hair and took a long look at myself in the bathroom mirror. *I look good to die,* I said aloud. I sat in my bed with my back propped up against the headboard. Again I thought, *as soon as I finish this drink I'm going to put the Walther PPK 9mm handgun against my chest over my heart and pull the trigger. Not much mess and my head and face would still look good in the picture, no head shot for me!* I had borrowed the gun, after begging, from my then partner, Norman Stamp. The police department had confiscated my off duty .38 caliber, two inch barrel, Smith and Wesson revolver as evidence in the Lancaster shooting, and I had to turn my service revolver, a .38 caliber six inch barrel Smith and Wesson revolver, over to Colonel Burritt when I was suspended without pay.

I had one half a drink left in my glass and the Valium's effects had kicked in. Just then the phone rang. *Shit!* I muttered. I answered the phone. It was my brother Tim on the line. "How ya doin brother?" He said. "Fine Tim." I replied. "You don't sound good Dan, I'm coming over." He said concerned. I persuaded Tim to stay home, assuring him that I was fine. I hung up the phone and glanced at my drink. *A few more swallows and I'm out of here."* I thought. Five minutes passed, the phone rang once again. I hadn't time to finish my large drink. This time I said and thought nothing, I was numb and didn't care whom it was. It was my longtime friend, Roseanne. "Hi Dan," she said cheerfully! "Hi." I murmured. "You sound bad Dan, what's wrong?" "Nothing." I said sadly. "I'm only a few blocks away, I'm coming over."

Roseanne later told me that she could feel the sadness and hear the emptiness in my voice. She was worried for my life. Little did she know at that time how right she actually was. I hung up the phone and realized that what I was thinking was definitely wrong and what I was about to do was unacceptable. I began thinking, *how dare I turn into a coward by ending my life! My family and friends loved me. They had been there for me, supporting me, since I fired that first shot at Lancaster, saving my life. I won't do this!* I said aloud.

I got out of my bed and poured my drink down the kitchen sink, opened the two bottles of vodka I had in the cupboard and poured them out also. I then went into the bathroom and dumped all the Valium's into the toilet and flushed it. Tim and Roseanne had inadvertently saved my life. They bought me just enough time for me to come to my senses and become strong and sane again.

I was to continue to abuse Valium and alcohol throughout my trials, but not to the extent I was abusing at this time of desperation. Roseanne bought pizza with her; we sat together and ate quietly. I think she knew, after all, I had shaved and cleaned up myself, dressed nicely and had cleaned my apartment at 11:30 p.m. I had looked good to die, but had not . . .

The Trials

August 1983; not more than a month after the death of Booker Lancaster I was indicted for manslaughter and use of a handgun in the commission of a felony. I received no counseling, therapy or guidance, the only help I received was from a beer bottle. Presently, if an officer merely shoots a suspect, not killing him in a seventeen inch struggle to someone's death, Lancaster's, the officer receives psychiatric counseling, is placed on administrative duty, *with* pay, and taken off the street until he or she is found to be fit for duty and able to cope with the incident.

In July 1983, I was given no help. The States Attorney, Kurt Schmoke, unintentionally, and inadvertently gave me therapy, "You have been indicted.," was my therapeutic utterance. Then, The Baltimore Police Department, the same department that had awarded me with three bronze stars and a silver star for NOT overreacting and NOT using deadly force when it was necessary and would have been justified, handed me their special treatment, "You're suspended *without* pay!" How was I to survive? I was a police officer since I was eighteen. I was now thirty.

Was this how the police department was helping to rehabilitate me and assist me in coping with my pain, anxiety, terror and anguish? I had shot two suspects prior to Lancaster, then all alone became directly responsible for taking another human life, a life that expired and was extinguished in my arms, by me! I think not! I HAD NO HELP!

So, the first trial begins. For six weeks from February 1984, until March 22, 1984, I was on trial for the murder of Booker Lee Lancaster, and the use of a handgun in the commission of a felony. I was extremely confused with the latter charge for I was mandated by the Baltimore Police department to carry a weapon within the city limits when on and off duty.

I was off duty when I shot Lancaster, however, police department rules and regulations, as well as procedures, state I must carry a weapon. How could I be charged with this if I was an off duty city police officer? Ultimately this so confused the jury that the jury became, hung, or deadlocked. A mistrial was declared.

November 1984 I was tried a second time for manslaughter but the handgun charge was dropped for it allowed me an additional four strikes, or not allow a person not of my liking to be on my jury of peers. By dropping this charge at the onset of the second trial, then State Attorney, Kurt Schmoke, insured himself and his assistants that I would not get an all *white* jury. There were three remaining *black* jurors to pick from and I still had four strikes to utilize. Kurt Schmoke seeing this, called for an immediate recess and upon entering Judge Thomas Noel's chambers stated that he wanted to drop the charge of use of a handgun in the commission of a felony. "Why now. Mr. Schmoke?" Asked Judge Noel.

Suddenly it dawned on the judge that I would lose four juror strikes and would not have an all *white* jury. Judge Noel's reply. "I am well aware of the reason you have decided to drop this charge Mr. Schmoke, and it sickens me. However Mr. Shanahan and Mr. White, I have no choice than to drop the charge and take away four juror strikes." "That's bullshit your honor!" I said loudly. Judge Noel and my attorney Jim White both immediately admonished me and warned me against any future outbursts. I stared down Kurt Schmoke, who lowered his head, not being able to look directly at me. Not being able to look directly into my frightened and angry eyes due to the fact he knew in his heart that he was attempting to ruin me, put me behind bars, and sabotage my career as well as my chances for a fair trial.

Those four strikes would have ensured me of acquiring an all *white* jury that I was certain to receive if the charge remained, even though Schmoke said in front of the news cameras the night the first trial ended and I was granted a mistrial. "There are no racial overtones in the Shanahan case." BULLSHIT! NO RACIAL OVERTONES! The six *white jurors* wanted me found not guilty and the six *black jurors* wanted to vote guilty. This is definitely a racial split!

Both trials had racial overtones and both trials had political overtones. Billy Murphy was running for Mayor against incumbent, William Donald Schaffer. Murphy was black, Schaffer white. Murphy was interviewed the night I shot Lancaster and proclaimed, "Are we going to let these white police officers kill our black citizens in our neighborhoods?" This along with the misinformation and negligence of then police department spokesman, Dennis Hill, combined to make an accusation of, "police cover up" An accusation that initiated my nightmare.

The *blacks*, especially Billy Murphy, were claiming that I placed the knife under Lancaster's body after I killed him, that the knife was mine and that Lancaster didn't have a knife at all. I murdered him for no reason, came the cry from the *black community*.

All this thanks to shoddy police work by Dennis Hill, and the aspirations of a Mayoral candidate that had political desires but had no solid platform to run with other than attempting to crucify a *white* police officer that just happened to kill a *black* motorcyclist in a *black* neighborhood.

All BULLSHIT, LIES and FALSE ACCUSATIONS, all at my expense. My expense emotionally, mentally, and at the expense of possibly losing one of the things I loved. Being a Baltimore City police officer. May you all rot in hell.

THE END OF MY CAREER

BAD COP

The first trial had ended. It was February 1984. The outcome was a hung jury. The six *whites* on the jury voted not guilty, the six *blacks* voted guilty, which constitutes a hung jury. Most definitely and obviously the jury split along racial lines. This was obvious to everyone except Kurt Schmoke and The State Attorney's Office. Kurt Schmoke was the first black States Attorney in the history of Baltimore, taking William Swisher's spot. Kurt Schmoke appeared on television the night of the verdict and stated, "there are no racial overtones in this case and we will try Shanahan again." I was sickened and disgusted! I made that perfectly clear to the press, the citizens of Baltimore and Kurt Schmoke. I was infuriated and it showed.

My Attorney, Jim White, had done a fabulous job and performed wonderfully for the justice system and me. It was a stellar performance on his part. His secretary, Rita Jacobs, had done so much work and investigation; her research was instrumental in my final acquittal. I had to admire her. She and Jim were a marvelous team. They had worked wonders and compiled a near perfect defense for me.

The first trial lasted nearly two and one half months. The second trial was to begin the end of 1984. Kurt Schmoke assured the black community, the same black community that Billy Murphy, black politician, who was running for Mayor against the incumbent, William Schaffer, white politician, that, "Shanahan was guilty!" The same Billy Murphy that so easily and eagerly turned and incited the *black* community against me. Why didn't Schmoke and Murphy go to the same lengths and extremes to assure the *white* community of my guilt? After all, in 1983 the city was only forty percent black. Did Kurt and Billy, in their infinite wisdom, forget about the remaining white people? Did only the black citizens in Baltimore, "feel I was guilty," or as Billy Murphy stated on television, "how can we let these white police officers kill our black citizens right here in our community!" White people lived in the community also. Why didn't a white politician appear on television and say, "are we going to let these white police officers kill our citizens in our communities and neighborhoods?" This didn't happen because Schmoke and Murphy wanted the case to become racial, wanted it to become political. Because by my being found guilty, my demise would nicely benefit their jobs, careers, and reputations. But, what about Danny Shanahan? How about the fact that he was a highly decorated police officer that worked diligently in that same black community and saved lives, black lives, as well as placing his life on the line so many times throughout his career. Danny Shanahan didn't matter. He was unimportant. He was a, *casualty of war.*

Well I was going to matter. I was going to be important. Those two were in for a rude awakening. Something was going to occur, something they could never nor would never comprehend or grasp, "justice would prevail!"

The months that passed from the first trial to the retrial were difficult months for my family and me. I had no income; I was suspended without pay, in order to *appease the black community,* as Colonel Woody Burritt was instructed to advise me. I was forced to wax and detail cars in a small shithole body shop on Fayette St., not far from the headquarters building. The fundraisers I attended netted over $27,000.00. The owners of several bars and restaurants that myself and five brothers frequented, all assisted in raising money for my defense and me. Bobby Rush and Tim Barger, owners of the Barn restaurant, went over and above to help me, as did Buddy Winters and Walt Bushman, of The Emerald Tavern, and Jimmy, from Jimmy's Seafood on Holabird Ave. There were so many more that were on my side and did what ever it took to help me. Many I didn't know, they were sympathetic, and they sincerely cared.

So many officers were on my side, both white and black. I feel that very few fellow officers were actually against me, or felt I was guilty. After all, it could have been anyone of them in my shoes. *For the grace of God there goes me.*

Fortunately, for Kurt Schmoke and Billy Murphy, unfortunately for me, the officer was white, me, the suspect black, Lancaster, and therefore a golden opportunity for them to shine in the eyes of their co-workers and friends, black co-workers and friends especially. A golden opportunity for Schmoke and Murphy to boost their careers at my expense, this white boy's expense.

Police departments all over Maryland supported me and showed their support. My own department was turning its back on me due to political and racial pressures. That was total bullshit! The Baltimore City Police Department's higher echelon knew this and decided to ignore that fact.

Twenty-eight letters of commendation, three Bronze Stars, and one Silver Star, all add up to a highly decorated and successful police officer, especially after only eleven years. It was proper to commend me for all the good I had done, but this one time, this Booker Lee Lancaster shooting time, I was absolutely forced to save MY life by firing at a suspect threatening to kill or seriously injure me. I had no idea that the bullet would ricochet off Lancaster's arm bone and pierce his heart. I just wanted to stop his violent and unlawful advances and to keep myself safe, not to take his life. God forbid I look out for my safety for a change! Lancaster died in my arms, He was a bad guy but nonetheless I had to hear his last words and that death gurgle, me, no one else.

The end of my career came quickly and quietly. I was waxing cars on Fayette St., two blocks from the headquarters building. I was in between the first and second trials. I walked into this dump of a body shop and opened the door to the office. I saw approximately $3,000.00 in bills strewn over the owner's desk. The owner was, at that time, one of my best friends. Enough of a best friend that I let him handle my entire legal defense fund money. The Fraternal Order of Police didn't want to help with my case. It was too racial and political; that sounded familiar?

The owner was on vacation when I walked into his office and saw the money. I looked at Mark and Gomer, "where did you guys get all this money?" I asked. I noticed nothing out of the ordinary, everything seemed normal. "We sold that boat trailer and Mark's Cougar." I knew that these two were somewhat shady but they did have a trailer and a Cougar and both were gone. I had no reason not to believe them. I knew that they had been arrested for various misdemeanors, but, so what! I had my own serious problems and I really didn't care about them and their money. No big deal! Besides, Colonel Burritt had suspended me without pay and had taken my badge, ID, and gun as well as suspending my police powers. I had no authority to question them, plus, I had a bad attitude and a lot of animosity towards the police department.

"Do you and John still want to sell your boat?" asked Gomer. "Damn right! You know I need the money Gomer!" I replied. "One thousand dollars, right?" He asked. "Yep, $500 for me and $500 for John. I replied. "Here Dan, one, two, three, four-fifty, five hundred, there's your half, I'll put John's money in an envelope until he gets back so Mark and I don't spend it." "Okay by me." I said. John and I had a 1935; thirty-eight foot Matthews's motor yacht. I needed the money so we decided to sell it.

I jumped on my motorcycle and deposited the money in the municipal credit union. I had NO idea or inclination that this $500 was stolen in a bank robbery.

As the FBI questioned me about the $500 I asked them this; "If I knew the money was stolen bank money, why would I have immediately placed it in the credit union?" The bills could have been marked or the serial numbers could have a look out on them. It made no sense to put stolen bills into a bank or credit union. I would have put them in a hole in the backyard or spent them immediately if I was doing something illegal. I would have left NO paper trails.

Why didn't I take money from the defense fund? The fund raising money passed directly thru my hands. I counted all the money before personally handing it to Jim White. That was over $27,000.00, not a measly $500.00. Makes no sense. Makes no sense because I didn't accept $500 to allow these two to rob a bank. It wasn't so!

The FBI told me that my fatal mistake was not getting a receipt or bill of sale. Due to my notoriety from the Lancaster trial, I was being looked at very closely. Had I produced a simple bill of sale for the $500 I would not have been charged. I really didn't understand. Many times in my life and especially as a police officer I had purchased items for different amounts and I never asked for a bill of sale. I didn't think it was necessary. It was in this case!

The owner of the body shop returned home and was given his $500.00 in cash. All was as it should be. He didn't receive a bill of sale, he also wasn't charged with receiving stolen bank money. Why? I was.

That following weekend John and I took Mark and Gomer out on the boat to show them how to operate the forty-year-old boat and how to handle any small problems like docking. We drank all day and enjoyed all of it. On the way back to the marina at the end of the day, Mark and Gomer told

John and I that they had robbed a bank to get the $1,000.00 to buy the boat. "Sure I said" "You two are full of shit!" Any police officer will tell you that people like to confess their sins and crimes when drinking. It had happened several times over the span of my career. "Hey Dan I hit a car last night and left the scene." "Hey Dan, look at this gun, I got it cheap, think it's stolen?" Questions like that I passed off as bullshit, bar talk, with some false bravado. I just didn't take it seriously, just as I didn't take Mark and Gomer seriously. We laughed about the bank robbery and continued to have fun, drink and party. It was soon forgotten.

A week later I happened to be in the company of a robbery detective, John Gavirilis. He handled all bank robberies on the eastside. He would later become Police Commissioner and leave in disgrace. He burned a lot of his friends on the way up, guess he got what he deserved. I just had to ask about the hold up that Mark and Gomer told me about, what if they really had done this. I cornered Detective Gavirilis, "John, was there a bank hold up on the eastside last week involving two white males, one older, one younger?" After a moment he said, "Yes, there was a holdup involving two white males, no guns were used, a letter was, and no one was hurt. Why do you ask?" *Could this be true? Naah, no way.* "Why do you ask Dan?" John asked again. I told him that maybe, just maybe I knew the two guys involved but really wasn't certain. They could have read the newspapers and could be lying to me. "What do you think I should do John?" I asked. "I am coming up on my second trial and it would make me look very bad in the eyes of a jury, hanging with bank robbers, besides, Schmoke would love to dirty my reputation and this could be the vehicle he used." John looked at me and said, "You're right Dan, besides, no guns were used, it was a note, and no one got hurt, I'd leave it alone."

I had no idea what had just transpired here. I was reaching out for direction, help. Detective Gavrilis knew that I possibly had two suspects that may have robbed a bank but was advising me to, "leave it alone." Wasn't that malfeasance in office, neglect of duty, and obstruction of justice? I was confused, apprehensive, and had a bad feeling about all of this. I should have handled it differently but I had to look out for me. People in high places wanted me in jail.

As I was leaving the headquarters building I was in deep thought. I decided that Detective Gavirilis was right, leave it alone. He should have followed up on my statement, he didn't. I too handled things inappropriately.

I was torn about my decision, but all the uncertainty quickly disappeared as I walked away from the building. I walked slowly towards the body shop, the body shop I was forced to work at to make ends meet. The police department had turned its back on me; it had taken my coveted badge, my ID, my gun and also all my police powers. They may have just as well have taken my heart, I was tremendously upset. I was infuriated.

I stopped and turned towards the headquarters building. I looked up at the top floors where the upper echelon worked and made all the big decisions and I said aloud, "I have NO police powers, NO ID and NO gun! I should turn these guys in but, FUCK YOU!" I again yelled, "FUUUCCCK YOOUUUU!"

My anger, hurt, resentment as well as my bad attitude towards the department was about to cost me my career. That moment was definitely a, "defining moment." In my life and career. I was a human being, not a robot, a Robocop. I had all these emotions, feelings of despair and loneliness; I had all these questions but went nowhere to get answers. I desperately needed answers.

My animosity had closed my eyes to what was right and just, and to what I should do.

Several weeks passed and the second trial began. The State Attorney pulled at straws and fumbled the ball many, many, times this second time at trial. Jim White, my attorney, sensed this and pounced on the opportunity. When the time came for Jim to present my case, the case for the defense, Jim stood up, faced the judge and said, "your honor, I feel as though the State has not presented enough evidence to find my client, Officer Shanahan, guilty of any wrongdoings, the defense rest!" I loved that part!

I was acquitted. I had won. I also had made Kurt Schmoke appear inept. The defense had rested without even putting on its case and the States case was so weak it didn't stand on its own. That's unacceptable in the world of law and lawyers. Kurt Schmoke and Billy Murphy had failed. They had been defeated and were embarrassed about it.

I was put back to work in the days that followed, not on the street on patrol, but back where I started as a police cadet. I was put back into the communications division. I was a police dispatcher again. I was also a hero, a legend. I had beaten them all; I was the fair-haired boy in other police officers eyes. I enjoyed every minute of it too.

A week or so later I was settling in, all was quieting down. The celebrating, congratulating, and handshaking were done, over. I was hot stuff but was beginning to cool off.

I was working the 6 a.m. to 2 p.m. shift on that fateful, career-ending, day. I was dispatching the citywide channel. All hot or emergency calls such as shootings, stabbings, armed robberies, bank robberies, etc., were given to me over a small squawk box located to my left and that was connected to 911 operators headsets that were taking the calls. These operators sat directly behind me. We were separated by a large piece of glass. I would receive a call from one of the 911 operators, decide which districts needed to know of the emergency or hot call and broadcast the necessary information. There were times when I couldn't hear the information given out over the four inch, by four-inch speaker clearly. I had to turn around and look for the operator that had just given me the information and ask them to repeat the address. No big deal, this happened to all of us and quite often, especially on a busy shift. It didn't matter how experienced or how good you were, human error did occur.

Then it happened. "500 North Co_____on, for a bank robbery in progress!" I hadn't heard the street correctly. I turned and yelled thru the glass," was that Collington or Conkling?" The operator had not given me Street or Avenue. Had she said street I would have known Conkling Street, if she had said Avenue I would have known, Collington Avenue. There was no Conkling Ave., and no Collington St. It happened. I wasn't sure of the address. I couldn't hear what the operator was trying to say. Being so confident I took it on my own to give out an address. If it was incorrect, no big deal, OR so I thought. I broadcast 500 North Collington Ave. as the address for the bank hold up. I worked Collington Ave. in the Eastern District for eight years, but further North. 800 block to the 1800 block of North Collington Ave. I wasn't familiar with the 500 block, which was in the South East District. Maybe that's why I gave out Collington, not Conkling. Collington sounded more familiar and I had used that street name many times as an Eastern District officer. Besides, if I were wrong an officer on the street would correct me. I had made this type of mistake before. LITTLE DID I KNOW I WAS PUTTING ANOTHER NAIL IN MY COFFIN. I did not hear the correct address.

"Dispatcher, there is no bank in the 500 block of North Collington it must be Conkling!" Came a voice from an officer in the South East District who was on the scene in the 500 block of N. Collington Ave. I immediately rebroadcast the correct location. "Attention all units, the bank robbery in progress is not, I repeat, is not, on Collington Ave., it's at 500 N. Conkling St, 500 N. Conkling St." This was acceptable police procedure. No questions were asked. My sergeant and lieutenant were monitoring the channel and all was well. I had done as I was trained and had done nothing wrong, nothing wrong, YET!

Shortly after I had broadcast the proper location, a Southeast District officer asked if I could take a description of the hold up suspects and rebroadcast it out for other officers in the vicinity. "Certainly 221, go ahead with your description." It read, and I broadcasted something like this. "Attention all units, wanted for armed bank robbery at 500 N. Conkling St. are two white males. Number one white male is approximately twenty five to thirty years of age, five foot six inches to five foot eight inches tall, wearing blue jeans, white shirt and brown coat. Number two suspect is a white male with a baldhead, five foot nine inches to six foot tall. Approximately forty years of age. These suspects were last seen driving a light brown Chevy with a dark brown vinyl top; the . . . I stopped in mid sentence. *Oh my God, Oh Shit!*

it couldn't be, no fucking way! The description sounded like Mark and Gomer! And it sounded like they were driving my police officer girlfriends car! JoAnne's car was getting a dent fixed and she had dropped it off that morning. She had a light brown Monte Carlo with a dark brown vinyl top. *It couldn't be!* I thought. I quickly glanced over the remainder of the description and immediately felt faint and sick to my stomach. I began to quiver and shake.

I knew I had to make a decision, and make it quickly. If it was Mark and Gomer this time and they had my girl's car, my police officer girlfriend's car, there could definitely be serious consequences; *this could be a major fucking problem.* I thought. I was coming unglued. I knew all the phones in the communications division were taped, all calls, incoming and out going were constantly being taped. I had known this for years. But, I had to know; I had to know if this was in fact Mark and Gomer.

I picked up the phone and called the body shop. John answered. I was very excited and my insides were in knots, I was stressed. "John, it's Danny, where are Mark and Gomer?" "They went to lunch." "Went to lunch!" I said excitedly. "Where did they go to lunch and what are they driving?" I asked. John replied, "I don't know where they went but yes they are driving JoAnne's Monte." John knew that when Mark and Gomer said that they were going to lunch that it meant they were going to rob something. I had no clue as to this code name shit. John knew they were robbing a bank with a police officer's car, and let them do it, plus it was my girlfriend's car to boot.

Jesus Christ John! I said. Had John known about the other bank robbery that I questioned Detective Gavrilis about? *They must have committed that one for real, Oh my God!* I thought. *This is very bad, very, very bad.*

I had to broadcast the description a second time, usually this is done after a more detailed and thorough description is obtained from additional officers on the street and at the scene of the crime. Knowing the phone I was talking on was being taped, I didn't care. I instructed John to listen to the description I was about to broadcast. I laid the phone down on the table with the earpiece facing me, so he could hear the description. I repeated the same description; I picked up the phone and said to John, "Well, what do you think?" "Shit Danny!" Was his reply. "Shit!" I repeated, "Christ John this is not good!" I told him to call me when the two assholes returned. Then, I did it! I ruined my entire career! And maybe my entire life. I COMMITTED THE CRIME! Had I had stopped there, at that point, and called my lieutenant or sergeant, and explained what had transpired it may not have looked good but it would have been the truth, no deceit. To that point nothing illegal had occurred. I had done nothing wrong, committed no crime.

What was I going to do? What if Mark and Gomer get stopped and a gunfight ensued? They were armed this time, that's what I was told. What if one of my buddies gets shot or killed? Or, two of them for that matter. Should I help them get away so no one gets hurt and deal with them later, or should I tell someone where they are going and maybe risk a gun battle, a deadly gun battle. What am I to do?

You as the reader, maybe a police officer, have to make the decision before you finish reading this paragraph. What are you going to do? Are you going to assist them in getting away and maybe stop a gunfight, maybe a deadly gunfight, or are you going to tell your supervisor that you know where they are headed and have you friends, buddies wait for them at the body shop and risk one or more of them dying. Are you going to tell the wives and kids of a dead police officer that you did this, you caused their loved ones death because you didn't send them away and deal with the repercussions later? I didn't know what I was going to do. Do you? What is your decision?

I decided to help the two bad guys get away and avoid a possible shoot out with my friends and buddies. I decided and acted on that decision. Why didn't I ask for help? Why didn't I call someone? I don't know. I did the WRONG thing, I made the WRONG decision.

Here is my crime, Here is my three years in Federal Prison, here is my disgrace as a police officer, here is the disgrace to my family name, here is my fall from the top, here is my 100% total FUCK UP!

I began to change the description of the vehicle I changed the direction the vehicle was traveling enabling these two fuck ups to get away, to escape. That way no gunfight could come about and none of my police officer friends could get injured or killed. If I don't do this and a friend of mine got killed or disabled, how could I face his family?

"Danny, why didn't you get the two robbers out of the area? If you had, my husband and their father might still be here. Why Danny, Why?" I played this hypothetical scene over and over in my mind. I made the decision. No dead police officers today, no sad wife and kids this day. *Get them out of there Dan.* I thought.

"Attention all units, in reference to the bank robbery at 500 N. Conkling St., the vehicle has NO vinyl top, (wrong), and is traveling South on Conkling St., not North. (wrong),. Those words sealed my fate. I had confused the officers on the street. They had trusted me; they had trusted my description to be correct and true. I had let them down; I had let ME down too. Almost immediately an officer from the South East District came over the radio and tried to correct me. I purposely ignored him and his corrections. I wonder what he was thinking as I ignored him. I felt so bad but I had to do what I decided. It would give Mark and Gomer more time. Again the Southeast District officer attempted to correct the description, this time I broadcast the proper information but the lapse had given the two robbers time to get away. It was done . . .

I was ruined, I was sick to my stomach. I asked the lieutenant if I could go home early. He said yes, after all I was the fair-haired boy, my lieutenant gladly let me leave. I immediately went to the bathroom and vomited. I left the locker room where I changed and grabbed my things. I rushed out into the hall and called the body shop on the public payphone. "John, are they back yet? You know they robbed the fucking bank don't you?" John replied, "Yes Dan I know and yes they are here." Tell them to stay there until I get there, I'm going to fuck somebody up if they leave! Hear me John!" I hung up the phone.

The deed was done and the damage was irreparable, no one would believe me, no one! Not with these set of facts;

1. Mark and Gomer had robbed a bank two weeks prior to this robbery. Had told me and I opted not to say a thing, powers or no powers I should have looked into the robbery.
2. I did absolutely nothing, fuck Det. Gavrilis, I did nothing.
3. JoAnne's car was used in the second robbery, she was a police officer, and they knew that. That's why they took it.

4. I was dispatching while they robbed the bank at gunpoint. Mark and Gomer had heard my voice on a police radio when one of my friends stopped by to say hi to John. I actually said hi to John over the radio that morning. I had no idea Mark and Gomer knew I was dispatching. No one was going to believe that either.

5. I sent responding officers the wrong way to insure Mark and Gomer's safe getaway.

6. I lied about the car having NO vinyl top

7. I received $500.00 from the first holdup, most likely it was stolen and I had no bill of sale.

8. I used a taped phone to talk to John.

9. It was quite obvious that I was aware at some point, that Mark and Gomer were the correct suspects.

10. WORST of all, I totally and completely FUCKED UP! Dead cops or not, I fucked up, I AIDED and ABETTED. No one was going to believe that the $500.00 from the first robbery was just for the boat, I'm certain Mark and Gomer told the FBI that the money included the second robbery also. It Didn't! I took no money other than for that boat. I could have taken thousands of dollars from my defense fund, why didn't I. This is, and was, all-irrelevant. I had nobody on my side to listen. I have no reason to lie now, this is the TRUTH!

I reached the door to the shop. I entered and slammed the door behind me. "What the fuck did you just do? "Do you know what you have done to me?" "Fuck you both!" I pushed Mark and Gomer into the wall. I had my gun out and had it pointed the barrel at Gomer. I had known him the longest, I somewhat trusted Gomer. "I should blow you're fucking head off!" "You asshole, you too Mark, Fuck you too."

"I'm going down, I'm done. I should shoot both of you!" I left; I left in JoAnne's car. The FBI would tell me later that Mark and Gomer had robbed several banks, including two in Virginia. They robbed the banks then came back into town to attend my fundraising affairs! I had no idea, not a sniff. Besides, no one would believe me anyway.

John was just as guilty as the other two and myself. He knew all along about the first robbery and kept it from me. He allowed me to put $500.00 of stolen bank money in the credit union. When he told me that Mark and Gomer had, "gone to lunch," he knew damn right well that they were robbing another bank and, in a police officer's personal car! He knew of all the circumstances and allowed it all to occur. When the heat came down on John, he pussed out, rolled over and told the FBI all they wanted to hear and then some.

He was obviously given immunity, no charges placed against him in return for all his knowledge, and cooperation. Fucking pussy snitch! Of all four of us involved, John was the only one that didn't go to jail! I know why now, the rotten snitch bastard put me, Mark and Gomer in so he could avoid any jail time. What a best friend! Hence, "keep you enemies close but your friends closer."

He lied about the extent of my involvement to save his sorry ass. Why else would he be the only one not sent to jail? He also helped Mark and Gomer paint one of the getaway cars a different color after the first robbery. With full knowledge that he was covering up evidence. His involvement and degree of aiding and abetting made my extent of involvement seem minimal. Yet, he received no jail time. It's quite obvious why.

As of July, 2001, John belongs to a motorcycle club that was started by police officers, and still has police officers amongst their ranks. Members that know me and of John's involvement, snitching, lying and cooperation. "Ironic or sick?"

I noticed the FBI following me; I thought I was good at my job, I pale in comparison to the FBI. They knew my every move and knew exactly what I was doing and going to do. They are impressive.

No one was going to believe my side of this story. Not even my Attorney, Jim White. I offered to take a polygraph and to this day still would if asked. Jim wanted nothing to do with it. He said, "Danny what you just went thru with Lancaster is nothing compared to this bank thing son." I seriously damaged him; he really looked out for me and was instrumental in keeping me alive and sane thru all of this chaos. Jim died of cancer when I was in prison in Texas. I never had a chance to say goodbye to him, I broke his heart.

I was sentenced to three years in a Federal Prison Camp in Big Spring Texas. I actually served two years and twelve days. It was one the most difficult times I had to endure, one of the loneliest times in my life. I don't care how much movement you have, being away from your family and two year old little girl was extremely difficult to deal with.

I believe Mark and Gomer are still incarcerated, I hope so. I'll never forget Judge Black's words to me when I pleaded guilty to receiving $500.00 of stolen bank funds and to violation of Federal banking laws. "Mr. Shanahan, you've had a taste of how the system works for you in the Lancaster shooting case, now let me show you how the justice system works against you! THREE YEARS Federal Prison, court adjourned."

I was sent to Big Spring Federal Prison Camp in Southwest Texas. The FBI was sympathetic and understanding. They sent me to the nicest prison camp in the country. They were looking out for me, plus I had contracts out on my life from members of Booker Lee Lancaster's motorcycle club. The FBI was also protecting me. They treated me better than my own department, the same department I had worked so hard for to become a great police officer. Now, I am a convicted felon and ex-cop with no career. With some help, I had orchestrated the end of my career.

FEDERAL PRISON

FEBRUARY 1985
BIG SPRING, TEXAS

I n February, 1985 I was sentenced to three years in a Federal Prison located in Big Spring Texas. This prison is located in Southwestern Texas not far from New Mexico. I was charged with, and pleaded guilty, to receiving $500.00 of stolen bank funds.

I was allowed to self commit, or turn myself in, on May 25, 1985. I would not walk out of this minimum security prison until June 6, 1987. Two years and twelve days after my brother Tim boarded an airplane and accompanied me to Texas to turn myself in, to the prison authorities. Tim and I were extremely emotional as we hugged goodbye. He was leaving his little brother to sit in a prison that neither one of us knew about nor what lay in store while I was incarcerated there. I was solemn, sad, and very nervous. I had no idea what to expect. I went from a decorated police officer to a convicted felon in a matter of ninety days. My entire world was turned upside down. As Tim drove away alone, he was so frustrated and upset that he pulled to the side of the road and beat on the steering wheel of the rented car until the wheel actually bent. I'm sure that my entire family felt his pain as well. I let them down and now had to pay the price. It was a stiff price to pay too. All the shiny important things in my life were tarnished. My shiny career, my shiny badge, my new shiny marriage with a shining new little girl. All dull, tarnished and gone.

I attempted to show restraint and be a man about this but inside I was frightened. For six hours I was fingerprinted, photographed, initiated and oriented into prison life. Those six hours seem like lost in time, a blur, for I don't recall much of that first taste of my freedoms being taken from me, the sour, bile tasting, unpalatable taste of prison. Usually I took other peoples freedoms, not this time; it was my turn to experience the opposite side of the criminal justice spectrum.

I was given a blanket and a pillow and was escorted by a fellow inmate to my room. I was assigned to the sunset building room 348. This was located on the third floor, far end room, in one of the two buildings housing approximately two hundred and fifty to three hundred inmates in each building. The other building was called the sunrise building. Each was named for their location. I watched some very beautiful Texas sunsets in my stay there. It always seemed so very ironic, and I wrote my mother often to that effect, how the spectacular sunsets temporarily lifted my spirits and how it was saddening that I had to experience such beauty in such an ugly place. At least an emotionally ugly place.

The full moons were breathtaking as well. I would lie out on the grass in the middle of the compound and stare at the bright round sphere wondering if anyone in my family or any one I loved might be looking at the moon at that exact moment so I just somehow might feel not so very far away from home. I especially missed my two year old daughter. I wouldn't see her for quite some time and this was destroying me as was the entire disgusting situation. I was very lonely, dejected, and depressed.

Up to that point in my life, the two years in Texas were the loneliest time in my life and was, to that point, the most difficult situation I had to handle and to accept. Of course, I had no options, and the diaper room hadn't touched my life at that point in time.

I was to be incarcerated from the time I was thirty until I turned thirty two years of age. I missed Christmas, Thanksgiving, Easter, and the other family holidays that I enjoyed.

I was completely devastated, humbled, embarrassed, and belittled. I was placed in a room with three former police officers from New Orleans. They were three of the infamous Algiers Seven. Seven police officers that were found guilty of violating a black mans civil rights, unjustly, and were incarcerated for seventeen months. Upon their attorney's advice, they chose not to see the parole board until they had some time in prison. Finally after fifteen months the parole board hearing was held for all three simultaneously. The parole board examined the case and told the three that there had been a mistake, the parole board told the three that they didn't belong in jail and that they could return home. Three police officers that lost their entire careers and spent seventeen months in federal prison weren't supposed to be there. They were furious and bewildered. After returning home the New Orleans police department would not allow them to return to the police force, they were, convicted felons. Sorry, tough shit!

These three officers, Steve, Dale, and Mac, all read that I was being incarcerated at Big Spring Prison Camp, pulled some strings and had me placed into their room. I cannot explain how much easier this made my very first day with no freedom, family, career, or confidence. My first day of being a convicted federal felon. They welcomed me, assured me that this was most likely the best prison in the country and that I would be fine. I was very uneasy, but somehow felt secure with police officers such as myself that had fallen out of grace. Federal prison, Big Spring Texas housed mostly white collar criminals. Police officers, judges, government officials and many, many attorney's, make up a large portion of the inmate population. The remaining 25 percent, or so, consists of criminals coming down off of lengthy prison terms that have been locked away and are in need of some freedom, such as a prison camp, like Big Spring FPC, which has no cells, fences, or walls. It allows a smooth transition into the community. Alot of witness protection inmates lived at this FPC also.

My first night of incarceration there came a knock at the door at room 348. I did not answer, however, Steve did. I overheard the person at the door ask if a police named Shanahan was here. "Who's asking?" Said Steve. "My name is Terrance, I was a cousin of Booker Lee Lancaster, the guy Shanahan shot and killed." My heart skipped a beat and I nearly choked. *How in the hell did this guy know I was here and what is he doing here from Maryland?* I wondered. I knew I had to act like a badass or there would be repercussions, I knew this. I walked to the door and glared at Terrance. "What's the problem?" I asked sternly. "Nothing." Came his reply. "I just wanted to see the cop that murdered my cousin, Lee." I nearly shit! My first day in a Federal prison, four thousand miles from home and Booker Lee Lancaster still haunts me. *What the Fuck!!* I thought. I said to Terrance, "Look Terrance, Lee, made me shoot him, I told him to put the knife down, he didn't. He forced me to shoot him. You know this!" "I know but I still don't like you." He said. At that point, Steve, a hardened homicide detective from New Orleans along with Dale and Mac, who were his Sergeant and partner, came to the door. Steve said, "Look asshole, all of us were cops and you don't want to come to this room again or you will get fucked up! Understand Teeeerrrrannce!" Terrance said nothing and walked away. I had no problems from him until the day he was leaving, three months later. He walked up to me in the dining hall and said, "See your white ass in Baltimore, Shanahan!" I had been there for three months now and was gaining confidence. "Fuck you! See your black ass at the fucking Baltimore City morgue Teeerrrraaancce!" He left and I ate.

I met and sat with Senator Michael O'Keefe from New Orleans, Assistant Secretary of Defense, Paul Thayer, and met Billie Bob Harris, who was a millionaire and involved with inside traders information that ultimately caused the downfall of Paul Thayer. Three very important men that were only allowed ten dollars in quarters a week to buy sodas, candy, popcorn or goodies to eat after meals and while watching late night television. Each inmate was only allowed ten dollars in quarters per week. However, I learned to turn my tall floor lamp upside down, remove the felt false bottom and insert another roll or two of quarters so I could eat more or trade off for other items I needed. Prison is a constant bartering system, everyone barters. You need soap; I want a Snickers bar. You want an apple, I want two quarters. Bartering is the prison way. It is the way to comfort and satisfaction.

For some unknown reason I kept a daily diary of my time in Texas. It covered and spoke of the ups, downs, good and bad, that I went thru daily. It covered my daily routines and my job at the kitchen scraping food off of inmate's dishes after meals. The smell was horrible and I rarely ate after my shift, I ate before work. The diary also covered my inner most thoughts and feelings, what I was feeling at that exact moment in time. It talks about my first New Years Eve. Myself and my three roommates placed sodas and ice on the shower floor so the melting ice would drain. We placed an iron upside down between two books like a stove burner and put metal cans of cheese on top so we could have melted cheese and crackers. We concocted something called a, "hook up". Which consists of noodles from cup of noodle soups, cheese, sausage, tuna, and other items we saved from our once a week grocery shopping trip that we were allowed. Then at the stroke of midnight each of us had a Haagen Dazs ice cream that was such a delight that we savored every delicious bite. We each had one pint of this special ice cream. This was the same each holiday. We tried to make it special in our own small, convicted felon, way.

Once a week we sat and huddled together eating this delectable treat, "oohing and mmmming," as we tasted the smooth ice cream we waited for all week long and had to stand in line for usually two hours. The commissary was so very small and a two hour wait was the norm. But, if you wanted the essentials, such as shaving cream, razors, soap, etc., and sweets and goodies, it didn't matter. We all were there to waste time, do time, pass time. A two hour wait was two hours closer to freedom. Passing time was the essence of doing time. It took me an hour to clean and lace my sneakers, and hour to do a small load of laundry, an hour to walk a half mile around the track, an hour to eat as slow as possible. Anything to waste and pass time. After all, I had time to do, and plenty of time to do it, two years and twelve days.

After one year I was allowed to return home for a one week furlough. I discovered this after nine months. I had to have had no, "shots," or infractions, a positive report from my employer, and a place to stay in Maryland that could be documented. I was giddy with excitement. However the next ninety days took a lifetime or it seemed.

I was amazed. The Federal Bureau of prisons was allowing me, a convicted felon, to fly home to Baltimore, stay a week, and return on another flight, all with just my word and that of my family that I was staying with them. Then, I would return to the prison and do another year. Amazing, but GREAT! I made it home for Christmas, 1986. One week with my family and a few left over, "real friends." I was definitely ready for sex, beer, family and friends. After a year away from all that mattered to me, e.g., family, I was delighted and bewildered. I didn't care, I was home. I was going to see my little girl after being away for a year and I missed her tremendously.

The one week passed quickly. I thoroughly enjoyed being with my family. Getting back on a plane to leave once again for a second year was terrible. However I did get to come home. I was depressed for a week upon returning

to Texas, I learned that this was normal due to enjoying a taste of freedom
then having to relinquish that freedom once again.

I stopped drinking two days before I returned for I was aware that I
would be subjected to a piss test to insure the prison officials that I had no
drugs or alcohol in my system since I was out of the prison environment.
The entire time I was incarcerated I was tested just once. Drugs and alcohol
were available. The fastest runner in the prison would collect quarters from
inmates, bills were not allowed in the prison, then, he would run nearly a
mile to purchase alcohol at the closest convenience store, only to run back
as quickly as possible before he was missed or an **emergency count** was
conducted. The convenience store employees were well aware of their inmate
customer but did not care.

A **count** is just that, all prisoners must return to their rooms so the guards
could assure that all inmates were accounted for. These **emergency counts**
were conducted for no special reason or if a guard, (hack), as we referred to
them, felt that a prisoner had walked off.

At Big Spring Federal Prison Camp, there were no walls or fences, just
a six inch curb. But, if an inmate stepped over that small piece of concrete
he was considered as an escapee. So, the six inch curb could have been a
one hundred foot tall electronic fence with barbed wire, for traversing over
it would be taken as an escape. I was not chancing being placed in a higher
level prison for stepping over a small curb, or for a taste of alcohol. I didn't
partake in drugs.

Reflecting back, the time I spent in prison was just a flash or blink in my
lifetime. However, the time I spent there dragged on so very slowly. I still

dream of fouling up and being returned to the prison, only to awake in a sweat realizing that I was still free and this horrible dream was a nightmare, not a dream and that I was still a free man.

I have no idea or understanding why I kept a diary the entire time I was a prisoner in Texas. I read over the entries and secretly I am scared and afraid, scared and afraid that I may have to return to the loneliness and depression I suffered through for two long years and the even longer, last twelve days.

Upon my release I remained on Federal Probation and had to report to my Probation Officer monthly. I had succeeded in staying out of trouble for nearly 3 years, yet was unaware I was soon to be NOTORIOUS once again.

NOTORIOUS

"SMILE FOR THE VIDEO CAMERA DAN"

I was with a male friend who was employed at the medical examiner's office. His job was to pick up the dead bodies from all over the city of Baltimore, the city with three hundred homicides a year. What a job! What could possibly be the highlight of his day? What satisfaction and enjoyment did he derive from that, fucked up job? Just like his job, Billy was, fucked up in the head. No wonder! Who wouldn't be, picking up the dead and mangled bodies of babies, the elderly, and the "innocents." As I referred to them. As well as the bad guys, robbers, murderers, drug dealers etc. What could possibly make his day? I can only imagine Billy coming home to his wife, "Hi Billy, how was your day hon?" "Oh, just fine, only two burned up kids, one headless homicide victim seventy years old, and oh yeah, that seventeen year old boy that crashed his car into a tree in Leakin Park, we had to take him out in pieces, fucking mess! But other than that, I had a great day!"

Christ! What a job! Billy and I had reputations of drinking too much. It was obvious we were in the midst of a great performance that night. It was a stellar performance!

"Smile for the video camera Dan, and say happy birthday to Jane!" Said her boyfriend Joe as he taped Jane's birthday party at The Bowman restaurant in Parkville. My five brothers and I meet there often after leaving our separate jobs or if there is a death, birth, any type of necessity for the family to get together. We usually meet at The Bowman. Happy or sad all six of us would huddle together to be sad or happy as a family should.

The filming continued nearly half an hour off and on. I was obviously intoxicated. It was obvious that this woman was trying very hard to get close to me. She had heard of me, thru my past, and liked the fact that I was the *notorious*, Danny Shanahan, bad boy. The local papers always started their articles concerning me with the phrase, "the notorious Dan Shanahan." I didn't like it much but I must admit it was flattering. "Jesse James Shanahan, Baby Face Nelson Shanahan." Not quite.

This woman hanging on me was very homely. I was married to a pretty woman. I wanted nothing to do with this girl. It was very evident by watching the video. I wanted nothing to do with her. I did notice that she seemed to know the bartender well. I also knew her well. I was shitfaced and having fun. I was in my glory! Drunk, happy, life of the party, somewhat famous, and of course, *notorious*.

"Will you leave me alone!"? I said several times to this ugly dog of a woman that continued to hound me. She was a tire biter; I wanted nothing to do with her. She sat on my lap, touched my face, put her arms around me and it was obvious to the other partygoers and on the video I was repulsed and continued to thwart her advances. Billy was angry with his wife. It was their anniversary and he wasn't going to sleep at home. He had a woman hanging on him but didn't seem to mind. I didn't care. We weren't best friends, merely acquaintances. Let him have some fun.

Billy pulled me to the side, "Dan, I got a chance with this chick, drive us to the hotel." "Okay Bill, come on I'll drop you two off where do you want to go?" Let's go to the Towson East on Joppa Rd. You can come in and have a beer with us." I turned, said my goodbyes and exited thru the front door. Billy met me at the car approximately a minute later. Him, his date, and for some unknown reason, this girl that wouldn't leave me alone.

She was a friend of Billy's so called date. His, "I'm pissed off at my wife on our anniversary, date." "Come on, let's go." I said disgustedly. I eyeballed Billy and mouthed to him, "Thanks Asshole!" We stopped for beer, twelve pack of Coor's Light for me and a twelve pack of Budweiser for Billy. He also bought a bottle of wine for his anniversary date.

I drove very fast and quite badly to the Towson East Motel. I was inebriated. Billy paid for the room as I grabbed some ice and cups from the front office. We were given room #223. I'll not forget that room number. I went into the room. Neon lights, king size bed, television, refrigerator, heart shaped bathtub, and a Jacuzzi. *"Nice!"* I thought. *It should be for eighty-five dollars a night!* I entered the room and was surprised. The beer was in the fridge, the music was on, an x-rated movie was on the television, and Billy and his date were in the hot tub sloshing around in the bubbles.

I was sitting at a small table by the front window with this obnoxious woman. She tried to pull my zipper down, I pulled away. "Sorry dear, not at all interested" She was angry. I continued to drink and watch the x rated movie on television and the real one in the tub! "Great tits! Billy! I slurred. He grabbed his nipples, "Thanks honey!" He yelled back. "Not yours asswipe, hers!" I laughed. I didn't even know her name, or for that fact, the name of this monster in front of me.

I consumed at least seven more beers. I knew this because later the police told me that they found seven Coor's Light cans with dents in them strewn about the room. I would drink a beer, throw it against the wall and get another. They were mine. They stayed where they landed.

Hours later I remember Billy shaking me. "Dan the girls want to go back to Bowman's, I'm taking the car." I didn't care about much at that point. I was in a drunken stupor. I heard the door shut. I was alone. It seemed only minutes when I heard the door open again. I looked up thru my blurred drunken eyes. "I'm back, Mr. Party pooper!" Billy said." Did you do her?" Billy asked. I shook my head no acted like I was puking and laughed. Billy laughed and I passed out again.

Bang! The door flew open! I was being shaken and not shaken gently. "Shanahan! Dan Shanahan!" The voice boomed. I opened my eye to six police officers standing in the room around me and out the door. I recognized the police radios crackling in stereo. "Dan get up! You're being arrested for rape!" "Rape! What fucking rape! I yelled in a panic. I had my shirt and Down vest on but no pants or shoes and socks. I was drunk, slumped in the chair, a warm beer in my hand and every thing hanging out for the world to see.

I recognized several Baltimore County Police Officers. These were my friends and acquaintances. One officer was my brother, Pat's brother in law, Danny. We were friends and got along well. I was to find out later that Danny received the original call but after checking the name at the office register asked his sergeant if he could pass on this arrest. After all I was his sister's brother in law. I also found that several other officers refused and asked not to handle the rape call. They didn't believe the allegation.

Finally the sergeant had to find an officer willing to handle the call that worked in another precinct. He found an officer that disliked me to do the honors. Officer Meyer had a dislike for me and me him. I knew his ex-wife from school and officer, Dudley Do Right, Meyer, was more than willing and eager to ruin my life. The allegations were false and ridiculous. But, I was the *notorious*, Danny Shanahan.

I was dressed and had to be bodily carried by two officers down the steps to the back of the radio car. They were kind enough to handcuff me in the front. Billy was also arrested and immediately taken to the Towson Precinct for the investigation. Billy continually told the police that I had done nothing.

As I sat in the police car still dazed one of my friends asked if they could search the room. I said NO! "Why not Dan, hiding something?" I really wasn't,

I was confused, angry, drunk and being difficult. "I had not committed rape, and I didn't do drugs!" I said angrily. I was detained in the car for over an hour while a search warrant was procured. I slept thru the entire search. Nothing was found of consequence. I was taken to the Towson Precinct also.

I would find out about two weeks later that I was the brunt of many jokes between four officers that were golfing. They all knew me. Three were at the scene that night. Evidently it was quite funny to them that as the police rushed thru the door to apprehend a rape suspect and his accomplice all they discovered was Billy sleeping and me all fucked up, head down, a warm beer in one hand and holding my dick with the other! Very Grotesque! But hilarious to these officers, "Sick Fucks!" I said when I heard. Then I too laughed. I'm sure I was a sight to behold. *I'm just as sick!* I thought. Sadly, I was.

I was held for over six hours. I was handcuffed to an eight foot long two inch in diameter brass pipe, which was affixed to the wall. I could walk the length of the pipe dragging the cuffed wrist along with me causing a loud scraping metallic sound. Frequently I would pull hard at the cuff causing slight pain to my wrist. I was angry, irritated, and it showed. I knew I didn't rape anyone, especially dog face. I was extremely upset with myself.

Evidently my actions were annoying a young, very thin, pussy looking rookie officer. He came over to me and pushed me to the bench. "Sit down and shut up!" he yelled. I jumped to my feet, he dropped back quickly, "Fuck You Asshole!" I screamed. I was furious and coming down from my drunken stupor. *I did nothing wrong, I'm not a rapist!* I thought. "Fuck you, you skinny pencil neck little fuck! Do you know who I am? I was a City police officer and you wouldn't make a pimple on my ass rookie!"

I blasted him. I was releasing all my pent up fear, frustration, and anger onto this young cop. "Where's your gun you pussy?" I yelled. He had on a holster but no gun.

Three other officers came into the room. They too had empty holsters. "Doesn't anyone carry a fucking gun in here?" I screeched. I wanted a gun, and I wanted one desperately. The police must have known this ahead of time and prepared for the situation. I was in the frame of mind where I would have grabbed a gun from anyone at that point and immediately with absolutely no hesitation blown my fucking brains out right then and there! Nothing neat and clean like the near suicide at my apartment on Juneway in 1983, (Look Good to Die.) This would have been violent, messy and definitely deliberate. I would have it no other way. I did not rape!

I could not get a gun. Pat's brother in law, Danny, settled me down. The young punk police officer disappeared, wonder why? Somebody was thinking. Someone saved my life and probably didn't even realize it, procedure. I guess. I would again discover later, after the fact, that these officers knew of all my past tragedies and were alert and astute enough to have all the guns put away, fortunately for me. I really wanted to die. I had a strong desire to die hard and violently. I was ashamed, depressed, scared, embarrassed, and I could not believe my present set of circumstances. I had done *nothing* wrong or illegal.

Evidently, after Billy had finished with Fido number two I had passed out. Fido number one, my dog, took my pants socks and shoes off as I slept. She tried to arouse me to no avail. I not only turned her away sexually, I kicked her across the room when I realized she was touching me. She became angry. She was horny and upset! I wasn't playing. She told her girlfriend to get out of bed and made Billy take them back to Bowman's.

I was told later, as soon as this bitch entered Bowman's she threw herself on the floor and started flopping around like a fish and yelling hysterically. "I was just raped! Danny Shanahan just raped me!" All the waitresses, the female owner and the female friend bartender rushed to the Fido's aid. "Call the police!" Someone yelled frantically. Then all the females gathered around Fido and tried to comfort her until the arrival of the police department. It was a great performance, for a fucking dog!

After the air cleared and the investigation was completed, on all the stages of this horror movie, or should I say dog show, it was discovered that this woman was a certified schizophrenic, she was also bi-polar and had been under heavy psychiatric counseling for these disorders as well as for a documented case of dual or multiple personalities for years.

Afterward I was in the company of several officers and we discussed the dual personalities of this woman. Of course, one of the officers on the scene that night asked, "So Dan, which one did you Fuck!" "You are all sick bastards!" I said to them. We laughed and one officer began to bark. Only a seasoned, experienced cop could say something to that affect. You have to have experienced much horror, death, destruction and violence, as a police officer to develop that sick sense of humor. Like the scorecards being held up by the officers after the suicide jumper in Towson hit the ground. It's a safety check valve, a very necessary release valve.

I was not booked, photographed, or fingerprinted. Several of my brothers came to get me and take me home. My wife was totally bent out of shape.

Sad, angry, upset, embarrassed, and feeling betrayed. Fortunately, for my marriage, and me JoAnne was somewhat open minded, even in the most serious of times and situations. Partly due to her years as a Baltimore police officer in the Eastern District, and partly because of her love for me.

The videotape clearly showed the investigating officers and detectives that this woman was the advancing party, my obvious disgust with her, and obvious attempt to keep this lying bitch away from me. Billy was released after a few hours. No charges were filed against him either. I was released hours after him when everyone concerned were certain that I was settled down and back to a state of some normality. They wanted to be certain I wouldn't do anything to harm myself. That had passed.

A week passed. I was a complete mess. I knew I did not rape Fee Fee. However a declaration as to my innocence in this alleged rape would have been acceptable. It was an absolute necessity in my wife's eyes. It was a difficult week. Accusing female eyes, whispers, and the crude and snod remarks from other guys that I acted nonchalant about, but were actually ripping at my insides. However, the one remark, and incident, that tore me to pieces emotionally and made me feel so very bad about me. My father's remark and comment was the most difficult to swallow and accept.

Several days after the alleged rape of Fee Fee, I asked my dad what he thought and why he was so quiet towards me. He looked at me coldly and said IT. My morally righteous churchgoing, usher, sire of seven children, and great husband, said some of the most devastating and emotionally damaging words I think I ever heard. "Why did you have to rape her?" He said in a stern, condescending, hurtful, and negative tone. I stared at him with my mouth open and my eyes wide. My own father, my daddy, my hero, teacher, and guide most of my young life, the man who was so proud of me as I crossed the stage at Police Headquarters so many times to receive honors for doing what was right and just, the man I admired and adored had just accused me of a rape, a heinous felony that I didn't commit. It was if he had reached into my mouth, down my throat, grabbed my heart and snatched my soul on the way out and threw them both to the macadam stomping them to pieces as I stared in disbelief and disappointment.

I stared at my dad. I was speechless, shaking, and my eyes were welling up with tears of hurt. I looked him directly in the eyes and said in a weak, I give up, low tone of voice, "Fuck you, you asshole." I immediately left. I grabbed my car keys got into my car and drove away. I drove away a broken man, a shattered little boy. I wept, no, I cried out loud in the car. All the pressure was building. I sobbed uncontrollably like a three year old with a burned hand from touching the stove or a hot pot. I had to stop my car. I wept.

A few weeks after that incident I received a call from the Baltimore County Police Sex Unit and the State Attorney's Office. No charges were to be filed against Billy or myself. All was forgotten and forgiven in the eyes of the law. I called JoAnne and told her. "I'm so glad Danny, I'm so glad." I was definitely relieved and happy that the detectives had done their job to clear an alleged suspect not to convict, as was the usual case.

Days after my father's accusations we spoke. He apologized and admitted that he was wrong for doubting me, and that he felt badly. It was awkward. I don't recall my dad ever apologizing to me. We hugged and that was that. My dad died on June 14, 1996, Flag Day. I was as sad as I was when he said those words to me about the alleged rape. It severely impacted me, as did his death.

One month after this rape incident and me being detained for questioning, an article was printed in the Sun Papers. It started out, something to the effect, the notorious, ex-cop, ex-con, Dan Shanahan was arrested. I couldn't believe what I was reading. A month after the fact! Where was the big news flash! This was old news! I was livid. I had become familiar with most of the news writers thru the Lancaster trial. All were fair and true journalist, or so I thought. I called the writer of the article, Richard Irwin. I said, "Mr. Irwin, this is Dan Shanahan." "Yeah, what's up Shanahan?" He said coyly. "I was reading the article you wrote about me, are you aware that this took place over a month ago, and I was not charged?" "So what Shanahan, every time you fart, its news, you're notorious!" "It's not newsworthy! Can you print an article as to my innocence?" I said angrily. "No Shanahan, that's not newsworthy!" "So let me get this right Richard, An incident that occurred a month ago is newsworthy, but the fact that the man is not guilty of that charge and that fact recently came to light is NOT newsworthy? I want to clear my name!" He answered in an evil, fuck you, tone of voice. "That's not the way it works Shanahan, no one cares if you're innocent!" I paused in disbelief and anger. Then I spoke. "Your first name Richard is an appropriate name for you. You are well deserving of it, Riccchhhaaarrrdd! Because you are definitely, most definitely, a big DICK!" I hung up the phone. After all, *us notorious ones can do that!*

Good Cops, Bad Attitudes

On several occasions since I was charged, found guilty, and sent to Federal Prison in Big Spring Texas, for receiving stolen bank funds and banking violations, I've had many chances to be involved with police officers both in the city and Baltimore County. These *run ins* were not at all pleasant. I left both incidents disgusted and angered. I was, for the first time in my life, able to understand, and therefore developed, a general dislike for, and mistrust of, police officers, by the general public, and at times, by myself.

Christmas time 1999, my brother Shawn called me from his house. It was approximately 11:00 p.m. "Danny, I need you right now, I'm going to be arrested!" He said frantically. "What's happening Shawn? You know you're not supposed to be there!" I said angrily." Shawn had been drinking heavily. It was obvious. Looking back I should not have gone to his aid. I was almost certain I knew one of the officers present and I wanted to help my brother. Maybe I could talk Shawn out of being arrested. I was on probation from my shooting incident and I should have thought of my wife and kids. Of course I had no idea the situation would turn ugly.

I had to go, my little brother needed my help, and I lived only blocks away, I was certain I could handle myself, appease the police officers, and be the hero again. Wrong! Shawn's wife had taken an ex-parte out against him. He was to be nowhere near his house or wife. Shawn had the Christmas blues and was lonely. Add alcohol, and a dilemma, or as police officers refer to it, a situation arises. Shawn had removed half of the rear sliding glass door on the rear deck. A meddling neighbor was aware of the ex-parte and was kind enough to stick her nose in Shawn's business by contacting the police and advising them of a, burglary in progress.

When I arrived five police cars and a wagon crowded and blocked the small street. Upon entering the house I observed five police officers in Shawn's home. One black female at the front door, and four white officers in the kitchen with Shawn. Shawn had not been arrested yet but was in cuffs. I knew all four officers in the kitchen. One disliked me and I him, the other three had been in my company and to parties with me over the years. I considered them acquaintances. One officer, Tommy, had worked a radio car with me. I felt safe and at ease. We were glad to see one another.

It was very hot in the house. I was in the kitchen with the four officers I knew. As we were talking and I was attempting to keep Shawn from being arrested, the black female officer entered the kitchen bitching in a loud shrill voice. "Let's go! Either lock his ass up or don't! I have things to do, I have a date tonight!" I was appalled by this officer's actions. I couldn't believe this smart-ass bitch was talking to her sergeant, my friend, like that. Let alone being that rude and uncaring. She was insensitive to the situation unfolding in that house. *Not very professional.* I thought. "Settle down officer, were trying to work this out." I said calmly. "Who in the fuck are you?" She cackled loudly, like the chicken head that she was. I was disgusted with her bad attitude and her tone of voice. I had done nothing wrong, I didn't deserve that type of treatment. Chris sake it was Christmas. I said sarcastically, "Why don't you go outside? You can get home to your hot date as soon as possible, maybe he'll shove a dick in your mouth and shut you up!" I knew that was wrong to say, but she initiated the foul language and attitude. I became incensed. The officers in the kitchen said nothing. I feel they agreed with me. She left the room and went outside.

"I know he's not supposed to be here sarge." I said to my friend calmly and with respect. I had helped this sergeant in a time of crisis. He had left his service weapon in a car I had cleaned and I got it back to him personally without involving the department. That's a serious foul up. He hadn't been aware it was missing. I saved him much embarrassment. He was a friend and he understood that he owed me one. I was hoping to cash that chip in this night for Shawn. I continued, "He was just dropping off these presents for his daughter." I was facing the sergeant and the remaining three officers were standing to my right and left side. All was calm and civil

The phone rang. It was Shawn's wife. She explained to one of the officers that Shawn didn't belong in the house but it was okay with her for now as long as he left before she returned home. As the officer on the phone was relaying the message to the sergeant, I pulled my sleeves up due to the warmth of the house. I normally pull my sleeves up. It's a habit when I'm warm.

Suddenly and without warning the officer that was standing next to me, the officer that didn't like me, removed his pepper mace and sprayed myself and his sergeant with a full force stream of mace into our faces. *Holy shit! What's happening?* I thought surprised. I had no clue what was taking place or why. "What the hell is going on?" The sergeant yelled! We both went to the floor. One minute we were talking calmly and without provocation or cause, both the sergeant and I were pepper maced. Nothing had occurred to escalate the situation to that level, nothing; it was totally uncalled for and unnecessary. I was totally caught off guard, as was sergeant Star.

I grabbed my face and was pushed to the floor again. Shawn became scared, nervous, confused, and bolted out the back door and across the yards. He cleared the four-foot fence with handcuffs on! The sergeant was yelling, I was yelling, total chaos had replaced total calm in only seconds. I could see nothing. My eyes, nose and mouth were on fire! I tried several times to open my eyes to no avail. They burned so badly. I was incapacitated and extremely confused as I lay on the kitchen floor. I was grabbed and flipped over. Someone was handcuffing me! "Chris sakes! Why are you handcuffing me! Asshole! I haven't done a damn thing! What the fuck is going on!" I was extremely confused and angered. I knew the law! I had broken no laws and had done nothing to cause an officer to utilize his mace.

My mind raced! *What had I done? Did I say something threatening? All I did was pulled my sleeves up! What is happening here? Why was I maced!* A splash of cold water hit my face. "Fuck you! You asshole!" I yelled, "What's this about? This is bullshit and you know it, whoever you are!" I knew it wasn't sergeant Star, he was yelling too. Then I heard it; I heard the words that explained all of what had transpired in that kitchen. I heard the words from this prick cop that sprayed me. "That's for the bank robbery muvafucker, fucking traitor!"

That's for the bank robbery? I thought in amazement and anger. *That's for the fucking bank robbery?* I was completely taken aback, surprised! I was under the impression that the two years and twelve days I spent alone in a Federal Prison in Southwest Texas, missing two birthdays, Thanksgivings,

Christmases, my two-year-old daughter, and my family was enough punishment as well as losing my police career, wife, self respect, self esteem, and feeling utterly terrible about myself since that all took place was enough, obviously not.

All of this punishment was not satisfactory in this officer's eyes to cleanse me of my crime. On top of all that pain loneliness and suffering I had to be pepper maced for no fucking reason! *That will show me to rob another bank!* I thought bewildered.

As the officer splashed water on my face I reared back and kicked him across the kitchen. I heard him hit the kitchen sink and the knives and forks rattle. For some unknown reason I wasn't charged with assault on an officer, gee! Evidently what had taken place was this officer's small way of getting his payback for his moral support during the Lancaster trial, giving me five or ten dollars towards my defense fund, or maybe purchasing raffle tickets for my fund. This was his personal payback for me betraying him. "I hope you feel better asshole!" I yelled in disbelief and disgust.

He had single handedly caused a calm situation to escalate out of control. I was enraged. This was not at all necessary. Had I seen or had access to a butcher knife in that kitchen, I would have slit this fucker's throat and plunged the knife into his cold, revengeful heart! I wanted to spit in his face as he flopped around the same kitchen floor like a dying fish gasping for water. I was that angry and infuriated. He was judging me, not fair.

Cold water hit my face once again. It felt so refreshing and cool. "Who is it, I can't see you." I said. "It's me Tommy. Don't worry, asshole's outside." "What the hell happened Tommy?" "You knew he didn't like you Danny, when you pulled up your sleeves he said that was a combative move so he maced you!" What? That's bullshit Tom. I had my back to him!" "I know Dan, I know. Now sit back and let me clean you off. Sergeant Star is still washing off too, he got a face full of mace also."

Shawn had gotten scared when the mace started flying, he couldn't understand it either. He ran two blocks hurtling over fences while handcuffed. They found him in the bushes. I was assisted to the paddy wagon and placed inside alone. Shawn was taken in another vehicle. The officers wanted me alone. I could hear Sergeant Star reprimanding the officer that maced me and disciplining him for his actions and for totally overacting.

It became quiet. I felt the rear of the wagon dip down; I knew someone was standing on the rear bumper. "I'm sorry Danny." This prick cop said to me ever so quietly and discreetly. "I was wrong," He continued. I savagely kicked at the back door several times in anger and disgust for his actions. "Fuck you punk! You asshole! Fuck you!" I screamed. I was crushed, hurt and angry. *Will this shit ever go away, will I ever be forgiven and absolved? Haven't I paid my dues yet?* I wondered as the paddy wagon drove off. *Back to Central Booking!* I felt disgusted.

I appeared in court a month later. My attorney, Dave Love, had the charges; hindering a police officer and failure to obey the lawful order of a police officer, placed on the *stet* docket. This means the charges are dropped but the case can be reopened at any time if I foul up again. Actually it's an agreement that what took place *MAYBE* shouldn't have, on both sides. David Love has done wonders for me. He is aware that there is a grudge against me by certain officers and especially by the State Attorney's Office. Dave evens the score for me.

I haven't seen any of these officers since this fiasco. When I see an officer that I worked with and may have contributed to my defense, I wonder what they may be thinking and if maybe, just maybe, they want to take out their frustrations on me also. I don't need the bad attitudes. I'm certain they have no idea what being in a federal prison for over two years does to a former police officer. It was one of the loneliest times in my life and one of the most difficult situations I had to face. They just don't know. No one let me down, disappointed me or embarrassed me more, than me!

I should have contacted The Police Department's Internal Affairs Division to make a complaint. I could have caused this officer big problems. I decided against it, after all I couldn't shit on a police officer, it was an unwritten code, and it was unacceptable. Who was I to judge this officer, I'll leave that to him, and obviously he was much better at that.

August, 2000, I pulled my car in front of my apartment, which was located in the Northeastern District of Baltimore city. It was ninety-eight degrees with a one hundred and ten degree heat index. It was humid and extremely hot, a typical late summer day in Baltimore. I pulled the car to the curb but the car was facing the wrong way. Everyone in the neighborhood parked as they pleased. I was no different. I left the car running with the air conditioner on. My brother, Shawn, was with me. He exited the passenger's door and headed for the apartment. I locked all the doors except for the front passenger door, which I left slightly ajar. I was taking precautions, but, in retrospect, I should have turned the car off.

There was an electrical brown out in the area and my downstairs neighbor called me to tell me he was concerned about my six-month-old puppy, Harley. It was hot in the upstairs apartment for a young puppy. I was stopping home to retrieve the dog. I was in the apartment for approximately two minutes. Enough time to climb the steps, get the dog and come back out.

As I exited my front door I noticed a Baltimore police paddy wagon parked next to my car. I was unaffected, I knew a lot of officers in this district and they knew my car. I assumed it was an acquaintance, or a friend of mine that had recently been transferred to the Northeast District and was assigned to the wagon, Norman. He had been transferred because he helped me find a special parking spot at Oriole Park at Camden Yards; I had tickets for the baseball game. This action angered a smart ass, arrogant, racist, prejudiced, black officer who disliked me—and me him, very much. We had words many times over the years. He too was a motorcycle officer. Both officers had an argument on the street and one officer shoved the other. This is totally unacceptable and conduct unbecoming an officer. Both were transferred out of the elite motorcycle unit. Norm was my former partner and friend, he was doing what all of the officers do for friends, put them in a special parking spot during large events.

I had called Norm the night before the game and he instructed me where to meet him. The day of the game I pulled up to the intersection Norm was working. He moved the stanchion and directed me to a parking spot. I got out of the car, thanked Norm, shook his hand, and we began talking. "What are you doing Norman?" Boomed a deep black man's voice. It was smart-ass. He and I had a severe personality conflict. I hated him and he me. This was well known in the squad. It happens. Norm said, "I'm parking a friend." "A friend!" yelled YoBoy. "He's a fucking ex-cop and an ex-con, he don't belong here!" I had been out of Federal Prison four years but not shot yet. "Fuck you!" Norm said angrily and in my defense.

Yo walked directly up to Norm and pushed him forcing him back. Norm pushed Yo back and it ended. Words flew but no more physical touching took place. I thought it best to leave, I did.

This officer disliked whites as I did blacks back then. Even though he was a cop I considered him a typical YoBoy. All my years as a police officer I never thought of a black officer as a Yo, I had a mutual respect for all officers regardless of race or gender. Yo was definitely the exception. His dislike for us white boys was obvious, he didn't hide the fact that he too was prejudiced. He also had a bad attitude, not a healthy combination, prejudiced towards whites and an attitude.

I discovered this when I was informed that Yo only wrote traffic tickets to white citizens. I didn't believe this rumor. One day as I was relieving YoBoy I looked over the ten tickets he had written during his tour of duty. Sure enough all were traffic violations written to white people. I checked for three consecutive days and found the same disgusting evidence, all white violators. I was pissed. I don't know if it's because I didn't think of it first or because whites were being fucked over by YoBoy, or because it wasn't proper for a police officer to act in such a manner. Either way, I was out to avenge the white people.

I couldn't alleviate the problem so I joined in the fun. I wanted to play too! It was now a contest, except *black man Yo,* had no idea that, *white man*

Dan, was onto him. Since he worked the shift ahead of me I could look over his citations and count the number of whites written traffic violations. I wanted to see if he was steadfast in his outright hatred of whites. He was! He didn't disappoint me. I decide that if Yo wrote ten whites I would write fifteen blacks. If he wrote fifteen I would write twenty. The whites were always five tickets ahead. I was satisfied and Yo had no idea he was hurting his own. In my own sick racist mind the whites came out ahead each day I worked. Looking back I'm disgusted and embarrassed by my actions and his, but I was what I was, a racist. Times change, I've changed.

YoBoy instigated an investigation into the incident at the baseball game. Norm was well liked by his superiors and had much more seniority than Yo. Norm had been a motorcycle cop since the sixties. But a problem was a problem and this one was serious. Why? White and black, of course. What else constitutes a problem in an integrated police department?

Norm was sent to the Northeast District. This was known as vacationland. Not much crime and a much slower pace than the other eight districts. A lot of officers went to this district before retiring to ease back into some type of normality. This was a laid back mostly white district. Norm was devastated and I felt responsible. He was happy being a motorman and liked the perks that came with that job. The Northeast was not suitable to him.

Blackman Yo was sent to the Western District, which has always had a reputation for taking all the fuck ups and problem officers that pissed off the administration. The threat always posed to a rookie was, "Keep fucking up and you'll have a foot post in the Western District on the midnight shift!" This phrase stuck and I never wanted to be transferred to the Western district. The problem officers were sent there. It was a punishment to be sent there. The district was brutally violent, all black, and had the second highest homicide and crime rate in the city. Only the Eastern District was worse but it didn't have the bad reputation that the Western did.

I'm sure since the upper echelon of the department was mostly white at that time, that's why Norm went to the Northeast District and black Mo went to the district with the other misfits. I felt satisfied. He deserved it. However, I've met some fine officers that worked in the Western District but they either were assigned there from the academy, wanted to go to the Western District to learn how to be a *real* crime fighter, or transferred on their own. These officers didn't fit into the, "Fuck ups" category. They were seriously dedicated police officers.

Back to my apartment, hot day, dog, and Brother Shawn. I left my car running to cool down my dog. I was glad I did when I saw him. He was panting and had white foam around his mouth and jowls. I carried Harley to the car and placed him in front of the air conditioner vents to cool him. As I walked back to the paddy wagon I realized that Norman was not the driver but I recognized an officer that had an attitude towards me, a bad attitude. I had a problem with him once before. He felt as though I had let him down personally. He had stood behind me during the trials and put his ten dollars out for my defense fund. And I had the gall to make a mistake, or in his eyes, fuck up. I was a bad guy now. I was to be looked down upon, scorned and turned away.

He had run a motor vehicle check on me and found that the notorious Dan Shanahan didn't have a driver's license. He was itching for me to drive the car away so he could stick it up my ass by locking me up or writing several traffic tickets. "That would be payback, he would fix me!" The notorious, bad boy, bank robbing, ex cop, ex con, shot by police, suicidal, Dan Shanahan would suffer for his mistake. Dudley Do Right would see to that! I should suffer!

"Who's driving?" Dudley said in a low shitty tone of voice. My driver's license had been temporarily suspended for fleeing from the police during the high-speed chase the night I was shot. I couldn't drive, but was anyway. However this officer never saw me behind the wheel. I was safe as long as I didn't get into the drivers seat.

"I said, Shanahan, who's driving" He was being ignorant. I had to think quickly. I saw Shawn coming towards us. "My brother is driving, is that a problem?" Shawn looked at me nervously. He had been drinking. He mumbled, "Thanks a lot asshole." He was deathly afraid of receiving a drinking and driving charge. I whispered to him, "Just don't get into the car." "Give me *your* license!" Tough guy ordered Shawn. "I know you're not driving Dan, you're suspended." *Did your homework shit head?* I thought. Little did this shit know I was, in fact, driving. I had been driving for some time. Then he lectured, "You know better than to leave your car running and unattended Shanahan. It's against the law too. I'm writing someone a ticket! It should be you Danny!" He was being belligerent, cocky, and abrasive. *There was no need for this, Christ! Fucking Dudley Do Right sitting there telling me **I'm** breaking the law! This is such a minor infraction; it really didn't deserve anyone's attention and time. After all I had been thru, all Dudley had to say was, Dan you know better than to leave your car running, I sat here until you came out so there* *would be no problems, next time, just shut it off.* I thought in disgust. But NO, this asshole had to get his personal retribution. I deserved to be reprimanded but didn't deserve a stinking bad attitude and a smart-ass answer.

I was extremely sensitive around police officers that knew me and of me. Always overly concerned about their thoughts and feelings towards me after the Federal Prison stint. Not all officers treated me badly, just a certain few. I guess the ones that NEVER make mistakes. I shouldn't care about what other officers thought and felt about me, and my misgivings, but I was mired in doubt, distrust, and shit! I really *did* care. My downfalls and shortcomings over the years haunted me, especially in the company of police officers.

There I stand ninety-eight degrees outside in the sun, sweating, my shirt soaking wet and temper fired up hotter than the one hundred and ten degree heat index at this officer's inflammatory remarks, words and suggestions. At this time, I was slowly healing from some very serious psychological and mental problems caused by my third suicide attempt, which was the shooting I survived. I was fragile.

There I stood, listening to this fuck head cop lecturing me over such an insignificant charge that I could easily beat in court, a simple fucking traffic charge. No way was I listening to this bullshit, I had enough of cops with attitudes, especially after being maced by another asshole cop not many months prior to this idiotic, senseless, revengeful, bullshit, traffic stop.

I went off verbally, I vented. I walked directly up to the paddy wagon window where the officer was sitting. "Look you fucking asshole, you have no right to talk to my brother like that and I'm certainly not going to put up with your stupid shit, you fucking moron. Tell you what fuck head, write your goddamn ticket before I shove your ticket book up your wise ass!" I was becoming unglued and not very cautious.

The psychological medications I was taking to keep me settled, Paxil and Buspar, weren't doing their job. The officer broke in, "Shut up Shanahan, or I might just tow your car too!" He was taunting me. I fumed, "Is that right! Well I'll tell you what dipshit, how about I pull you out of that wagon and stick your fucking head up your ass to shut you up so when back up arrives and all the officers WE know get here they can see just how much of an imbecile you are! Write the FUCKING ticket asshole!"

I had to walk away, I was *seriously* thinking of following up on my threats. I was knotted up inside and an anger welled up inside my head. It's as if I was having a fistfight in my head and wanted the fight to spill out of my ears all over this prick, arrogant, loudmouth. Of course, I knew how far to push this officer, hopefully.

Dudley continued to talk to Shawn like me, a criminal. "That's IT! I've had it!" I said. I walked up to the officer and said sternly, "You need to get a supervisor here. I want to speak to your sergeant, NO! I want the fucking shift commander!" When a citizen request to see a supervisor an officer must oblige and call for his supervisor, unless the officer arrests the citizen. Then everything changes.

"Dan you've got to settle down, we'll be arrested." Shawn said quietly. "I can't Shawn, this guy is wrong and out of line, totally!" Fortunately for both of us Shawn walked me across the street while we awaited the shift commander, which is usually a lieutenant. As I attempted to gather myself I was staring at the bushes near the ground. I was very seriously contemplating pulling this officer out of his wagon and beating him. I began to picture the episode in my mind. That was a danger sign. I was extremely close to following thru on this mental threat. I was that upset and *unstable.*

I was beginning to fear the dangerous thoughts going thru my mind. Am I capable of such violence, such violence against a police officer? Violence against the very same individual I used to protect and help no matter the danger to me? I really want to harm him and make my point. I paused in my thinking then continued. What point, and Dan, what is the point? I had come back to my senses, back to the reality of the situation. I was wrong and he was a police officer. I took a deep breath and settled myself down. I had defeated myself. I looked up and around. I came back to normality.

"Dan, what's the matter, why do you want to see me?" It was Lieutenant Thomas, an acquaintance of mine. "Hi Bill, I said dejected, quietly and in a subdued voice. I was emotionally drained. I wasn't aware that the supervisor had arrived. I was in my own world. The events of the past twenty minutes, the rise and fall of my temper, emotions, and feelings of anger, had drained me. I was defeated. I was suddenly lethargic. I began to think of all that I had lost, especially my wonderful, exciting, fulfilling career. I missed my job immensely. I missed *all* of it. I stared at the ground as if mesmerized. I couldn't look up or away, my gaze was frozen.

How did I get to such a bad place in my life? What had happened to me? Why did I have to be the one to suffer thru all of this? Why me? I was sad in my mind. My whole being was sad and melancholy. My shoulders drooped, my head hung down and I felt lowly. I wasn't the angry, belligerent, arrogant man I had been only moments ago. "Dan, what's the problem?" Bill asked once again. I turned to face him. It was obvious that I was deeply upset and unsettled.

I had tears in my eyes, one streamed down my left cheek. "Jesus, what's wrong Danny? What's wrong buddy?" He knew I had been thru a tremendous amount of hard times in the past and was sympathetic. "Nothing Bill, nothing." I stated. "I received a call for a supervisor's complaint, do you have one Dan?" He asked. "I don't Bill, I really don't." I seriously wanted to make a complaint, but to what end? It would have been futile. I was the fallen dark angel; I was all that and more. I had become overwhelmed by all of the occurrences that morning. The tears flowed because I was reliving all the bad that had happened to me since I shot Lancaster. Usually when I get to this point I'm thinking of my shooting and how desperate I had become. I'm still angry and disappointed with myself. I had missed all the signs of impending suicide. Now, I was letting one individual upset me and open all the wounds again. It seemed as though every six months or so my wounds would somehow be reopened and salt ground into them by other people. I would become devastated and slightly disabled, both emotionally and mentally. However, I managed each time to pull myself out of the gutter of despair. At times I would think I was merely feeling sorry for myself. I had survived being dealt several dirty hands but always pulled myself together and healed both mentally and physically enough to continue on to deal with another dilemma. I was blessed. I still feel as though God has something very important for me to do, why else would HE continue to keep me alive and able to cope with the memories, wounds, reminders and *the past.*

I believe that Lieutenant Thomas realized what had transpired in front of my apartment. He looked hard at the officer in the paddy wagon and didn't bother to stop and talk to him and inquire as to what had taken place and what had initiated the supervisor's call. He understood. He left.

I walked across the street and sat in the passenger's seat of my car. I didn't look at, or acknowledge the officer. I sat in the car with my head down. Shawn got into the car and we drove off with his fifty-dollar ticket, a ticket for leaving the car running while unattended. A fifty-dollar ticket that very well cold have ruined me forever and most likely would have caused me serious injury, for I wanted so badly to injure and maim this officer at the height of my tirade.

An, assault on a police officer charge, would have completely damaged me both in the eyes of the law and more importantly, to my, once again, fragile, weak, and delicate, psychiatric condition and personal welfare. Not to mention the personal welfare of the good cop with the bad attitude.

Back to Jail

July 5, 2001 9:00 a.m.; I'm going to criminal court today to answer to the charge of VOP, or, Violation of Probation. I've been on supervised probation for three and a half years for my shooting. The shooting where I wanted to be killed by a police officer and was shot eight times only to live. I have done well these three and a half years. I have followed the rules of probation with only a few minor infractions. That is, until, November 24, 1999, Thanksgiving Eve.

I was away from my wife for the fifth time but was attempting to reconcile again. I was cooking turkey legs to take to my kids at my house. I was living in an apartment in Baltimore City.

I had been dating a woman for one month and realized that I wanted no parts of her and that I wanted to return to my family. I told her on November 23, 1999. She was in denial and didn't want to accept this. This woman knew where I hid a spare key to my apartment and at approximately 7:00 p.m. she forced her way into my apartment by breaking thru the screen door and using a key that I didn't know she had to enter my apartment. I was extremely surprised to see her. She was yelling, "You're not going back to your wife! You're not!" *How did she get in here? I told her to leave me alone! Why is she here?* I wondered. I was angry.

I told her to leave but to no avail. She began hitting me with the pans on the stove and I defended myself. I called 911 and requested help. The sounds of the pans smashing on the kitchen floor could be heard over the phone. I grabbed the woman by the arm to take her down the steps. She pulled back and her blouse ripped. Five officers arrived due to my notorious past. I really didn't want to be shot again and was somewhat calm. When the police arrived they talked to me but were unable to talk to the woman. She was feigning unconsciousness. She was fine until she heard the police call up the steps then she slowly got down on the floor and closed her eyes. When the police saw this they called for a medic. I knew she was faking but the police did not.

The ambulance arrived and checked out the woman. One of the paramedics pulled an officer aside and told him that the woman was play-acting. It made no difference. One of the officers looked at my hands and saw markings. "What are these Shanahan?" He asked. I explained that they were from blocking the hits from the pans. He thought that unacceptable and instructed a black officer that didn't like me to cuff me. Before he cuffed me he said something smart and seemed to want to instigate a fight. I tapped on his badge three times and said, "I put my life on the line for that badge for many more years than you rookie, you have no right to talk to me like that!" I was pissed.

A third officer interrupted the exchange by telling me, and the black officer, to settle down. That officer said "I'll cuff him, you settle down, let me take him." This officer put the cuffs on in the front and whispered in my ear, "I've got you Dan, its okay, come with me." He was being kind and understanding.

The woman went to the hospital and was immediately released. She had no injuries. She was lying. She was also diagnosed as bi-polar and schizophrenic. I went to Central Booking for processing. As I sat in my holding cell I was given charging papers. I was charged with second-degree assault on the woman, and assault on a police officer. I was livid. I was charged with assault on a police officer for merely tapping his badge three times? *That's bullshit!* I thought. I was bailed out by my family, once again, three days later.

The case went to court in June 2000. I was given PBJ, or, Probation Before Judgment, which is basically a not guilty charge. Also, the charge cannot violate someone's probation, it did mine. My Attorney, David Love, also had the assault on a police officer charge dropped. There was insufficient evidence to convict me the Judge stated. The case was dropped.

I was relieved. However, my probation officer had to notify the judge that put me on probation originally, Judge Evelyn Cannon, of my arrest. Normally a Judge will issue a Show Cause summons to the offender, in this case me. A Show Cause summons is just that. The offender must **show cause** why the judge should not violate the original probation. Normally this is done by a summons, not a warrant. A warrant is issued only if the offender has a past history of not showing for court, or, failing to appear charges. I had none of these. But, Judge Cannon issued a $75,000.00 warrant for my arrest! I had never missed a trial or not shown up for court. A warrant was totally unfair and out of order. She issued the warrant in spite of this. I was totally upset. Judge Cannon was out of line and was causing undue hardship on me to satisfy her. I was certain. I had to borrow $7,500.00 from my family to get bailed out of jail after a three-day stay in Central Booking, which is not a nice or comfortable place. Fair is fair and she was not!

Here I stood in front of the unfair and vengeful, Judge Evelyn Cannon. My attorney, David Love, is at my side as he has been so many times. I had taken two Valium and had two drinks this morning to settle me down. I was extremely nervous and was fearful of going back to jail for the original three and a half years. I was very wrong to drink. This not only fogged my mind but the mixture put me on the defensive against Judge Cannon. It was obvious. Mr. Love was extremely upset with me. I was hindering my chances of remaining free and hindering his ability to keep me free. It was a personal affront to him and I fully understand that, NOW. He usually wins his cases. I was causing him to fail and *fail* was not in David Love's vocabulary.

Mr. Love spoke to Judge Cannon. I don't recall the conversation. But I did hear her say, "I told him to stay out of trouble, and getting locked up is trouble, guilty or not!" Suddenly it was my turn to speak and explain to the judge about the charges at my apartment. I stuttered, repeated myself, and slurred my words. It was at this point where I couldn't talk properly that I realized that I had made a fatal mistake by medicating myself. As soon as I finished slurring, Judge Cannon said, "One year, Division of Correction!" I was in a stupor. A court officer immediately cuffed me and the cuffs were extremely tight. I yelled at him to loosen the cuffs, he pulled harder. "They're too tight asshole!" I yelled. "Shut up!" The officer replied back. I was screaming at Judge Cannon. "Can I speak judge?" "No, get him out of here!" She ordered in her arrogant loud voice. "This is bullshit judge!" I yelled again. "Fuck Yoouuu!"

The officer used my body to push the courtroom doors open. I was slammed against the wall. "Fuck you asshole, you don't have to do this!" I yelled. I then flung the officer against the wall and held him there with my body. He was nervous and shaking. "I said loudly, "You better call for help punk!" "I need a back up third floor Judge Cannon's room!" He pleaded on his radio. "You better call for two, shithead!" I said. I suddenly realized that this officer was extremely scared and was shaking uncontrollably. I realized what I was doing was very wrong and it was not like me to act in this manner with an officer. This was very wrong.

I immediately let the officer off of the wall and told him that I would stop if he did. His body became much less tense, as did mine. I stood side by side with him and told him it was okay and he could call off the back up. "It's okay now officer, it's okay." I said. "Call off the back up!" The officer said over the radio. He called off the responding officers. I said quietly, "I'm sorry officer, I know better." I felt bad about my actions. I was ashamed. I did all the wrong things that day.

I was rushed down the hallway by two officers and down the stairs to the back of the courthouse and taken away in a van immediately. An hour later I was placed alone in a holding cell at Central Booking and Intake. Section Five, Segregation Unit. Usually former police officers are placed in segregation. I was no exception. Segregation meant just that. I would sit in a cell alone for twenty-three hours a day with absolutely nothing to do. I was in that cell for nine days.

I found out a few days later from a guard that knew me that not only was I in segregation because of my former employment I was also on suicide watch due to the incident in 1996 and after spending five days in the Psychiatric Ward in 1997. The guard asked me if I was suicidal. I told him no that I was fine, just depressed. I was let out of my cell for one hour to shower and to make phone calls. My wife worked during the hours I was let out and my children were in school. I was unable to talk to them. I was lonely without them. I did however call my mother and brothers when they were at home. That was a relief.

I wore an orange jump suit. I had no idea what time of day it was unless I looked out my five-inch by five-inch window that faced west and overlooked Interstate 83, The Jones Falls Expressway. A large amount of cars in the morning coming south meant it was approximately 8:30 or 9:00 a.m., a large amount of cars headed north away from the city meant 4:30 or 5:00 p.m. I was so bored and lonely. *What had I done to myself again? When was I going to settle down and learn to do the right things and act properly?* I talked aloud in my cell.

My cell was a ten-foot by ten-foot room with block walls and a steel door, no bars. The door had a small slot in the middle for food trays to be slipped thru. I looked forward to meals because I was very hungry and I knew another mealtime had passed and time was passing, but passing so very slowly. I guess that's why people are sentenced to jail, to reflect and to appreciate freedom. I did reflect and I wanted desperately to be home and free. This was nothing like Federal Prison in Texas. I had no movement and no one to associate with, just me.

I had nothing to do but time. After three days I was able to get writing paper and a pen from a guard that liked and knew me. I studied my cell and surroundings. There was restaurant style butter pads stuck to the ceiling. There were one hundred and seven butter pad squares. I counted three times to pass time. The name, "MOC," is spelled out in pads. "MOC 4 ever." Is written in pencil all around the cell in the middle of the blocks. There is an excellent drawing of a thin rabbit carrying a bank bag with $ signs on the bag. The rabbit is running from a bulldog dressed as a cop. The cop has his nightstick in his hand and the name, "Ruckus," written on his left bicep. A drawing of a small bank, labeled, BANK, is in the background. The caption reads, "You can't catch me muvafucker!" The drawing is extremely detailed and professional.

Every concrete block that is at eye level has writing on it, e.g., "I miss you mom, I'm sorry mom." "I'll be home soon." God is the way." "I'm outta here nigga, going to shine my .45 and roll my blunts." Hi-Hat Bar, Eager and Wolfe, my night out nigga." "Goodies, Montford and Oliver." "You caught me once pig, had to shot me, next time you die." "My niggers, Milton & Biddle." Every block had something on it there was no room for me to write. Besides, what would I write?

It was ironic and seemed to me strange; every street mentioned in that cell was located in the Eastern District. I knew these streets personally and up close. Now I was sitting in a jail cell reading about these streets. I wondered if I might have sent any of the cell writers to this cell?

There are eight other districts and I'm incarcerated in a cell with only street names that I walked and worked as a police officer. Milton and Biddle, Eager and Wolfe. Why these streets? Why this cell?

I prayed most of the days. I prayed to get help to clean up my act and to straighten out. I talked to myself quietly in my mind constantly. *One year is a long time. What of my business, my marriage, kids. Could I do this time? Am I man enough? Tough enough? Mentally strong enough? Could I do this? I have to. After all, I put myself here! No one else, me all by myself! How long will I be kept alone? When will I be set free? I have no answers, only questions. I'm so very sad. Dan, be strong. This is not the diaper room. You handled that! Just do it Danny.*

July 13, 2001. I'm eight days in this cell alone. The only highpoint of my eight days was watching a severe thunderstorm coming from the west and headed directly at my building. I watched the sky darken, the winds pick up, the driving rain, the lightning strikes, the thunder, and the raindrops sliding down my small window to the outside world. I was enthralled that I could hear the thunder and thrilled by the lightning. Never before in my life did a simple thunderstorm keep all my attention and place me in awe. Plus, it passed much time with excitement.

As I awoke this morning it dawned on me that eighteen years ago on this very day, July 13, 1983, I shot and killed Booker Lee Lancaster at 9:23 a.m. How strange. I would never have dreamed that eighteen years from that day, in the year 2001, I would be sitting in a jail cell, a disgraced ex-cop, nine bullet holes in my body from an attempted suicide, and have done two years and twelve days in a Federal Prison in Texas for banking violations. I could not have dreamed this scenario or nightmare. Here I am. Did you plan this Booker?

I am a broken man again. I have no fight in me. No self-respect, self-esteem, or any type of self. I am as I was in the DIAPER ROOM, only this time, warm. I eat very little though I am hungry. I'm nauseated, I'm constipated, light headed, scared, sad, and depressed. I believe I'm on suicide watch once again due to not eating. The guards must document my activities. I really don't care at this point. I also have not been given my anti-depressant drugs that were prescribed for me, and that I have been taking for four years. They must help. I do feel extremely depressed.

I am able to read, my favorite guard continually gives me the books he is reading at his lonely station. I wonder at times, is he incarcerated also? Is he just me, stuck in this building, only in a uniform? There is an excerpt in one of these books that I wrote down in hopes that it will make me stronger, for I am feeling sorry for myself. "Sympathy! You want sympathy? It's in the dictionary between *shit* and *syphilis*. If you stand by and do nothing this world will roll right over you. Stand tall, be a man. It's when times are bad that shapes the character of a man." I constantly read this paragraph, it helps, and I am weak and insecure both emotionally and mentally.

Maybe I'll hear something from someone tomorrow? Maybe I'll be moved? Eight days is a long time to be alone, sad, lonely, and to feel the way I do. God, will you help me once again? I weep quietly and in my pillow.

THE DIAPER ROOM

1996

I have attempted to write this chapter at least three times now. At one point, due to the experience of the diaper room, I stopped writing completely for months to put this chapter out of my mind, to forget it. The sheer intensity of this chapter and the plethora of emotions and feelings that this time in my life evokes are overwhelming to me. This singular fifteen-hour period in my life overshadows anything that I'll write in this book. My emotions are at an all time high, my eyes well up with tears attempting to put on paper, to share, what had occurred mentally, emotionally, psychiatrically, and physically to me in fifteen lonely debilitating hours.

God spared my life on the night of November 2, 1996, or should I say cheated me out of dying. He and the heroic efforts of one doctor and his medical staff at Hopkins Bayview Hospital, Dr. Mark Ott, pulled me back from the throes of death, not once, but two times. During that ten to twelve hour life saving surgery, I say that God, *spared*, my life, but maybe I mean *cheated*. Maybe all those entities combined, both spiritually and real, cheated me out of my wish and attempt to finish my life and end my depression.

They took away, and cheated me out of, keeping that unbelievably intense feeling of overwhelming peace and solitude, that warm inner peace that lifts all the burdens and pressures of living, by DYING. I had been shot at fifteen times by two Baltimore County police officers. Eight of the eleven bullets struck me. Five of the 9mm shots fired could have been fatal. This took place after a ten mile, high-speed chase, ending only after I crashed into a parked car and jumped out of the car I was driving. After my car could be driven no further I pulled my Glock 9mm automatic handgun out of my waistband and began waiving it in the air. As I expected, and, at that point in my life, wanted, I was shot out of fear. I knew that the police officers would view me as a threat and protect themselves. I had counted on it. After all, I was a former police officer, I was armed, suicidal, and I had fired shots earlier.

All the earmarks of an attempted suicide by someone who had mentally snapped. Two bullets destroyed my left leg, three hit me in the chest and three or four grazed me. I should have died on that street corner sprawled over the sidewalk. I was so intent on dying that a Baltimore City police officer that was a friend of mine had to handcuff me because I was kicking the paramedic away from me, yelling the entire time, "I want to die, let me die!" Paramedic, "Doc," Watson is the person that started all the cheating and stealing by saving my life and stabilizing me on that night on the sidewalk at the corner of Eaton St. and Gough St.

February 1997, The Baltimore City Police Department and State Attorney's Office contacted my attorney, the well known, and highly respected, Howard Cardin. These agencies were ready to arrest me for handgun violation and assault on several Baltimore County police officers. I was still in very bad physical shape after being shot and grazed by bullets nine times. I was on crutches and was waiting for my left femur to heal, a plate had been surgically screwed and attached to it in an attempt to piece it back together and make the leg functional once again.

The black talon round had shattered the bone in a blow out type of fracture. The bullet still remained in my leg with the x-rays showing several fragments of bone and bullet strewn about inside my leg. The largest piece of bullet resembled a small car fan blade. That's exactly how a black talon bullet is designed to perform. It strikes matter, expands, and sharp jagged edges rip and tear at other bone, tissue, and organs. They are extremely deadly. I still had a colostomy bag attached to the right side of my abdomen. The bag was definitely grotesque. Emotionally and physically, I was a mess, and it showed.

Howard Cardin advised these agencies against taking me into custody. He stipulated that if they took me into custody that they became responsible for my health and ultimately, for my life. They conceded and decided to wait until I was physically and emotionally stable before allowing me to turn myself in to authorities to satisfy their outstanding warrants.

April 1997, I was allowed to turn myself in at headquarters to satisfy the outstanding warrants. I arrived at 8:30 a.m. sharp. I was to meet a detective I had known for years. He would walk me thru all the booking procedures personally. This would expedite matters and at least make me feel comfortable. I wasn't sure what type of reception I would encounter. Fortunately he was understanding and compassionate.

A lot of officers that knew me realized I wasn't the same Danny Shanahan after killing Booker Lancaster and him dying in my arms, after the pressures of the trials, the political and racial aspects of the entire situation, and the bank robbery.

The detective placed me in his unmarked radio car and drove me to Central Booking and Intake. He didn't handcuff me out of respect and courtesy. He said it wasn't necessary and I was pleased. I hated being handcuffed; it is very degrading and humiliating to me.

The detective made certain that the correctional officers were aware that I was a former Baltimore Police Officer and that I should be handled properly and with respect. I felt so much more at ease and still had a small amount of self-respect and self-esteem left.

I was fingerprinted, photographed, and sent directly to the city jail psychiatric ward. I went directly to the prison psychiatrist. Before seeing the prison psychiatrist I was walked down a one hundred foot hallway to a room at the end. As I was being escorted down the hall, I passed a room that immediately caught my attention and caused my heart to skip a beat then speed up considerably.

Ten men, seven black and three white, walking around a small room that had steel grates and bars everywhere I looked. Nothing or no one was out of the correctional officer's view. An officer was assigned to watch the men in this room constantly. The officer could see the toilets, showers, and the entire room. There was no privacy in that room.

All ten men had absolutely nothing on except for and adult diaper, a Depends! Two men were standing on their, bolted to the floor beds, staring at the wall. The others were milling around. All were talking to themselves or yelling profanities. "My God!" I said softly. I had heard rumors of this room but never believe it existed. The DIAPER ROOM at the Baltimore City Jail psych. ward.

These men closely resembled caged animals. They paced, stared out blankly into space, were aloof, spaced out, and seemed not to be in touch with reality, or as my dad would say when myself or one of my brothers came home intoxicated, "on queer street!" All ten were most assuredly, on queer street, most certainly not in contact with the real world.

What am I doing here? My suicide attempt was over five months ago. I was receiving counseling, was on anti-depressant drugs, Buspar and Paxil. I was okay! I thought. *I had no need for a FUCKING DIAPER! These ten poor bastards were on 24/7 suicide watch, a current suicide threat or attempt, not an attempt that took place five months ago!* I thought angrily.

I was not going in that room, and I definitely was not putting on this white plastic, cloth and Velcro waisted, fucked up diaper! NO FUCKING WAY! I screamed in my head. It resonated loudly all about my brain, cranium. *NO FUCKING*

WAY! I was scared and somewhat petrified. I had a knot in my stomach that would not go away and I felt sick.

"I'm Doctor Tom Kite." The voice said. I recognized the last name. "Any relation to Officer Kenny Kite?" I asked. "Yes Dan, He's my brother." I was immediately relieved. Kenny was a friend of mine. His brother wouldn't allow me to be placed in a diaper room. Doctor Kite liked me and right about now, I was in love with him! I took a deep breath and settled down a bit.

I was interviewed and asked several pointed questions about my suicide attempt and my present state of mind and mindset. I felt I did well. After all, I was fine I had become emotionally stable over the last five months. The counseling by former Baltimore County officer Craig Kalman and a very efficient and caring counselor, Meadow Lark Washington, along with the medication I was taking, was helping tremendously. I had no desire to harm myself.

Dr. Kite and I talked, I was feeling relieved of my pending gloom in the diaper room and the situation seemed to ease somewhat. I was comfortable again and felt relatively safe and certain that no diapers were in my near future. Dr. Kite left his small office and returned fifteen minutes later. It seemed so long a period of time. Two guards accompanied him.

My face flushed, my stomach turned. "I'm sorry Dan, I have to place you in the *diaper room*" "Why?" I pleaded, "Why?" There was no macho tone in my voice, no manliness. "I can't take the chance Dan, what if something happened to you tonight while I'm home?" "I'll never forgive myself, neither would your family." "I must take this precaution Dan." "It's been over five months since my suicide attempt!" I said in a pleading tone. "I would be dead if I wanted to by now." "Sorry Dan, take him officers."

I was slowly and quietly led out of the office. I couldn't be angry, but I most certainly was mortified and petrified. *I did not belong with those animals, those sickos, my God!* I was walked down the hall to a small laundry room. I was given my diaper. "Take all your clothes off, give me your medal and your eyeglasses." The devil said. "Can I keep my Saint Michael medal, it's always protected me?" I said softly in a futile attempt to keep my precious medal given to me by my wife, JoAnne. I wanted to keep anything that would protect me from, that room, that cage, that HELL! "No." Came the reply. I was escorted directly across the hall and placed in a twenty-five foot long by ten-foot wide room alone.

Nothing was in the dark, dank, hole of gloom. Not even a toilet. "Dr Kite said you didn't have to be confined with the other *diapers*, you can be alone." The officer said. "What if I have to go to the bathroom?" I asked. "It's a diaper! Remember?" He said as the door slammed shut. A hole covered with dark tinted plexi-glass approximately four inches by four inches was all I had to look thru. It really made no difference I couldn't see anything thru it anyway. There were no windows anywhere. *I'm supposed to shit and piss myself!* I thought in desperation. "No way! I'll burst before I wallow in excrement like a fucking infant, like a fucking animal!" I said aloud.

I was given no blanket, no pillow, no sheet, nothing. However, I did find a threefoot wide, four foot long, by one inch thick, piece of worn out black foam rubber, once my eyes adjusted to the darkness at 5:00 in the afternoon! Also I found a second piece of one-inch thick foam rubber in another corner that measured two foot by two foot. The foam pieces were thin on the edges, had chunks missing, and small holes, it was quite evident that they had been used over and over again; they were worn out pieces of nothing. *What the hell are these for?* I thought. *My bed! That's my bed! Holy Shit!*

I sat on top of both pieces of foam with my heels up to my butt. I rested my chin on my knees. I slowly sank into depression, it seemed like a depression that I had never before experienced. I had no eyeglasses, therefore no clarity of vision, no St. Michael, and no clothes. Just a dark, dingy, blurred, tomb to lie in, to me it resembled a tomb. I began to sink into my thoughts; nothing could pull me out of this severe state. I wept.

After being involved in two street shootings, and shooting a man with him dying in my arms while his eyes were fixed on mine, after the Grand Jury indicted me for murder, after losing a career as a police officer that I loved, the two lengthy trials, two years and twelve days spent in a Federal Prison in Texas, hundreds of miles from my loved ones, especially my beautiful two year old daughter, Jacquelyn, after my divorce from her mother whom I still loved, after marrying JoAnne who lost her job as a police officer because of me, after only three months out of prison because she was pregnant, after my father's death and my grandmother's death the very next day, after bankrupting my seven year old business, after surviving a personal financial fall, after leaving my wife three times prior to the night I got shot eight times in an attempted suicide, because she told me she was taking my kids out of state and away from me, after surviving that shooting and nearly losing my leg, after surviving two other attempted suicides, after having a colostomy bag for months to have it reversed and dealing with the severe abdominal pain associated with the reversal, after two extremely depressing and physically taxing weeks recuperating in a rehab in West Virginia no where near my family or proper physical care to nurse the three gaping holes in my chest from being shot, after all that and countless other horrible things that had happened to me since I became a police officer in 1973 that I can't recall, nothing, NOTHING, I had experienced and that had caused me to become hardened and callused over my police career, could touch the difficult time I was having trying to cope with wearing one single article of clothing in this darkened, cold, dismal, room, *a plastic diaper!*

I could sit up no longer, I felt as though I had no backbone, no spine. I felt like a blob of jello. It was so cold in there. They kept it at a very low temperature so that a patient was so preoccupied with being cold he wouldn't think of entertaining suicidal thoughts. It was working. I was curled up tight in the fetal position on the larger piece of foam. I tried to bring my body as tight together as possible so as to get warm. The dark block walls were exceptionally cold.

The smaller piece of foam wouldn't stay atop me to hold in any warmth, to small. I put half of it against the wall to insulate my naked bare back from the cold, and tried to wrap the other half over my curled up body to get some type of warmth. My efforts were fruitless. I couldn't get warm.

I lay there and prayed. *Dear Lord, why would you allow me to get past and survive all those times of suffering and also allow me to survive all those bullets and live, to let me lie here like a baby animal that cannot get warm? Why would you let me suffer like this? Haven't I suffered enough? You know Lord I never once complained to anyone, not even to you thru all the pain and agony. Being shot so many times and having to deal with the pain of a steel plate and screws being placed*

in my leg, as well as dealing with that colostomy bag, that shitbag, and the pain

associated with it along with the humiliation and embarrassment. Why are you

doing this to me? I see no sense in it. Why would you put me in HERE, to suffer

in a diaper, in shame, when you could have just let me die that night? I know it's

said that you do things to us for a reason, but what possible reason do you have for

doing this horrible thing to me?

No Answer, I never would receive an answer this day. *Why couldn't I have*

died? I was so cold! I got up and knocked on the small plexi-glass window,

I was shivering. After five minutes a nurse came to the door. "Please can I

have a blanket?" I asked. "I can't do that." She said. "Can I have a sheet or

even a news paper anything, please?" I was begging. I felt no shame at this

point, no self-respect or self-esteem whatsoever.

The nurse must have seen the desperation and anxiety in my eyes and

the sadness on my face. She bought me back a thin blue plastic medical

shirt. It wasn't going to keep me warm but I wanted anything. I thanked

her profusely. I quickly slithered to my corner, my dark corner of one-inch

foam, desolation and misery. The plastic surgical shirt did nothing, it was

so thin it immediately ripped into little strips. "JESUS CHRIST! FUUUUCK

THIIISSS!" I yelled at the top of my lungs. It was a scream of release and

resignation. The door suddenly opened and a male guard came in and said,

"I'm sorry, you can't have that plastic." He took it from me. He had to pull

it out of my cold hands. The door closed. I sunk into my small piece of

foam. I sobbed, I shivered and quivered. I was defeated, humbled, beaten,

felt hopeless and helpless. What a difference from being the sharp dressed, respected, confident, somewhat cocky, Officer Daniel J. Shanahan, motorcycle officer. I thought in anguish.

For another fourteen hours of seeming eternity I laid in that room freezing, whimpering, and begging *God to let me go to sleep, or let me go to sleep and never wake up.* I lay there wide-awake, unable to sleep. I was staring at the floor in a mental state of suicidal depression. It was like remembering what had occurred on the night I was shot, I was once again experiencing this blow with full blunt force with all my senses. Nothing could numb the ever so sensitive thoughts and feelings that this one room and one piece of clothing were so cruelly and relentlessly doling out to this broken man, this piece of flesh and bones curled up in the fetal position on the floor.

I had no sense of being. I was just a blob of shit, sniveling and sobbing in a cold lonely, dismal, dark, *Diaper Room.* An evil diaper room that was consuming me. Totally and completely consuming any good *positive* thoughts or feelings I had nurtured and established throughout my lifetime. No good thoughts could pull me out of this hell at this point. I lay there motionless, thoughtless, mindless, only shivering at short intervals. I kept repeating to myself, *I want my mom, where are you mom? I need you NOW mom.* I stopped praying

I stayed in this room from 5:00 p.m. until 8:00 a.m. the next day. Those fifteen hours temporarily broke me down as a man. It took every fiber of my being to mentally survive that room. Physically it was taxing due to the coldness and sleeping accommodations but that passed ten minutes after I had my clothes on, however, mentally, emotionally, and psychologically I struggled. This will not fade from my memory, Its been five years since this occurred and I can remember those fifteen hours so clearly and vividly that I wrote this chapter with no reserve and much clarity. This experience has made an indelible mark in my mind.

There is no diaper room anymore at the Baltimore city jail. It's called something else now. The patients wear thin blue shortened clothing. No one believed this story, they didn't believe me at first either as I was telling them about this room. But, as I told of the degradation I experienced it became obvious that I could never make up a story such as this one I was sharing; they believed. The magnitude of loneliness and sadness is difficult to explain. I think that the small tears that come to my eyes as I speak of the diaper room, just like the tears that are slowly rolling down my cheeks at this moment and dropping onto the keyboard are a convincing sight. I seldom speak of this experience, it devastates me.

The next day the guards came for me. I was given back my eyeglasses, sweat pants and shirt, as well as my tennis shoes. I was elated to have my clothes back. I put my, Michael The Archangel, medal, back around my neck. I slowly warmed, both inside and out. As the guard stood by watching I slowly pulled off my diaper and placed it in the sealed trash container.

It was over, my fifteen-hour diaper was *dry*, not soiled or stained. The only parts of me that were soiled, stained, dirtied, or damp, were my *memory and my heart*. I was taken to the Baltimore City Psychiatric Ward, upper level holding cell. The, NUT WARD, as it's referred to. I was happy and relieved to be free of both the *diaper* and the *room*.

Psychos, Murderers, Rapists, and ME

What do the Baltimore City Jail Psychiatric Ward, Joe Metheney, accused serial murderer, Bob, from Hopkins Hospital, also a murderer, Spookie, a serial rapist, and a former police officer, ME, have in common? *Absolutely Nothing!* However, the city jail, powers to be, decided that the former police officer, ME, would be better off being held in this ward with these people when I turned myself in to the jail, and after surviving the, *diaper room, which is located there.*

I was placed in this ward thirty minutes after I came out of the diaper room. I felt ecstatic! I had survived that horrible unspeakable night of terror and fear. I had no idea what situation I was about to be placed into. But I had on real clothes and I was warm!

Joe Metheney was an accused serial murderer. Joe was a big man, six foot six inches tall, weighing two hundred eighty pounds, lots of tattoos and a baldhead. He looked intimidating. Metheney had murdered four prostitutes and buried their bodies in and around a vacant pallet factory that he worked at located in South Baltimore. Metheney lived in a small trailer located on the factory premises.

Joe explained to me that he never would have gotten caught if he had of taken his time to bury his fourth and final victim. He killed for the drugs. Evidently he was so engrossed and anxious with getting money for his drug habit that he had no interest at all in any type of sexual gratification. He needed drug money. "The last whore had only $3.75 on her." Joe explained.

I killed her. He went on to say that he was so interested in getting his drugs and getting them as soon as possible that he half assed and haphazardly buried his last victim. He didn't spend the time to bury her deep enough.

The shallow grave was quickly and easily discovered. Once Joe came down off his drug high and was questioned and interrogated he confessed and showed the homicide detectives where the remaining three bodies were buried.

Contrary to the crimes he committed, Joe was a quiet, gentle, humorous individual. He seemed nothing like a serial murderer to me. However, I had never been in company of a serial murderer. Actually, not more than four hours after I was placed in the psych. ward, all thirty or so inmates in there with me knew I was a former police officer. This was not good, not good at all! I could feel the tension level rising, especially when the tier was locked down but not the individual cells. Everyone could walk around the entire tier; we weren't locked in our own individual cells.

Policy dictated one man per cell. I guess two crazies in one cell aren't feasible. We came out of our cells for afternoon open cell time; Metheney walked up to me, placed his hand on my shoulder and addressed the thirty or so psychiatric criminals and inmates.

Joe was both feared and respected by the other inmates. Mostly due to his size, demeanor, huge presence, and the fact that his crimes were the most newsworthy, famous and heinous. Also, Joe had nothing to lose. He had committed four murders and was never to be set free. I feared Joe Metheney. There I stood with nine bullet holes in me, no strength, fifty pounds lighter than my pre-shooting weight, presently nursing the reversal of my colostomy and most definitely petrified, standing next to a notorious, violent, mass murderer. I was scared shitless.

I most definitely could not have protected myself. Whether I have never been intimidated, nor let *anyone* intimidate me, is or was irrelevant. I was in no shape mentally or physically to defend or protect myself. Joe Yelled. "SHUT UP!" They did. "This is Danny he is MY friend and no one is to fuck with him!" "He was a cop, but the cops shot the shit out of my friend, no one fuck's with him!" I felt a little better but then I wondered what Joe wanted in return. After all, he would never see freedom again. Both he and I were well aware of that fact.

Joe looked at me and said in his quiet voice, "there you are officer, no problem. Let's get some tea Dan." Joe must have noticed my sigh of relief and the change in my facial expression from fear to relief. He said, "Lighten up Dan." At that moment I knew I would survive this horrible ordeal safely. *After all*, I had *a serial murderer* looking out for me!

I was a hero and popular after that, all the inmates wanted to see my bullet holes and scars. They were extremely impressed. The days that followed I was treated like a king and I will not, and dare not say, I felt at home, for I didn't. But mass murderer, Joe Metheney, was kind to me and showed me respect. I was fortunate.

The next five days I had no contact with my family, I wasn't allowed to write or call. My family knew I was in the city jail but had no idea I was in the psychiatric ward. The jail officials told my family they had no idea where I was. It wasn't until I made bail that I was able to talk to or see my family. I was very upset and needed my family. I wasn't where I belonged.

While in the so-called, "nut ward," Joe showed me how to melt styrofoam cups to make black ink to be used in jail tattooing. How to place two pieces of lead from a lead pencil into each opening of an electrical socket and how to bridge those two pieces with a third piece of pencil lead that was protruding from a shaved wooden pencil causing a large short or spark. This large spark was utilized to ignite a small piece of toilet paper that was fluffed and flowered so it immediately caught fire giving us a light for our contraband cigarettes.

He also showed me how to roll toilet paper into the shape of a fat tire, igniting the sides and then placing a tin cup into the center of the rolled toilet paper which burned ever so slowly due to the tightness of the rolled paper, which heated the contents of the tin cup or can. I also was taught how to make a *stinger* to heat water for coffee or tea. Cut an electrical cord; pull it apart so you have two separate ends. Place the ends into a cup of cold water and plug in the cord, instant hot water.

I learned something all five days of captivity in the ward. Joe taught me how to sharpen the point of a Bic pen to a needle sharp honed tip and how to use this, coupled with a small HO racing car motor, and lots of rubber bands to pull the tip back quickly, immediately after the small motor forced the tip forward mimicking a tattoo like device. Dip that tip into the black ink from the melted Styrofoam cup, touch the small motor wires to the ends of an AA battery and you have a tattooing gun. I was enthralled, extremely interested and amazed. *Every police officer should go to school and learn the ways of the street!* I thought. *Naah, guess that wouldn't happen, not in my lifetime.*

Joe and I talked at length many times. Every time we were allowed out of our cells Joe or I visited each other. He is a sensitive and caring individual; drugs transformed him into the murdering monster that he had temporarily become. Joe explained to me that he hated what he had done to those four prostitutes. He shared with me that his sister was the sweetest, nicest, most caring person he had ever known. She was a Girl Scout mom. She baked cookies and performed community service out of the goodness of her heart. Conversely, Joe hated and despised himself for his actions and atrocities.

Joe went on to explain that on three separate occasions he had attempted to take his life, commit suicide. He explained that on the first attempt he threw a rope over a large tree limb, fashioned a noose, stood on a trashcan and then kicked the can out from under his own feet. He said, "The fucking trash can hit the ground, the limb creaked, cracked, then broke hitting me right on the fucking head. Shit Dan I had a headache for three days! But I didn't die!"

The second attempt at his life Joe got one of his syringes and fired up a large quantity of Clorox bleach into his veins. He waited to die but told me he only had a bad taste in his mouth for a day or so. He was so disappointed. I can't recall what Joe's third attempt was, but obviously, it didn't work either. Joe finished his story saying, "I'm such a fuck up that I can't even take my own fucking life Dan!"

The next day I awoke to the tier being loud and buzzing with activity. Once the large doses of Elavil that were given to the inmates the night before, wear off, they become like caged animals, wild. They bark, howl, screech, and scream for no apparent reason. It occurs at no particular time, it's sporadic.

The sights and sounds were scary and unnerving. Especially for me. But, at 6:00 p.m., when, "Meds," is called all the inmates rush to the hospital desk on the second floor to receive their doses of Elavil. After fifteen minutes the entire ward becomes quiet and all the inmates settle down for the evening like infants dozing slowly off to sleep after a warm bottle of milk.

I asked, "Spookie," why was the tier so loud and buzzing with conversation. He explained to me that Joe had been taken to court for a bail review. "A bail review!" I shouted. "Yeah, a bail review for the fourth murder. Maybe they'll reduce his bail and let him out? RIGHT! We've been laughing about it all morning, Joe just left." I was astonished and confused. But, the law is the law. Maryland law requires that each inmate receive a bail hearing, a review of the charges to decide whether to drop, lower, or increase the bail set earlier by the court commissioner. Joe was no different, he could not be overlooked, and he had his rights, mass murderer or not.

Joe came back hours later. Everyone gathered around him. He was on television at noon and in the papers this April morning in 1997. He was, after all, a celebrity in this section of the jail, the nut ward. Joe settled in and went on to explain to his captive audience the proceedings that he had just gone thru. Joe Explained, "I got up before the judge and the States Attorney began to read the statement and particulars of the fourth murder. The judge looked right at me and asked me what I had to say. I looked back at her and said, "I hope your tits fall off bitch!" Joe then told us that the judge denied bail. REALLY! All of us laughed hysterically. I shook my head in bewilderment and went to my cell laughing. *My God!* I thought.

I haven't followed Joe's trials; I have no idea what happened to him. I do know that he was kind to me and kept me safe. He provided me with sanctuary and solace from the dreaded diaper room and from the thirty plus psychiatric criminals in the City Jail Psych. ward.

Bob was in the ward for murder also. Bob was a Hopkins Hospital fraternity socialite. His family was wealthy. Bob was well known and respected at the University. According to Bob, who also took a liking to me, his best friend, who was Asian, turned gay and approached Bob in a homosexual advance. Bob was repulsed which made his best friend extremely angry. They slowly became bitter enemies.

Bob was running for president of a fraternity at the University. His best friend, now turned enemy, began a smear campaign against Bob and also decided to run for president against Bob. Bob was infuriated. One night at a debate meeting, Bob left the meeting abruptly just before it ended. He traveled half way across the campus to his dorm room and retrieved a .38 caliber handgun that he had been hiding. He then proceeded back to the meeting hall.

Bob entered the room and slowly walked up to the podium where his ex-best friend was talking and deliberately shot him in the head, point blank, directly in front of a room full of students. Bob explained to me that his, now dead friend's, parents were very good friends with Bob's parents. They did not believe that their son was gay, denied all the other accusations and wanted Bob to die for killing their son.

Bob and I ate our meals together often. I was bewildered and perplexed by his eating habits. We had been given turkey, gravy, mashed potatoes and corn for dinner. I sat down next to Bob. He was slowly and methodically rearranging his food. He moved the potatoes away from the corn and the turkey away from the stuffing and that away from the corn also. He wanted no food item to touch the other food items on his plate. He was totally engrossed with this procedure that was performed immediately upon sitting down to eat. Bob would not look up or speak. He was in a trance-like state.

The total attention to his plate and his total lack of interest in my presence made it much easier to observe his behavior. Bob would, after meticulously separating his foods, arrange them in neat piles. Then he would begin to eat. He ate ever so slowly and deliberately. It was if he was counting the amount of chews, then swallow before eating another bite so as not to mix the foods in his mouth either. I dared not ask him if was counting his chews.

Bob systematically and intentionally placed one spoon of corn in his mouth. As he was slowly chewing he would carefully gather any stray corn that may have been misplaced from its neat little pile and replace them where they belonged in their original spot. The mashed potatoes were expertly formed in a neat little square. After removing a section of potatoes from the square mound he would repair that portion that he had removed to eat, and once again heap the potatoes in a neat square, minus 1 spoonful. Bob ate his entire meal, and every meal, in this fashion, never letting one food touch another, never letting the foods mix in his mouth, and he would gage the exact amount of liquid to drink during his meal so when finished eating all of his food he had exactly one sip of drink left to cleanse his palate.

I found myself eating very slowly counting my chews and intently studying my plate of food. I was becoming Bob at the dinner table. I stopped eating with Bob. I was, after all, the only individual in that spaced out, weird place, that was sane, or so I thought.

Spookie was the serial rapist. And he was just that! Spookie! He wouldn't tell us how he came to be known as Spookie, and I wasn't sure I wanted to know. He did all the jail tattooing. He and Joe Metheney were always together. Spookie did all of Joe's tattoos. I would sit for hours and watch the procedure, watch in awe, amazement, and intently. It was an art, especially with a hand made tattoo device. Spookie was a jail tattoo artist. That's how he made extra money or had extra food items in his cell.

Spookie had many tattoos covering his body. Including two tear drops tattooed under the outer corner of his left eye. Spookie was involved with several motorcycle gangs. A teardrop under the eye signifies the amount of people one killed. Spookie had two. I honestly believe he had taken two lives. I didn't talk to him that often, I was *spooked*. He never spoke of his crimes; everyone else did it for him. I have no idea as to the particulars of his serial rape charges; I really didn't want to know of his criminal activities.

After five days my family bailed me out. Actually, the bail was posted on the very first day I was there. The jail personnel told my family that they could not find me, that they had no clue as to where I was being held. RIGHT! I guess not, I was, after all, not in this world, or so I thought, not in a real life setting. I was in an abyss. It's no wonder I was not to be found, I was being confined with inmates that the jail wanted and desired to lose track of.

Once home I threw my clothes away and took a long *hot* shower. A bath wouldn't have accomplished the thorough cleansing I wanted and needed, for my body, soul, and mind. I then shaved. I was attempting to wash off the entire ordeal and experience. Especially the fifteen hours in, "The Room!" I finally felt normal and clean after the second day of showering. The ordeal, however, will never be completely cleansed from my mind and memory, NEVER!

THE MARYLAND
PENITENTIARY

JULY 14, 2001

J uly 14, 2001, a guard awakened me at 4:00 a.m. He had been instructed to escort me to DOC, or Department of Correction. The past nine days I was in a holding cell at Central Booking and Intake, which is evidently different. I was handcuffed in the back and taken down several floors to a dark, dank, smelly, basement. It felt wonderful to be let out of my cage and to actually walk more than ten feet. As I sat in my plastic chair a small mouse ran past me and not long after a roach approximately one and a half inches long scurried past my foot. I worried that this is where I would spend the next year. *My God! How could I survive this? Mice and roaches! Jesus! There must be rats too!* I was in a room with a television. This was the first news or information I had received about the outside world in nine days. I had no idea what current events had taken place in over a week. It was nice to hear what was happening around me.

I was then taken to a small holding room where I was re-handcuffed in front but with a gadget that holds the cuffs at an angle so that your hands are about three inches apart with the right hand on top, left hand on bottom, with palms up facing each other. Next a six-foot length of thick chain was placed around my waist then threaded thru a small opening in the piece of hardware separating my hands. The chain was cinched tight then leg shackles were placed around both ankles. There was absolutely no way I could reach my face or knees and definitely no way someone bound in this fashion could attack a guard or another person. I was amazed and at the same time thinking how I came to be in this situation and position. I knew, but didn't want to face my own thoughts. I watched television.

My thoughts drifted from the television and I began to think of the black man on E. Eager St. that I had so severely cuffed and inflicted so much pain on. Payback? I'm not certain. I was placed into a step van and driven out of the overhead door that separated Central Booking from the street and from the cell I had occupied for the last nine days. We turned left out of the gates and drove one block. I was assisted out of the van and taken thru a green fenced door. As I passed thru this door I saw it!

My eyes were wide open, my face was expressionless, or I'm not certain, I must have had a look of total fear and that of being stunned. I entered the yard of the Maryland Penitentiary. I was at a loss for words or feelings. I was completely in awe and speechless. My heart most clearly seemed to stop. I gasped and not only was taken aback, I stepped back. I stopped walking, as did the fifteen inmates walking with me. It was as if we were one unit or person experiencing the same picture. None of us had been in the Maryland Pen in our lives. It seemed as though we were breathless all at once. "Let's go!" The correctional officer, or, C.O. interrupted. "Let's walk!"

After all I've been thru, after the diaper room, both shootings, five days in the city jail Psyche Ward, after all I've seen and experienced, nothing could have prepared me for unbelievable and intimidating sight at which I was gazing, mouth wide open. The Maryland Penitentiary. The monstrous size of the walls made of six foot long by three foot wide black stones that were laid one hundred years ago, when the Maryland Pen was a train station

The yards and yards of coiled, shimmering, barbed wire and razor wire atop that. Forty-foot walls and forty-foot fences with very small chain link so that even a small finger couldn't fit so the fence couldn't be climbed. Seven courses of two foot in diameter barbed wire plus another row directly on top of that wire. Then, another fence twenty-five feet past the first one with more barbed and razor wire atop that fence. Black stone cell blocks adorned with large letters describing what block it was. "A BLOCK," "C BLOCK," "D BLOCK". The guard towers sitting twenty feet above each corner of fencing that surrounded the entire complex and reaching sixty feet above the ground. The C.O., (Correctional Officer), pacing slowly back and forth along the fifty feet or more tower walkway, with his pump shotgun cradled in a menacing display, across his chest waiting for a problem to arise.

The single tower at the far end of the yard approximately one hundred feet in the air that appeared identical or similar to the tower that Merlin lived in with his owl Arcamedes, in the Disney film, The Sword and the Stone. The hundreds of inmates, young and old, milling around, playing handball, volleyball, basketball, or lifting free weights in the sunshine. The entire view of the Maryland Pen from my standpoint resembled scenes from the famous films, The Shawshank Redemption and The Rock, minus the water. Two yards very large in width and approximately two football fields long with A, C, and D blocks situated at the far end of these yards, forming a block in itself.

B block was situated alone, for this was the segregation block utilized for inmates that couldn't get along with others or continuously fought with the jail guards. B block was a horrible place to be kept in. Twenty-four hours in your own cell for three days in a row. No books, only three meals, and no extra food from the commissary. One shower in three days, one phone call in three days.

The Maryland Pen not only had me captured, it had captured my imagination. It was completely surrounded by some type of building made of these huge blocks of black stone, metal roofing, pointed end caps, and a one hundred foot cupola. The buildings formed one large block.

The A, C, and D blocks were sitting at the opposite end of the yard where I was standing. I could hear the C.O. yell, "Shanahan, A block, 310!" My eyes slowly looked out to the A block building. As dark, dingy and frightening as anything I had ever seen. *I have to go into that building and also walk two hundred yards past and amongst all these criminals and convicts.* I thought. *Dear Lord, please help me thru this, one day! What is awaiting me? What have I done to myself this time? How will I endure this?* My mind was swirling with thoughts, horrible jail thoughts. I was completely and utterly terrified.

This cannot be happening to me again! I had an empty sick feeling in my stomach, I was lightheaded and wanted to puke. With the first look at this monstrosity I seemed to be scared straight. *Never again!* I swore to myself, never again.

I walked the entire length of the yard to the A block building. I walked up three flights of steel stairs that had the corners worn flat and smooth. The diamond plated steps had been worn down smoothly due to the hundreds and hundreds of inmates that had traveled up and down these steps over the years, planting their feet on the corners, turning to go up the next flight of stairs, and continuing on.

I found my cell, number 310. It was six feet wide and eight feet long, with one bunk bed. I had the top bunk. The new guy always gets the top bunk. I placed my bag of clothes that were issued to me, on my bed and put my issued toiletries, toothbrush, toothpaste that taste like sand, a comb made of rubber, a roll on deodorant that didn't work well, and a rubber pen that was nearly impossible to write with, it flexed to much, next to my clothes.

"Hi. I'm Toby." Said the voice. He was black. Toby was thirty-eight-years old and had been sentenced to one year also. He had struggled with a police officer and took the officer's gun from him. He pointed the gun at the officer's chest and stood there until other officers negotiated with him to drop the gun. The ordeal lasted for thirty minutes. Toby finally dropped the officer's gun and was arrested without incident. He seemed like a nice guy and was easy to get along with. I dare not tell him I was a former police officer. That is something that any officer knows. I most certainly was not going to reveal that information, especially being incarcerated amongst eighteen hundred black inmates with only two hundred white, plus the fact that I may have put some of them in there.

The cell was very confining. There was no room for two grown men to stand, so one of us had to be in our bunks at all times. We sat in our cells the majority of the time. The door to my cell is three feet wide and made of solid one inch thick steel bars approximately four fingers wide. When exiting my cell I can take only one step before I come face to face with another set of steel bars. That is the width of the walkway along my tier. There are fifty cells on tier three with two men per cell.

There was only one stainless steel toilet and one stainless sink. The sink does not have turn on and off handles, there is a spring button that must be pushed that allows water to flow for ten seconds then the water shuts off. Someone had pulled the front panel off of the sink and rigged a toothbrush handle to the inner workings so that once the handle was turned and set into place the water would run continuously. This allowed the water to get hot enough to shave with or to fill the toilet with hot water to clean my clothes.

There is a central laundry that picks up inmates soiled clothes once a week at 4:00 a.m. If you don't get up at that time your clothes stay dirty. The inmates run the laundry, so if a nice piece of clothing comes to the laundry it usually doesn't get returned to the inmate. I learned this early so I was able to keep most of my decent clothes. I was allowed two pairs of pants, four pair of underwear, four socks, four tee shirts, one pair of shoes, and one winter coat. I was in the steel and block jail from July to January. In the summer months it is so hot that I cannot sleep, the sweat rolls off my face and down my back as I lay in bed not moving. There is no airflow and the foul smells of nearly twelve hundred inmates permeates the air, the smell is putrid. Of those twelve hundred inmates I inadvertently discover that four hundred and sixty seven have aids and are in the general population, as am I.

My family and a few friends sent me money once a week. I saved three weeks for a small fan. When I finally received it I felt like it was a Christmas present that I had wanted all year when I was a small boy. I was extremely happy. One small fan pleases that much in a hot stinky jail. I had air movement.

In the winter months there are very few blankets. I applied for one and was told that I was issued a blanket upon entering the jail. I was not for it was July when I entered, no blankets were needed. It took me three weeks to finally get a blanket and that was from an inmate being released. The heat didn't work very well so I had to sleep in my jeans and coat from November to January 12th when I was released. It was so very cold; I pulled my head down into my coat so my ears would stay warm. That wasn't so bad, it muffled the constant yelling and screaming of the inmates that never ceased. The jail was noisy all the time.

When I first arrived and wasn't accustomed to the high level of noise and couldn't sleep, I put toilet paper in my ears to lessen the onslaught of aggravating noises and screaming to my eardrums. My head would pound all night. After seven days my mind must have learned to accommodate the noise and I could sleep without toilet paper stuffed deep in my ears. The mind is wondrous, it adapts to any type of situation. Being alone for nine days, the diaper room, this jail, and other unfamiliar and frightening situations I found myself in over the bad years.

Since I learned not to send my clothes to the laundry I was taught how to take care of my own laundry. I shut the water off to the toilet and flushed. This left an empty bowl. I would use Comet cleanser to clean the bowl that myself and my cellmate had shit and pissed in all week. Then I would flush that out. After emptying the bowl a second time I would utilize the gadget that enabled us to get a continuous flow of water.

After a minute or so, the water began to heat up. I used a borrowed bucket that was passed up and down the tier and used by other inmates to fill the bowl with hot water. Then I placed a small amount of laundry detergent purchased from the commissary into the bowl with my soiled clothes. I used my hands to rub the clothes together and wash them. After washing the water was lightly wrung out of the item and it was placed on the floor until I finished the remainder of the dirty laundry pile.

When done washing theses clothes, the toilet was once again flushed and the soapy water was gone. I then filled the toilet with cold water and placed half of my clothes into the clean clear water to rinse them. After rinsing I would place a corner of the clothing article on a hook located above the toilet and twist the water out of the clothes. Then I would remove the shoelaces from my tennis shoes and hang them from the cell door to the opposite wall to be used to dry my clothes as they hung across the cell. Newspaper was place on the floor to soak up any dripping water that fell from the drying clothes. Not only do I shit in front of a stranger, I clean my clothes where I shit. Lovely.

After twenty-four hours, all the clothes were dry and could be put away until next week. I was allowed one drawer to put my clothes into, just one. I washed clothes on Mondays and Toby washed clothes on Wednesdays. Two days a week hanging, drying toilet cleaned, clothes, cluttered an already cramped and confining cell. After my clothes were folded and put into my one drawer, I was able to replace my shoelaces and walk with a normal pair of shoes with laces.

We were allowed to go outside two times a day. I had to walk across the jail yard to eat three times a day. It didn't matter the weather, thunderstorm, heavy rain, snow, and extreme heat, whatever the weather we had to walk to eat. If you're hungry enough, which I usually was, you walk.

I would sit in my third floor tier cell and think. Am I a criminal? Am I as bad as these other inmates that are here for drugs, murder, robbery, rape, and other felonies? I only violated my probation. Do I belong amongst the waste of society? Is my behavior aberrant? Am I a threat to society as many of these inmates are? I continually question myself. Each time I end by thinking the same words. I fouled up. I put myself here. There may have been mitigating circumstances, but inevitably, I put myself in this jail cell. I hang my head in shame and disgust and feel bad. Eventually I upgrade my attitude and go on to another day. After all, time cannot be stopped and I will be free some day.

As I was thinking these lowly thoughts one day in August, I happened to look up from my bed, which is located on the third tier which is also at street level allowing me to see passersby and cars traveling east on Eager St. only to see my old partner Norman ride by in his radio car. I had told him where my cell was located and I heard him hit the siren two times as we had talked about. It was Norman! He was outside my cell approximately one hundred feet away in a radio car we used to share waving at me. I was excited, happy to see a familiar face, and at the same time embarrassed and ashamed that he had to see my in this shit jail. I immediately became depressed and sad as he left. I took a deep breath and exhaled. I subconsciously longed for the old days when I was a decorated and respected human being and police officer. Not the piece of whale shit that I was now becoming and most definitely was feeling like. I was devastated once again. *Does this never end?* I think. I feel numb to my surroundings.

The jail itself is just that, a jail made of steel bars and concrete blocks. There is nothing warm and fuzzy here. It is all, cold, hard, and uncaring. There are no rooms or doors, all steel bars. Bars, bars, and more bars. There are five floors or tiers of bars. That's one solid wall of steel, one inch in diameter, bars reaching sixty feet from the floor to ceiling. The outside wall of the penitentiary is located merely twenty-five feet from my cell and directly across from me. The walls are made of white painted cinder blocks. There are many windows from the third tier, street level, to the top of the ceiling. Most don't open and are dirty. From floor to ceiling the total height is over eighty feet, eighty feet of bars and blocks.

As you walk outside of my six foot by eight-foot cell there is a three-foot walkway that stops at that sixty feet of steel bars. I can look down at the floor where the first rows of cells are located, three floors underground. To my right on the floor is a small six-foot by four-foot guardroom. From that vantage point the guard can see all the cells in his block, A BLOCK. This area of floor is called the "Flats." From this point the guard can use his issued bullhorn to yell, "Feed Up!" That means it's time for a meal.

Everyone faces his or her cell bars to await the opening, which is done by pulling a switch located at the end of each tier. Only one tier at a time is emptied to alleviate fights and human backups. Everyone wants to eat, and eat now! Most run to the cafeteria to get in line first. I usually walked for I didn't care much to eat beans, beans, and more beans.

Beans and rice, beans and cornbread, beans and ham with two slices of bread with butter. Beans and, "mystery meat," for we knew not what it consisted of. It appeared to be bologna. Most inmates don't care, they eat anything put in front of them, I never ate the so-called meat.

I walk around the razor wire yards frequently and all I do is think. Many times on clear days the Baltimore Police helicopter flies over and hovers slowly. I can read the large letters on the underside of the chopper, "POLICE". My mental and emotional wounds open and the helicopter seems to pour salt out of the sky into those wounds. It burns and hurts terribly. I think of the days I flew in that helicopter, and the day my police officer girlfriend, now wife, JoAnne, who was a helicopter observer, flew alongside of me as I crossed the Russell street bridge on my police motorcycle, blowing kisses and waving at each other. I was so very happy and content then.

I sob in my mind as I walk with my head down and my shoulders drooping from my pain and hurt. This is jail. This is confinement. This is horrible!

One Month

I've been in the Maryland Pen for thirty days now. I'm sitting on my bunk writing about my experiences here. I'm writing what I'm living and experiencing at this moment in my life. I'm beginning to understand why I was extremely prejudiced towards blacks when I was a young police officer. The same feelings and racism I had back in the seventies and eighties are beginning to surface again, and again, I'm struggling with this ugly beast. This is beginning to resurface due to this incarceration. I am generalizing because I have a few black acquaintances, and my children have black friends that I like immensely. I encourage their socializing with their African American friends. Eighty percent of the inmates that I have everyday dealings with are black. Whites are definitely the minority in this shithole. This is reverse discrimination at its best.

Some blacks seem to take pleasure in making things difficult for me and the other whites incarcerated here, i.e., a black inmate that I asked about the proper procedure for picking up clothes sent in from home. His job was to call out inmate's names when their clothes arrived. He worked with the clothing officer that distributed clothes and worked that job for over six months. He was absolutely familiar with the procedure. He told me to go to the back of the line and to wait for my name to be called. I waited one hour for my name to be called. I knew my clothing was in the clothing room, I saw the box my wife sent to the jail for me with the name, "SHANAHAN," written in large letters on the sides. I would have continued to wait for another hour until the clothing room closed down but a white inmate realized that I was in line for over an hour and inquired as to what I was waiting for. I explained to him the situation.

He smiled at me and went on to tell me that I needed a pass from my cell block officer to be called, no pass, no name is called. This black inmate would have let me stand in the hot July sun for over two hours, knowing quite well that I needed a pass, knowing I did not have one, and that my name would not have been called at any point while I waited. Paybacks?

Another example is the black inmate that distributed the ice to inmates at 8:00 p.m. The ice given out was supposed to last the remainder of the evening while locked in our cells in the July heat with no air circulation until the next morning. Therefore, ice was a must and each inmate was desperate to have a cool drink due to the extreme heat and humidity. Each black inmate received two scoops of ice while every white inmate received only one scoop. I watched this occur and reoccur each night this past thirty days. Not one white complained, including myself. I was outnumbered and disliked. Paybacks?

A black inmate talks on the phone for his allotted twenty minutes, but goes over ten minutes or so knowing a white inmate has been waiting in line for those thirty minutes to make a much needed and wanted phone call home to loved ones. Instead of giving the phone to the white inmate that deserves, and has waited for it, the black inmate gives the phone to a black friend he waves to, that has been playing dominos for the past half an hour. These ignorant and selfish acts took place many times these past thirty days, and many times to me personally. Paybacks? If so, paybacks for what? Is this treatment towards white inmates just the opposite in the Hagerstown prison? Or the Jessup prison, which are mostly white? I think so.

I was eating dinner at the cafeteria one evening; there is no selective seating in the Maryland Pen, and inmates sit wherever the correctional officer dictates. This is done so one group of inmates cannot gather at one table or section. There were three blacks at my table that seated four. Two older black males began talking about white police officers and racial profiling and how the white cops only pulled over blacks. There had been a problem at that time with the Maryland State Police. The story was in the news. It was quite obvious to me that these two were attempting to incite me. I felt as though these two were ganging up on me. They took advantage of their numbers, three against one.

I had no recourse. I could say nothing to defend myself, or white police officers. I would have created a problem plus given away my past as a policeman. That would not be an intelligent move considering my present situation. Their prejudices were being voiced loudly, angrily and were pointed at me. I listened, fumed quietly and bit my tongue. I did not racial profile my car stops, however I did write only black motorists for two months when I discovered the black officer was only targeting whites. I never pulled a car over strictly due to the driver's race. I only stopped drivers that were breaking the traffic laws. These two black inmates had to voice their opinions of whites and white police officers in my presence fully aware I wouldn't say a word to defend myself, or the white officers. They had free reign to mouth off to this white boy without implications. Discretion IS the better part of valor

Prejudice is alive and well! Racism is rampant in this jail and in this city! I experienced it personally as a cop and as the inmate I am at present. Reverends Jesse Jackson or Al Sharpton, as well as other politicians and

Washington socialites, along with the bleeding heart liberals, want to paint a pretty picture that prejudice and racism is waning in America. They are quite wrong, mistaken. I'm adamant and vehement about this. They are looking thru rose-colored glasses. This ugly monster is all too prevalent, especially here in this jail. I am witnessing it first hand, which I feel gives me the right to speak out on this sore subject by writing about my feelings and emotions.

Would I feel this anger and disgust if this prison were made up of eighty percent white inmates? I don't know, I've not been in that situation and certainly am not now. Unfortunately, there is a constant unrelenting pressure between whites and blacks here. This pressure slithers and sneaks all around and hides in the crevices like the roaches here, but it is constantly present, like a fucking demon, the devil, Satan.

I was waiting to see my counselor not long after I was sent here. Fifteen blacks and two whites were crammed into a small room, twenty feet long by ten feet wide. I was one of the white boys. All the inmates were waiting to see the same counselor. The entire two hours I waited, not one black said a single word to me, nor I them. The black inmates talked loud and called each other nigger and boy, which made me extremely uncomfortable. I shut my mouth and ignored all of them.

After all the blacks had been seen or left the room, and the other one white inmate had gone, only myself and a black inmate remained. Mere minutes after the last black left this remaining black inmate began talking to me. Shit, we were best fucking friends, or so it seemed. However he had not uttered one word to me the past two hours! Why? Peer pressure, ignorance, and racism? Beats the shit out of me.

Several times now, in this short period of time, I've been pulled aside by a black inmate, usually when there are only a few blacks around or none at all. They ask me questions about *their* cases. They'll show me *their* court documents and ask me to read them and give them legal advice. I'm no lawyer. Maybe this white boy looks like one. I'm white, wear glasses, have short hair, and look somewhat intelligent, and carry myself with some semblance of confidence, or so I'm told. Out of politeness or kindness that my parents instilled in me, I spend my time talking to them when I don't really care to. I don't want to know their problems and concerns. I have my own. I miss my family also, for Chris sakes. But I listen intently and act interested.

The very next day I'll see this same black inmate, individual, with a few of his black buddies, and I'll say, "Hey man, how you doing? Or, Did you get a hold of your attorney like we talked about last night?" The latter question based on a previous conversation that this guy initiated the night before. I either get no answer or a back turned to my face. *Fuck them!* I think angrily. Now I act stupid and don't get involved. *Not my problem! Let someone else save the fucking world and be the nice guy! Racism and prejudices Dan, remember?* Alive and well, especially here!

When there are three or more black inmates in a group and I must be thrust into their company for one reason or another, always a cold reception follows. As most leave and one remains he finally decides to talk to me. *No thanks! Fuck you! Be yourself and be a leader! I* think with disgust. I'm generalizing once again. Now and then I have been tolerated and talked to. It's extremely obvious here that most of the black inmates have a seething hatred for white people. How did this happen? I did nothing personally to the blacks here. However, I am suffering the consequences. Guess that's why there are prejudices among the black ranks as well as the white. There's no headway being made here on the racial hatred front.

The first four inmates to walk into the commissary building today were all white. With this 80/20 percent split, it's very unusual for this to occur. All four of us woke up extra early and put our food list in before anyone else. Then we were first in line to retrieve our food items and goodies because we awoke at 400 a.m. The first words yelled, as we four walked into the building, were, "All white guys! Should have known! White muvafuckers!" In a cynical angry voice. *Fuck you asshole!* I thought. Being white had nothing to do with being the first four in line. *I'd like to piss on that asshole's head.* I thought. There is a blatant verbal attack on whites here. It's quite clear that the blacks here blame the, "white boy," as they so quickly and eagerly state, for *their* shortcomings.

My thoughts and emotions are becoming uncontrollable here. *I didn't put these blacks here! I didn't sell the cocaine or heroin! I didn't rob anyone at gunpoint! I didn't hold up the store! I'm just an inmate too! It's not my fucking fault you're black! It's not my fault you're here! Get fucking real! I'm sick of this shit! I'm sick of the racial tension and racial slurs!*

Just as Baltimore's first Black State's Attorney, Kurt Schmoke, the man that prosecuted me, said after my first mistrial in the Lancaster killing where the six whites found me not guilty and the six blacks found me guilty, "there is no racial split in this jury decision, there is no racial overtones in the Shanahan case." That's bullshit and he knew it, I'm certain he still does. Racism and prejudice are here to stay. I feel as though it will not end or cease in my lifetime, definitely not anytime soon. Each one of us should have to spend one day here, in this setting and in these surroundings as a "white boy," or as a black inmate at a mostly white jail, and you'll agree with my angry and irate words.

One individual has given me a breathe of fresh air in my hazy and murky thinking about the prejudices here. Ms. Henary, a *black* counselor, has caused a break in the racial barrier. She has provided me with a release, a pressure valve type of release. She has gone out of her way to assist me in being released from jail early with a home detention agreement. She has spent extra time on my case and has listened intently to my concerns. She has called the powers to be, personally, in an attempt to help me return to my family and to freedom. She is a professional and was able to give me a small amount of hope when I had nearly given up on the racial tensions here and caused myself serious injury. I am outnumbered. This welcome release from the racism doesn't last long. Unfortunately, in a matter of minutes after I leave Ms. Henary's office, my thoughts turn racist again and my dislike for these black inmates once again surfaces. Not fair, not just, not nice, simply unavoidable and inescapable.

60 Days

September 5, 2001. I've been incarcerated two months today, however it seems like six. The time goes by ever so slowly in jail, just as it did in Federal Prison in Texas. Those two years and twelve days, eighteen years ago, seemed an eternity to me. As I look back, it was merely a spit, in my lifetime of forty-six years. I've settled in and accepted the fact that I am in jail. It took this long for me to mentally acknowledge my surroundings and situation. I've adjusted and have a routine I follow each day. However, each day continues to be a struggle especially with the racial tensions that don't seem to cease, the tensions are a constant.

I stood out in the prison yard today. I was at the far end, the end farthest from the six hundred inmates out for exercise time. I let my gaze slowly sweep the entire yard. I wanted my eyes to take in all the sights. Men playing basketball, volleyball, cards, dominos, lifting free weights and simply loitering together. I studied the sandlot baseball diamond, which consisted of stone, dirt, and rocks with a few patches of grass scattered here and there. The forty-foot razor wire fences, the ancient black block buildings that are so very drab, dreary and depressing in appearance. I slowly took in all the sights of this hellhole in one slow, deliberate, gaze. I sit on the ground and write what I am seeing.

I wanted to savor and remember this picture, setting, before me at this very moment. I purposely wanted to make an indelible mark on my brain detailing my surroundings. I want to be able to recall the loneliness, sadness, tears, fears, uncertainty, prejudices, bad treatment, smells and sights. I want to remember what I've been thru here. To slowly suck on the unpleasant memories like a sour Life Saver candy. I don't ever want to experience this or anything similar to this again. This place has taken a very small piece of my heart and soul, that's all I will allow it to take from me. Pieces of these two entities will remain here when I leave. They will stay where they fell, at the entrance gate, the day I arrived in hell, the hell that has taken its toll on me.

As I look over this eye opening, inner strengthening sight, my focus and thoughts are abruptly interrupted by, "Foxtrot," the city police helicopter.

The same police helicopter that assisted me in capturing many suspects as a young police officer in the Eastern District. The same police helicopter that chased me the night I was shot in a police assisted suicide attempt. The helicopter that belongs to the Baltimore City Police Department, the same department that has enabled me to experience all that I have shared with the reader in this book.

Suddenly I feel, and wonder, yes I'm sure of it, I feel completely and totally disgraced as I see the letters, "POLICE," on the underside of the helicopter, the same letters that adorned my badge and shirt sleeve. I feel like the convicted felon that I am. I feel mentally, as I am physically; scarred, stitched up, shot, broken boned, torn and callused. I feel sadness for all I've lost, such as my career, both by my own actions or by those of others, both good and bad, such as Booker Lancaster, Kurt Schmoke, Billy Murphy, Jim White, Dennis Hill, and Judge Thomas Noel, and others that I most likely am not aware of. I feel utterly humiliated, degraded, and embarrassed, as I stand in this prison yard amongst thieves, murderers, and rapists. I feel sick, but somehow this, to me, all seems apropos.

Prison Etiquette

I was under the impression when I became imprisoned that the inmates would act civilly and like adult men attempting to pass time as easily and orderly as possible. I thought as though each inmate would attempt to get along with one another so as to pass the time with some type of order, or in an orderly fashion.

I was definitely mistaken. I began to see just how ignorant, selfish, rude and disgusting, inmates act. In the hotter months the odor of men not showering and not practicing personal hygiene is quite obvious. With two men living so closely together in such a confined area you learn very quickly who showers and who does not. The guards attempt to get everyone to shower but certain inmates walk into the showers then walk out while the guard is not looking. They actually sneak out so as not to shower. In heat that reaches in the upper ninety degrees with little air circulation these inmates begin to stink quickly.

There are lines in jail for everything that an inmate needs or wants. Meals, clothing, phones, and commissary are a few examples. We were able to go to the commissary once per week and only if you had money in your account. The commissary carries all the goodies that inmates crave. Chips, candies, ice cream, sodas, with much more including the most favorite, Little Debbie cookies and cakes. Men trade for Little Debbies. Two fudge round cookies can get a soda or a soap powder, four zebra cakes gets two bags of chips. There is constant bartering in jail. If you don't want it someone will trade for it. One cigarette cost one dollar or that equivalence in goods. Ice cream is like gold, especially in the hot months. Just as a dog will walk away and chew on a bone or piece of meat to be alone, inmates get their ice creams, sit in a quiet corner or in groups and eat their prize away from the other inmates so no one requests a taste.

The lines don't remain lines after long. Certain inmates will work their way up to the front of the line and stand next to the first or second inmate originally in line. When the door opens everyone rushes in pushing and shoving to get what each one wants. "Yeah me! Fuck you!" attitudes abound. No one wants to start a fight over this petty bullshit so the weaker inmates let the bullies thru without question. Since there were twenty two hundred blacks and only two hundred whites, I had to tread very carefully and be very cautious if I became aggravated or angry. I was constantly biting my tongue and was very careful not to aggravate a situation by mouthing-off. I was the minority. I was most definitely outnumbered and the large amount of blacks took advantage of the lesser number of whites.

If an inmate was third or fourth in a line and only blacks were ahead and behind the white inmate, the blacks did as they pleased. Just prior to the door being opened five or six blacks would step in front of the white guy. This was a game for the blacks. If a black was on the phone and a white was next in line, the black when finished his call would hand the phone to a buddy and tell the white that he was holding his place. The blacks would use more than the allotted twenty minutes. Sometimes I waited the entire forty minutes of our out time and still couldn't make a call.

No one dare whine or complain to a guard, too many blacks would seek revenge. "When in Rome, do as the Romans!" Was my philosophy anytime I was incarcerated. That is the code and secret to survival, especially in a mostly black jail when you're white. I was most definitely the minority or token white in the Maryland Pen. The prejudice against each other is very obvious.

A black can call another black, nigger, but if a white says that word, a fight is inevitable. I became sick of the word. Nigger, nigger, nigger, nigger, nigger, was all I heard nearly all day long. "Hey nigger, give this nigger a soda." This nigger's hot!" "You niggers aint beating this nigger in cards." "How long does a nigger have to wait in this line?" This niggers hungry, let's eat." "Give a nigger a break man, give me the ball." I was amazed at the frequent use of this ugly word. I couldn't understand how the blacks used it as a common name but if a white even whispered the word, a situation quickly arose.

I asked my black cell mate why this was such a common word among the blacks and why it was used so often. He and I had a good relationship. He was intelligent and also was street smart. He looked at me calmly, seemed to understand my question and said to me, "They are ignorant and have no education or pride in themselves. I'm sick of hearing it too Dan." I never heard Toby say nigger to another black. I believed him.

Prison is never quiet. It's always loud. There is a constant buzz and continual yelling and screaming amongst inmates. The fifth tier yelling down to the flats for a soda, the second tier yelling up to the fourth tier for a magazine. Mostly, there were just bullshit conversations going on, some inmate trying to prove his manliness by yelling louder or uttering more profanities than others. It was very annoying and disgusting and continued throughout the night into the early morning. I was forced to utilize toilet paper in my ears to keep the noise to a minimum so as to sleep until I was able to buy a set of headphones to quiet my surroundings.

Inmates ask for anything you may have in your unlocked drawer, such as commissary items but give nothing in return. Inmates are stingy and selfish. I had items stolen out of my cell while eating in the cafeteria. One inmate keeps lookout while another sneaks into the opened cells on that tier and takes whatever he wants. Batteries, soap, pens, chips, whatever the thief can steal without getting caught is taken. No one complains, you just steal from someone else, I did.

While eating if an inmate wants to offer another inmate some portion of his meal it cannot be touched by anyone except the receiver. The giver holds his tray out and the item is taken. The giver never touches the food offered. Usually there is a trade involved, i.e. pudding for green beans, or meat for beans, etc. No hands touch anyone's food, if you hand two pieces of bread to another inmate it won't be taken and words are exchanged, no hands are allowed. That's how terse words are exchanged and fights begin.

An inmate is not allowed to reach across or in front of another inmate to get or give food. The inmates must stand up and make the exchange. I nearly became involved in a fight because I reached over a black inmate. He was aware I was new and made a big deal out of my actions. I told him I wasn't, "up to date," with the rules and apologized. A white inmate settled the aggravated inmate down and all was fine. However, for the next six months that inmate and I never ate together and we, "eye fucked, or stared," at each other whenever we met or passed. An inmate doesn't go out of his way to give another inmate his goodies on his tray such as cake and cookies. If that happens it's a sign that he is your "Bitch," and you are giving him something special to acquire something special from him later.

The tray is left on the table in front of the inmate you want to give your excess food to and the receiving inmate takes the givers tray back to the kitchen, something for something. That keeps things even no one owes the other, nothing is insinuated.

When the cell doors are open and inmates have time to intermingle the trading is vigorous. This is the time to trade for items needed or wanted. There are a few rules of prison etiquette that must be observed on the open tiers. You don't walk the narrow tier with no socks or shoes on with you shirt tucked into your pants, this is a sign to the homosexuals that you are available. I made this mistake and was immediately called down by my prison etiquette savvy cellmate. He stopped me before I left my cell. I was fortunate. By no means does an inmate walk out of his cell with just a shirt and underpants on. This is a sure sign that you are someone's girl and want sex. If you dress like a girl you get treated like a girl, a girl wearing her man's shirt, therefore a faggot, available.

Turning the bottom of your pants up several inches, especially jeans, is also a sure sign of being gay, as is wearing shoes with no socks with the pant legs rolled up. Any feminine look, smell, or action is misconstrued to be a gay come on. A straight heterosexual inmate must be extremely careful not to act in any manner than that of a macho, strong, "take no shit" man, or problems could arise at night or in the showers.

Most inmates shower in their underpants. I wore my cut off sweats *and* underpants to make certain I wasn't sending *any* type of mixed signals. When I returned to my cell, I removed the excess water from the sweats and hung them on the bottom of my bed for the next adventure to the showers.

Two televisions are on constantly. Each is on a different channel and usually I was forced to watch basketball or black sitcoms. The Cosby show was a favorite of the black inmates. No one was allowed to touch the television or to change the channel unless a vote was taken. Usually there were approximately forty inmates in front of each set. Since thirty-three were black, all black shows were watched. After sometime there, I didn't care. I couldn't hear the show anyway. Unless I stood directly under the set and made certain I wasn't obstructing someone's view I couldn't hear the show. I tried to watch the actor's lips but that became old very quickly.

Eventually I would go back to my cell, climb into my top bunk and put my headphones on to escape the noise, profanities, yelling, and overall sounds of four hundred on edge, aggravated and, angry at life inmates. I spent most of my time in my bunk, which consisted of a one-inch thick mattress and no pillow. I used my bath towel wrapped up in one of my tee shirts as a pillow for my entire stay.

Happiness is relative in jail. So much is taken for granted when free. In jail, a simple pair of tennis shoes, a single magazine, a pair of sunglasses, an apple, a banana, cup of good coffee, you own shirts, pants, socks, and underwear are major treats. Getting to the phone first and getting in line to fill your cup with ice before the ice machine runs out and to get the ice to your cell before it melts makes for a happy, content, satisfying night. Real soap, toothpaste, and deodorant, from the outside world are special. State issued items such as these, either burn, don't work, or tastes horrible.

Outside of prison, happiness may be a steak dinner and six beers, or a new car, or five hundred dollars. Incarceration lowers the standards of what happiness and being content or satisfied entails. An extra cup of juice at a meal, an extra large piece of cake being placed on your food tray, or an extra pint of milk, or a new razor blade with real shaving cream rather than soap that doesn't lather, makes an inmate just as happy, satisfied and content. It's all-relative to your present situation and circumstances.

It's extremely difficult being held in a jail like this. I have so much time on my hands to think. After all that's what jail is about, time. Passing time, wasting time, or doing time, it's all the same. Any activity that can pass the time is a desired commodity in jail. I have so much time to think so I become depressed, lonely, sad, and angry at my present circumstances. I miss my family tremendously, that occurred as soon as the first day passed. When I laid my head on my makeshift tiny pillow the first night I immediately began thinking of my family, especially my three children. Time drags, an hour seems like a day, day like a week, and a week like a month. Nothing seems to pass the time quick enough except talking to my family, family visits, or sleeping.

I assume that's why it is prison, so no one in their right mind wants to come back and return to the stench, dirt, ignorance, heat, cold, bad meals, noise, blatant disregard for another persons property, feelings, wishes, or desires. I hope and pray to never again have to experience this personal hell that I have placed myself in.

I learned much while sitting in the Maryland Penitentiary, words, phrases, and proper prison etiquette. Below are a few terms that I had to learn to be able to communicate with other inmates and to, at times, fit in to survive.

He has sugar—diabetic

On the hammer—lock-up

Blister—faggot

Play splitsies on the crap game—50/50 on the cocaine

Chicken heads—women

Starfish—asshole

The bookins—Central Intake and Booking

On California time—not in touch with what is happening

Feed up—time to eat

C.O.—Correctional Officer

Cell buddy—cell mate

Uptown—home

Yo, main man—I don't know your name but I need something

Yo, muvafucker—Hi

My peeps—My people or family

Send me a kite—send me a letter

My dog—my friend/buddy

Father's Day—Pay day for State employees

Car wash—blow job

Sling shots—Tighty whitey underpants

Alligators in the shower—New guys afraid to get in the showers

Fee Fee—Sock with Vaseline in it/artificial pussy

Wick—toilet paper rolled up to make a match by shorting out light socket

Turtle doving—hugging and kissing

Feel me?—understand me?

Gump—fag

Hopper—young inmate that's restless

Put the Columbo on it—Look into it

P/C—protective custody

Kick the bobo—talk

Bit—amount of time to serve

Downtime—amount of time in jail this bit

You need a loaded gun in your mouth—brush your teeth/breath stinks

Skit skat—got to go

Hit me off—give me something

Hook me up—give me something

Hook up—tuna fish, noodles and other foods to make a late night meal

Kiyow—shower

Jingle—money

Streetside—outside the gate the streetside of jail

Yardside—outside gate-yard side of the jail

911

September 11, 2001. Today the United States was attacked! Three planes were hijacked and suicide missions were flown. Hundreds of people died at New York City's Twin Towers and hundreds more at the Pentagon in Washington D.C. The jail is in, "lock down," due to the attack. I'm sure it's precautionary. As I sit in my cell I strain my eyes, ears and neck to watch and hear the television set that is situated nearly out of my sight. I am sitting on my bunk writing again. Now I am hearing that a third plane crashed in Pennsylvania. There are no other details.

I feel personally devastated, my eyes well up with tears since I've learned of this horrific act. I hide my tears so other inmates don't see me. I have taken this personally. I'm not certain why? Maybe because I miss my family and want to protect them? I feel vulnerable.

Most of the inmates here could care less. They crack jokes about the attack, are loud, uncaring and insensitive. I'm extremely upset by this behavior. However, there is nothing I can do about these selfish, arrogant, and disgusting persons, criminals, animals. I'm beside myself today. What occurred in our nation today is almost unfathomable. The carnage is unbelievable. My thoughts turn to the police officers, the firefighters, and the hundreds of American citizens that were killed attempting to save lives. I've been there. They never thought of themselves, they ignored danger signs and dangerous situations. They gave the ultimate sacrifice in return, their lives. They are now victims, statistics, and heroes.

I will never forget this day or where I was when this atrocity against our country took place. I am sad. Sad that I have put myself in this place and sad to have to witness some of these people, monsters, make light of this horrible occurrence. I want to beat, punch, kick, disable, and injure them. I cannot. I won't get home to my family if I act on these emotions.

Are these individuals that ignorant to their surroundings, that uncaring and self centered that they act in this manner? Or, are they that selfish? Are they feeling that since it doesn't directly affect them that they don't have to, or want to care? I don't know. I'm baffled, angry, and perplexed. It's inconceivable to me that someone could act this nonchalant in the face of such devastation, death, loss, and anguish.

Watching the horror unfold on television miles from me is causing all my emotions to well up inside. I cannot cover up or conceal these emotions. My eyes are moist and I want to stay in my cell even though the lock down has ended. I hurt for the victims, I'm feeling overly patriotic and I'm certain that this cowardly act will be dealt with swiftly and with the wrath of God and this great country.

I am struggling with the heartless indifference these inmates are displaying. It's a travesty, it's saddening, it's cruel, it's uncalled for and it's adversely affecting me more than I want it to. I am imprisoned as is my heart and my feelings. My heart is heavy and feels like it is bleeding. I would like to get the morons here to see and feel as I do but I'm aware that this is futile. I cannot, I will not and I do not dare. I have emptiness inside me. I miss my children I need to hold and hug my family and my children. I need to protect them, I need them, and I need their love.

Kill the Cop

October 15, 2001 the Lieutenant of the Correctional Officers awakened me at 6:00 a.m. Evidently a threat had been made on my life, overnight. I was taken into the captain's office and questioned. "How long have you been being threatened Shanahan?" I explained, "approximately two weeks." "Why didn't you tell an officer?" I didn't think it was necessary." I said. "You're in a bad place Shanahan, this is very serious! We received a note last night that read, (we are going to kill the cop in cell A310). This is so serious that I'm taking you out of the general population and putting you into C BLOCK for administration purposes immediately!" He spoke seriously.

I went back to my cell, gathered my belongings, said goodbye to my cellmate who told me that this was the best thing to do to stay alive. I was out and gone in five minutes. I was then taken out of A BLOCK and escorted by two guards, not handcuffed to the darkest, dankest, oldest Block of cells in the penitentiary, C BLOCK. C BLOCK was off limits to every other inmate and housed the inmates that stabbed, killed, and injured other inmates, basically it housed the inmates that couldn't fit in, didn't listen to the guards, and were in fear of being injured and killed while in the general population. Inmates such as me!

For the past two weeks I had been constantly told by my cell mate that he had been told to warn me to, (watch my back). That three inmates on tier four, 1 tier above mine had been planning on killing me out in the yard while lifting weights or in the shower. I was definitely concerned but thought it only prison bravado. Obviously I was wrong. However I became much more concerned when I was lifting weights yesterday and a new inmate that took a liking to me said, "there's a cop in A310, he's got a problem." I said back to him as I looked behind me, "I'm the cop in A BLOCK310, but I wasn't a cop I was a security guard. He seemed to accept that explanation and said; "I told them they wouldn't put a real cop in here." *I told the officers I was a cop when I arrived here the first day, that's why I was in isolation and segregation for the first nine days! Then they put me into general population for three and a half months! I assumed it was okay. But, assumption is the mother of all fuck ups!* I thought. I left the weight area and sat in a corner with my back to a wall waiting, just in case.

Six times I've been stopped by inmates this past two weeks and asked if I was a cop on the Eastside. I said no each time and explained that I was a security guard. I thought this would suffice to keep them confused, uncertain. Three days ago I became somewhat unraveled when a black inmate asked if I was the cop that ran a black guy down with my car and killed him, on Harford Rd. I denied that also. Booker Lancaster immediately flashed in my mind. I've been more and more concerned for my safety this week. I was coming down the fifteen flights of stairs from the auditorium located up top floor and I noticed that there were no guards at any of the landings. This is highly unusual because fights and stabbings happen on these narrow unguarded steps. There were no guards, I was very nervous, not a guard in sight. Something wasn't right. I had an eerie feeling.

I put a request in to see my counselor two days ago to explain my fears and the situation. Now I don't have to go, the threats have taken priority over the counselor meeting. I'm sitting in C BLOCK, Regional Segregation Unit. I'm alone in a cell once again, as I was my first nine days here. However, this time I am allowed out for one hour once every seventy-two hours. I'm locked down, no yard to walk, weights to lift, volleyball to play, television to watch, no cellmate to talk to, nothing.

As I spoke to the lieutenant and captain this morning they were quite surprised that I have been in general population for three and a half months.

I was told that if something would have gone wrong and I would have gotten injured, "heads would have rolled." They fouled up. Evidently the guards were talking about me being a cop and a few inmates overheard their conversation. That's considered juicy news in a jail, certainly this one.

A part of me doesn't care at this time if I were to be killed, but my three children, my five brothers, and my mother's faces continually cross my mind. I should want to stay alive for them if not myself. The fleeting thought disappears. I do have a will to survive. I have to remain strong and keep my attitude in check. Maybe I'm feeling sorry for myself or it's my subconscious way of dealing with the fear of being killed and not being able to see my children and family ever again.

In the past two weeks, two inmates have been stabbed to death, one in the shower. One inmate hanged himself where I am now, in C BLOCK, another inmate overdosed on heroin, and the fifth death occurred when an inmate was beaten with a dumbbell taken from the weight pile. This beating occurred upstairs in the auditorium. Was I to be next?

Segregation is difficult. I must stay in this eight foot by ten-foot cell alone for seventy-two hours. I'm allowed out for one hour to shower and to make a phone call. I haven't spoken to anyone in my family in three days; they have no idea where I am or why I'm not calling. I sit on my bed or the toilet to change scenery now and then.

I try not to sit or lie in bed for any extended period of time. I want to be able to sleep thru the night. At least those eight hours go by easily. I'm struggling with my time here. I thought passing time with a cellmate was difficult, this is pure boredom and solitude. The sink is backed up so I use my left over juice cup from breakfast and slowly empty the water from the sink to the toilet. I called maintenance five times, no response. So each morning after I shave and brush my teeth, the sink is full and it's time to slowly empty this disgusting soapy, toothpaste, water. This does pass time.

In A BLOCK, where I came from, I would pass on breakfast at 5:30 a.m.; the food was not worth getting up for. Waking up that early makes the day seem endless. I'm out of my cell at 9:00 a.m. to go outside for recreation until 10:30 a.m.; sometimes I can get a pass to the library and read for those hours. I do like that. At 10:30 I am back in my cell until 12:30 at which time I shave without a mirror, and rest. "Feed Up!" is called and it's time for lunch, 12:30. The cafeteria is a three hundred yard walk. The guards rush the inmates thru their meal. I'm constantly shoving food in my mouth as I get up to place my tray on the tray table for cleaning.

Here in C BLOCK I can take all the time I need, I eat alone and the guards don't care if you eat slowly, or eat at all. However, I had acquaintances or inmates to eat with in A BLOCK. After gobbling lunch down, we go back out for recreation until 2:30 p.m. I go back to my cell at 2:30 then at 5:00 p.m. we are sent to dinner. I shove my food in my face and return to my cell until 6:00 p.m. I sleep, do laundry in the toilet, or write. We are let out of our cells the last time at 6:30 p.m. until 8:00 p.m. to watch television, make a phone call, shower, or to sit around and talk on the, "FLATS". That is where the televisions, showers, ice, and large cooling fans are located. Nearly everyone gathers on the, "FLATS," in the evening. Then we go back to the cells at 8:00 p.m. until 9:00 a.m. the next day. Not so bad as I sit here for three days in a row in segregation with absolutely nothing to do, read, or see. It is somewhat ironic and silly, but, I'd rather be back in A BLOCK 310 with my goodies, mirror, and my talking cellmate than in this shitole. This shithole cell with only the mice and roaches to stare at, somewhat ironic I think.

C Block

October 16, 2001: it's 3:00 a.m. The noise level in this section has not only awakened me from a fitful dream but it is near deafening to me. In A BLOCK where I've been for the last three and one half months, there's a loudness that gradually lowers to a quiet constant hum before becoming very quiet and ceasing by 2:00 a.m. Then, the noise crescendos back to it's original loudness by morning. It's a cycle of sound.

IN C BLOCK, this much smaller black blocked building, which houses 100 inmates that start fights, argue with the guards, cause problems within the prison population or are segregated from the general population, like me, for safety reasons, there is no gradual decline in the noise level as morning approaches and passes. The noise is continuous and unending.

My body is quivering uncontrollably from the noise. I awoke to a level of noise that equaled that of a playground of three hundred school kids at 8:00 a.m. on a summer morning the last day of school. I hear no flow of conversation. There is no continuity to the words to form any type of discernable sentence. "Fuck you! Shorty! Nigger, toilet paper, Eager St., nigger slut, shut up, asshole, sister, C.O., yo, shit, kick your ass, eat, uptown, etc., etc., etc. No words even resembling any type of conversation. It's similar to a large wave of noise and words that never seems to come to shore, never peaks or climaxes. It's a wave of noise continually assaulting my ears and brain. I'm in awe. It's almost inconceivable to me what I'm experiencing this moment, 3:15 a.m. As I am lying in bed with my ears to my makeshift pillow, an oversized bath towel my wife sent to me two months ago rolled up to resemble a pillow.

I can hear my body quivering. I'm not shaking noticeably but my body is vibrating. The humming in my ears is making me sick to my stomach. I cannot make the noise cease.

One hundred inmates here are noisier than twelve hundred I left. They all are locked in their cells so their voices must carry at least ten feet to be heard at all. They yell up a tier or two, down a tier to the FLATS, thru a wall to the next cell, or across the entire block to converse. This goes on and on. It's causing my head to spin. I have to puke. I do!

I'm so glad I can at least get up and write. It must take a certain type of individual, a certain kind of person to be able to endure and survive this environment.

I cannot fathom or grasp the thought of having to spend five, ten, or twenty years in these surroundings, let alone a lifetime, having to suffer thru this horror. There is nothing that important to me that would cause me to want to stay here.

I'm in a slight state of agony. It's as if I cannot escape this constant noise, this onslaught of single words pounding my brain. I would guess that the human mind would adjust to this noise. I do know that I am not adjusting well at all. I cannot sleep, concentrate, or think clearly. I keep trying to picture my children, my family, and my wife, my mom. Anything to help cease this never-ending mental and emotional assault.

I pray, Dear Lord, Please! Please! Deliver me from this noise and thru this night!

Thursday October 18, 2001: I'm still here. I was supposed to leave Wednesday. Not only did I not leave, I was left in my cell all day Wednesday. I've spent forty-six hours straight in this cell with absolutely nothing to do. The sink in my cell is stopped up. I've filled it and emptied it twice to move around some. I pace my cell to exercise my legs. I did some push ups off the wall. The floor is to dirty. I am bored sick.

October 20,2001: This morning the inmates in this block went crazy, ballistic. Approximately one hundred inmates began kicking on their cell doors, walls, and bunks. They began screaming and yelling. It sounds like a jungle in here. The entire infrastructure of the building shook, lights flickered, and the floors rumbled. I have never experienced such a large violent, significant show of force. It is somewhat exciting, intriguing, but also, frightening. I am one of four white men amongst the over one hundred black inmates and they are pissed.

If these inmates would somehow get out of their cells I would have a major situation, problem, on my hands. Especially being a former police officer that killed a black man, and of course, white. The inmates are threatening to set things on fire to break out if possible. I can hear a lot of running outside, like the sound of soldier's boots hitting the asphalt, possibly reinforcements. None have come into the tiers yet; it's been over four hours now. The violence has been constant for hours. It doesn't let up. I'm not certain what may have caused this eruption of human feelings. It's breakfast, the ordeal has been continuing all night.

This tension has been slowly escalating all week. It seems from what I can gather, that an inmate hanged himself. This in itself is not noteworthy. Evidently the inmate changed his mind and called for help. He called for help over and over but no one came. It seems that also the inmates were screaming for the C.O.s to help this man but no one arrived to cut him down. He died gagging in his cell alone. He was a loudmouth and a troublemaker. Supposedly his family was notified that he died of *natural causes*

Two days prior to this, murder, as the inmates are referring to it, a young inmate was beaten and choked by a large black C.O. who was a sergeant. This sergeant doesn't wear a nametag. A few inmates witnessed this attack and screamed for the officer to stop. The sergeant continued the beating and dragged the young inmate around the corner and out of sight. Not long after his bloody and limp body was dragged along the tier and he was thrown into his cell on the top tier. All hell broke loose early this morning due to these incidents and the guard's bad attitudes, and the treatment of several other inmates'. This is quite scary and unnerving. I'm somehow feeling secure locked in my cell. This is ironic. I am feeling somewhat secure locked in my cell.

The instigators yelled and threatened violence throughout most of the early morning hours. They wanted all the inmates to refuse their breakfast trays. It seemed as though most of the inmates were convinced. They would not take a breakfast tray and would stand together and united. Their solidarity was strong, at least in words.

It's 4:45 a.m.; "feed up" was just called. The instigators reminded the inmates of their fast and rebellion. All the inmates ate their meals. There was no unification or solidarity present, no threat. The instigators yelled out, "Don't take your trays!" The reply from one of the inmates was, "fuck you, this nigger's hungry!" Other inmates laughed and everyone ate quietly. Some uprising! But, I still want out.

I spoke to the Captain of the guards. It seems as though I'm not supposed to be in this jail at all. I should have been sent to Jessup Correctional Institute from day one. Instead I sit here for three days straight with nothing to do. My radio doesn't work, I have no books or magazines to read, no reading material to pass the time. I sit on my bed and stare at the wall for minutes, hours, and days. I have no idea what is going on in the world or even in Baltimore. I have no idea of the weather, I cannot see outside so therefore I don't know if it's sunny or raining.

My routine in C BLOCK is simple, boring, and nondescript. At 4:30 a.m. the guards bang on the steel bars while yelling, "feed up!" Everyone wakes up to eat. My tray is slid thru the steel door bars. No walking to the cafeteria like in A BLOCK, no exercise here. I only eat the cold cereal, the fried bologna, eggs and mystery meat that I still cannot figure out what it's made of, all make me sick. I go back to my bunk at 5:00 a.m. and stare at the walls until 8:30 a.m. when the guards begin calling names of inmates that are leaving. I have been praying for three mornings now that my name would be called and I would be moved, moved anywhere from here. I brush my teeth, empty the sink with my cup and sit until 10:30 a.m., lunch is delivered. I eat the cheese and mayo, but not the mystery meat or the grits. The cake is good.

After lunch I shave without a mirror and with soap in the stopped up sink. After shaving I empty the sink once more counting the cups to see if thirty-one is the magic number each time I have to empty the sink. Each time it takes thirty-one cups, I'm thrilled. This keeps me somewhat occupied. I have stopped counting the ceiling tiles and concrete blocks for days.

When I'm done eating lunch I exercise by walking one hundred times across the eight-foot long cell, lots and lots of turnarounds. I do push ups against the walls for the floor is too damn dirty to lie on. From 12:30 p.m. until 4:30 p.m. I get into my bunk and think, then I get up to walk a few times, then I sit and stare at the wall and think some more. *How did I get to be here? Am I going to straighten up this time? Why did this happen to me?* I continually ask myself these repetitive questions and a plethora of others.

At 4:30 p.m. dinner is served. Spaghetti and two meatballs with real buttered bread. I can stomach this. I drink milk at two meals. At lunch we drink base. Base is a concentrated generic cool aid that tastes like shit, I poor it in the toilet. From 4:45 p.m. until about 9:30 or 10:00 p.m. I try to stay awake as long as possible so I can toss and turn all night as the inmates' scream, yell, and curse at each other all night long until breakfast at 4:30 a.m. Then they sleep. I guess the animal is satisfied and sleeps.

The BLOCK becomes quiet after breakfast. I enjoy this time. I can function and my brain is not yelling at me in my head. My rehabilitation is overwhelming me. I have changed so very much, now maybe, just maybe, I can actually fit into society and become a productive member, an asset. I have learned so very much in this jail. I'm certain I can put all my newfound knowledge to work for me immediately upon my release. I've learned to sit quietly for hours and days at a time, how to start a fire using a pencil, how to produce jail tattoos, how to remain patient as I stand in lines for ninety minutes or more, how to gracefully accept a racial insult without kicking someone's ass, how to not look into a jail guards eyes when he is belittling me in front of several inmates because he is having a bad day, and so much, much more. I am a walking *fucking* jail encyclopedia.

Thankfully I have become quite aware that I am in no way similar to the majority of these inmates. I am not selfish, ignorant, rude, dirty, or uncaring. If they can't steal it, take it, take advantage of you, rip you off, or step in front of you while you are waiting in line for an hour to get into the door first, they are not completely happy. I will never be as these individuals are. I am from a completely different world, planet, and universe. It matters not to me that I may have a criminal record; I am not a criminal. My demeanor, spirituality, and make up will not allow it. Plus, I don't have that mentality, *or so I hope?*

I don't know enough adjectives to describe to you, the reader, how uncomfortable, unsettling, and nasty it is being incarcerated. It's degrading, humiliating, lonely, and depressing. Prison strips you of your self-esteem, self-respect, dignity, and confidence. Incarceration is a type of mental, emotional and psychological rape. The degradation cannot be erased or forgotten, it stains everything that I hold near and dear. Prison makes it quite obvious and clear that we take our freedoms for granted. You have no one lying next to you at night keeping you warm and making you feel secure and loved, you cannot go into the next room and watch your children sleep or say goodnight to them, you cannot walk into the kitchen and eat whatever and whenever you desire, there is no freedom and no freedom of movement.

Having to urinate or defecate five feet from a stranger, or have them do the same five feet from you is most disgusting and vile. There is nothing speedy or fast in prison. You wait at least twenty minutes in a long line before eating every meal; you will wait an hour or two to get to the commissary to buy a new razor or a treat for yourself, some peanut butter or sweets. You will wait for the phone, to go to the library, everything in jail is a waiting game, and you will always lose.

If you are in law enforcement and might presently be on the wrong side of that Thin Blue Line, return to the proper side now. You won't fit in here, in jail. You will struggle emotionally and psychologically each day just to get thru that day. The guards don't like you. The inmates despise and loathe you for a list of reasons. You are alone. It's obvious and inevitable. Any freedoms you have will be a blur, gone. Get back on the right side. You have a great job and accomplish many good and just deeds. This is the complete other end of the spectrum of right and wrong. If you like yourself, job, family, freedom, privacy and life, remain on the right side of that Blue Line.

At 8:00 p.m. on October 24, 2001, I was taken out of segregation, protective custody. I was placed in handcuffs, shackles, and waist chains. I was taken out of C-BLOCK! I was taken outside for the first time in nine days. I was oblivious to the weather the last four days; I was only aware of day or night. I walked outside into a seeming paradise! Seventy-five degrees, clear sky, and a beautiful bright and brilliant spirit lifting half moon. I was mesmerized at the clarity. I had not seen the moon for four months. This was a feast for my eyes. The air smelled so very clean and fresh. I was absolutely delighted. I felt giddy, my heart leapt with happiness. I felt a tinge of freedom. Such a beautiful, crisp, and spiritually uplifting evening, I felt fortunate even though I was still confined, cuffed and shackled. So very different from what I had only moments ago left behind me. I had the feelings of a child seeing Mickey Mouse in person at Disneyland. My spirits, morale, and senses were at a high. I felt alive.

I thanked God quietly, and aloud, for allowing me to experience and feel this spectacular sensation. I cared not that I was cuffed and shackled and had a six-foot length of chain cinched tightly around my waist. I was under the impression that I was being transported and transferred to Jessup Pre Release Unit located in Jessup Maryland. Not such a nice place, but much better than the penitentiary.

I became aware two hours later that I was in fact going to EPRU, or Eastern Pre Release Unit located on Maryland's Eastern Shore only miles from the Chesapeake Bay Bridge. I had suddenly gone from total confinement and miserable surroundings to a wide-open country setting.

As I stepped off the prison bus the guard removed all my chains and cuffs. I was free to walk about. I was free to walk the one hundred feet to the intake building all alone and unescorted. As I entered a Correctional Officer that actually treated me with kindness and respect greeted me. There are no fences, barbed wire, cuffs, or harsh restrictions here. I feel as though I am in prison heaven.

It was 11:30 p.m. when orientation was completed. I was given two sheets, a blanket, and something I haven't had for nearly four months, a real pillow, and a soft, real pillow. I had been using a rolled up towel. I was escorted to a dormitory that contained approximately fifty pre release inmates. I lay in my bunk. The dorm was so very quiet I was unable to sleep, even though I had a mattress that was six inches thick, not the two inches I was accustomed to, but never comfortable with. I stared at the ceiling most of the night. The quiet was so very different. The quiet was upsetting my brain and body. It seemed deafening. After blocking out all the noise and loudness in C-BLOCK I've suddenly been placed in a normal sleep setting and I cannot sleep. It's 5:00 a.m. on October 25, 2001. I've thanked the Lord for delivering me from evil many times this early morning.

October 26, 2001, I am ecstatic. I have been taken from one extreme to the other. I awoke at 6:00 a.m. after a fitful sleep. I enjoyed real coffee, eggs, butter, toast, oatmeal with lumps, orange juice, and buttered bread with as much sugar and jelly as I could eat. I am flabbergasted. It seems like Christmas morning to me. After breakfast I walked around a quarter mile track four times, the entire time I was taking in the air, trees, leaves, and sheep across the field. A sheep dog was herding the sheep, I stared in disbelief. I had gone from watching roaches and mice walk across my cell to wandering at my leisure around a dirt track watching sheep and deer. I am like a different person here. The Correctional Officer took a Polaroid picture of me last night as I arrived fresh from the penitentiary. My eyes are red and I have dark circles around them. I look sickly.

For lunch I had tuna, fresh bread, corn chowder and a fresh salad with salad dressing. For dinner I had meat for the first time in four months, not mystery meat, a steak! I cannot get over the contrast in my life that I am experiencing. I am beside myself, giddy. I have been walking all day and actually talking to myself. *I can't believe how lucky I am to be here. I can smell fresh cut grass! I see sheep! Look, a leaf falling, and oh my look Dan, a hawk!* There is a washing machine and a dryer here, I don't have to use the toilet to wash my clothes, plus I can stay in the shower for as long as I like with hot water. I have access to six vending machines that contain all sorts of cakes and candies, I can carry cash, and I can visit with my wife and children for two hours, not thirty minutes. I can hold and hug my wife and children. My five brothers visited this week; I choked up as I hugged each one. I feel reborn, but I am still incarcerated. Even though I am incarcerated and one hundred miles from my family I don't care. I am somewhat free, free of the Maryland Penitentiary, A-BLOCK, the filth and dirt, but most importantly, C-BLOCK.

My spirits have soared. My attitude has changed noticeably. I am a person once again. I am an individual, not feeling as a rat or a lowly roach wasting away in a cell, alone. I am as happy as I can be in these circumstances. My wife and Attorney, David Love are responsible for the move. I am extremely pleased. Thank you Lord.

November 2, 2001. Five years ago today I lay in Hopkins Bayview Hospital with nine bullet holes in me struggling for my life after a ten-hour surgery and dying two times on the operating table. I was on life support and had no idea of what I had done to myself. I would survive this suicide attempt and I feel fortunate to be alive even though I am incarcerated. I am happy to be alive and healthy. I voluntarily attend two Alcoholics Anonymous meetings each week. I need the help and welcome the chance to handle this disease. Unbeknownst to the other inmates, my Aunt's husband, Ken, comes in twice a week to handle the AA meetings. It was so comforting seeing a familiar face. My face lit up when I saw Ken. I stayed late after the meeting to speak to Ken, He hugged me! I needed a hug so very badly. Thank you!

I will be released on January 12, 2002. I was able to acquire a job with maintenance. I help maintain the grounds and the entire unit. I was told to rake leaves my first few days in the unit and enjoyed it completely. I was in the cold fresh air and the sun raking leaves for hours. The job was pure enjoyment for me. My misfortune has changed me and I feel fortunate to be where I am, always knowing that no one can stop time and the time will come when I am released and free. Hopefully I can put this horrid adventure behind me and go on to pick myself up and be what I was intended or whatever God and fate has in store for me.

A MOTHER'S STORY

Like Mother, Like Son

Do you know that your soul is of my soul, such a part
That you seem to be fiber and core of my heart?
None other can pain as you, dear can do.
None other can please me or praise me as you.
Remember the world will be quick with its blame
If shadow or stain ever darken your name,
"Like mother, like son" is a saying so true.
The world will judge largely the mother by you.
Be yours then the task, if task it shall be.
To force the proud world to do homage to me.
Be sure it will say when the verdict you've won,
"She reaped as she sowed. Lo! This is her son.

Margaret Johnson Grafflin

A fter my mother read this book I pleaded with her to write this chapter. (A Mother's Story), is not mine to write. I, in no way, can portray to the reader what a police officers mother must go through each and every day that her beloved little boy/girl, her police officer son/daughter, begins his tour of duty on the streets of any state in this country. For that matter, any country in this world. Every police officer has a mother.

My mother doesn't want to rehash or relive what me, her son, and my brother, Mike, have done, not done, experienced, endured, or withstood. Also her grandfather, John, brother in law Skip, and daughter in law, JoAnne.

As I began to finalize this book, I understood fully why she wouldn't write about her feelings of being the granddaughter, sister in law, mother in law and mother to two sons that were Baltimore City Police officers. She never liked the fact of any one of us being enforcers of the law.

I was hoping **my mother** could reach out to the mothers of police officers so they too could identify with my mother. It's not to be. However, I can repeat some of what I have heard, not heard, and took notice of, throughout the years, the good and the bad years.

Each night when my brother Mike and I were scheduled to work as police officers, my mother would iron our white police shirts with the bright yellow and blue arm patch that displayed, "Baltimore City Police". With the near completion of every single shirt my mother would recite a, Hail Mary prayer. A prayer to The Blessed Mother of Christ that her sons would come home safely each night, and in one piece.

She would pray that both of us would use common sense and good judgment in carrying out our duties.

There were mornings when she would awake to see a bloodied shirt hanging on our beds or in the hamper. She would immediately enter our bedrooms to see if we were injured. Her eyes would search her son's bodies to look for any visible injuries. Then quietly wake us. I would always say, "Don't worry mom, it's not mine." Or, "its mine mom but just a small cut, I'm okay." If working, Mike and I would also call her a soon as possible upon hearing of the shooting of a police officer so she would be aware that her son(s) was not the victim. I cannot imagine the torture and trepidation that my mother and other police officers mothers endure. Most of the time it's for over twenty years until her son retires, and hopefully her police officer son makes it without becoming seriously injured or killed in the line of duty. How can a mother survive this?

When a police officer is killed in the line of duty, the press speaks of the three children he left behind, or the sobbing wife left alone to fend for herself. This is definitely a truism, and saddening. However, rarely do I see, or hear, of the grief stricken mother who carried this little boy for nine months, raised him well enough and righteous enough to become a police officer and uphold the law in such violent and uncertain times, a mother who lived with her son and provided for him for over twenty one years. A mother forced to bury her own heart and sole, at no cause of her own. *The fiber and core of her heart.*

No other can pain as you. Imagine the pain of losing a son, especially if he were the only son! I cannot.

Of course children, brothers, wives and dads are devastated also, but a mother is so very special. *The world is quick with its blame if shadow or stain should darken his name.* It is also her name! She will be judged by her son's actions or lack of. So will the father. He has to remain strong for his wife as his sons body is laid to rest or if the son disgraces the family name. He too must endure. How, how can the parents of slain police officers ever recover from this type of death, usually a violent death or a highly publicized shameful, embarrassing, or criminal action perpetrated by their son.

If a police officer does his mother proud, certainly she is proud and likes to bask in her sons or daughters accomplishments. However, how does a mother continue on when her son disgraces the badge, his family, her reputation? *Remember the world will be quick with its blame.* And, the world most definitely is quick with its blame, **I,** know this first hand, I am well aware what I have done to my family, notably, my father, and mother. I cannot *force the world to do homage to my mother.*

A mother will love her son unconditionally, no matter the downfall that her son is also suffering through. Unlike most long term so called friends, acquaintances and former coworkers. Most forget your name, talk badly about you, and behind your back, and during a time of failure and disgrace a police officer is quick to be criticized, ostracized and no longer accepted into his circle of lifetime friends. He is no longer looked upon as one of them He is merely discarded, as was I. But a mother, a mother will hold her son tightly to her and say encouraging and healing words as the rest of the world attempts to strip her son of any dignity and pride. *You're soul is of my soul.*

A police officers mother is also a true hero. She is a hero in all of our eyes. She has reared properly, and nurtured, a keeper of the peace, a guardian of the law, a man among men, woman among women. She has given the world another police officer to do the dirty work that not many can handle nor have any desires to handle.

She reaped as she sowed. Lo! This is her son.

FINAL CHAPTER

A song by Rascal Flatts

I'm Movin' on"

I've dealt with my ghosts,

And faced all my demons,

Finally content with a past I regret,

I've found you find strength,

In your moments of weakness,

For once I'm at peace with myself.

I've been burdened with blame,

Trapped in the past for too long,

I'm movin on.

This song seems befitting of my life as a police officer and the chapters of this book. The chapters I've written. However, I am not certain that I have dealt with all of the *demons*, the sights, sounds, smells, and experiences I have weathered as a police officer. These have had a major impact on me, my attitude, feelings and personal thoughts. These *ghosts and demons* have most assuredly taken their toll on me, mentally, psychologically, and emotionally.

I regret my mistakes but can do nothing about them. No one has let me down, disappointed me, or embarrassed me, more than myself. I cannot forget the bad which is much more prevalent in my memory, than the good. It's always present. No matter how well my life is progressing or how happy I feel, the shame, sorrow, and sadness of going to prison, losing my career, being in the diaper room, as well as the killing of Booker Lancaster, are always surfacing and resurfacing in my mind, thoughts, and feelings. Some of these heart wrenching thoughts and feelings never subside, never go away.

Months before I had help from the therapists, psychiatrists, social workers, psychologists, and Alcoholics Anonymous, I had to struggle to get out of bed. Also, it was a daily struggle to not get drunk and stay drunk. I was depressed. There are those out there that wish I would lie down and stay drunk and those that wish for me to pick myself up and go on once again. I continue to pick myself up due to a firm upbringing and a foundation laid down for me by my parents. My dad has passed, but he taught me solid values. My mom continues to be my anchor, assisting me in my struggle to live a Catholic lifestyle.

I am burdened with blame and trapped in the past. I blame no one, no one but myself, for most of the occurrences in my life. I have owned the downfalls, shortcomings and misgivings. I take responsibility for my actions and lack of. At times, and in portions of this book, it seems as though I am trying to seek forgiveness, make excuses, or attempt to exonerate myself. This is not the case. After reading over this book, even though it may seem that way, I am in no way blaming anyone but me, Dan Shanahan, for all that I have done. I **am** burdened with blame.

I most definitely *regret* the course I have traversed, the path I have taken. However, I constantly fight to keep myself on an even keel, to stay the course, to do what's expected of me by my family, real friends, and most importantly my three children. I have many regrets, but am aware that I cannot change the past, however, that was then and this is now. Life continues.

I **have** *found strength* suffering through *moments of weakness.* I am better for the adversity. But, the two years and twelve days I spent in Federal prison in Texas, not more than ninety days after resigning from the Baltimore Police Department as a highly decorated police officer, the horrible experiences of the three suicide attempts, the diaper room, and the six months in the Maryland Penitentiary, coupled with other sorrow and sadness I have survived, have made me stronger but at a monumental expense to me and my family, especially, me. I sit and think about of the diaper room and the suicide attempts. Recalling those exact hours and moments cause me great distress, anguish, and emotional pain.

At times, I cry the tears quietly and silently. As the tears well up, they speak volumes about their origins and endings as they slowly trickle down

my face. I emotionally crumble and collapse. However, I recuperate. I recuperate because I have a strong, supportive, loving family, and I am a strong individual.

I feel as though I shall never be *at peace with myself*. Writing this book has been excellent therapy for me. But the sorrowful memories somehow surface over and over again. At times I question my mental and emotional stability. I do have safety valves and checks in place to quickly prevent the horrible thoughts of suicide and self destruction I had in the past. These cannot occur again. My family and real friends assist me in my efforts to stay alive and mentally able to function properly.

Other than some help and guidance I received from my uncle, a recovering alcoholic, and Alcoholics Anonymous itself, I have narrowed, through my personal trials and tribulations and the encounters I have attempted to share with you, the reader, my success in returning to a safe and stable life to three succinct and specific entities

GOD; or, if you will, a higher power, for watching over me, keeping me alive and safe through all I've had to withstand and endure since July 30, 1973. My starting date with the Baltimore City Police Department, especially, on July 13, 1983, the day Booker Lancaster tragically died in my arms and my life began to disintegrate and collapse. GOD and my Guardian Angel(s), specifically, Saint Michael the Archangel, patron Saint of Police, have sustained me through all of the bad, evil, sadness, and grief.

Saint Michael was God's policeman in heaven. Saint Michael and his guardian angels cast Satan and his band of dark angels into hell, therefore

Saint Michael is, and should be, the patron of the police officer. GOD has blessed me.

COUNTRY; The pride I have in being an American, the duty I felt and still feel, to become and remain a good and righteous hard working loyal citizen of The United States of America. This country, the greatest and most powerful in the world, that I had a short opportunity of protecting and keeping safe it's citizens, and that I have a fierce loyalty to. I had a small chance to serve this country, not as a Marine, Naval officer, Army officer, or Air Force pilot, but as a soldier of what's fair, good and honorable, by becoming a Baltimore City Police Officer. I served my country as well as I was able and I am proud of that and myself.

FAMILY; My family has never, never, let me down, abandoned and left me forsaken and discarded, as many individuals that I respected, loved, worked along side of, and admired did, no matter the circumstances. Friends that I was certain loved and cared for me also, turned away from me, disposed of my friendship as if it were garbage, friends that I had a strong loyalty to. Friends I missed, but no longer miss.

Through all the bad, embarrassing, shameful, and belittling episodes in my life, my family has been a constant in my life. My family has been a beacon of direction, a light to guide me back to them and a caring, loving, comfortable environment. My three children, five wonderful brothers, my sister in laws, at times, my two wives, my nieces and nephews and, most assuredly, my mother and father have given me hope, understanding, encouragement and a love that I can find in no other place. The unconditional love that they and a few close friends have afforded me is nearly inconceivable. My family has picked me up, brushed me off and sent me back into an unforgiving and sometimes difficult world, filling me with pride, intestinal fortitude, and a sense of power that no one else could have provided.

I am loved and I know this. My family is my life and lifeblood, my family sustains me. I love you and thank you from the inner most reaches of my ripped, torn, tortured, but still salvageable heart and soul.